Mastering the OSCE CSA

Objective Structured Clinical Examination
Clinical Skills Assessment

Jo-Ann Reteguiz, M.D.

ASSISTANT PROFESSOR OF MEDICINE
DEPARTMENT OF MEDICINE
MEDICINE CLERKSHIP COURSE DIRECTOR
UNIVERSITY OF MEDICINE AND DENTISTRY OF NEW JERSEY-NEW JERSEY MEDICAL SCHOOL
NEWARK, NEW JERSEY

Beverly Cornel-Avendaño, M.D.

SENIOR FELLOW
DIVISION OF GASTROENTEROLOGY
DEPARTMENT OF MEDICINE
UNIVERSITY OF MEDICINE AND DENTISTRY OF NEW JERSEY-NEW JERSEY MEDICAL SCHOOL
NEWARK, NEW JERSEY

ILLUSTRATIONS BY MOIRA MCDONOUGH

McGraw-Hill
Health Professions Division

New York St. Louis San Francisco Auckland Bogotá Caracas Lisbon London Madrid
Mexico City Milan Montreal New Delhi San Juan Singapore Sydney Tokyo Toronto

McGraw-Hill

A Division of The McGraw-Hill Companies

Mastering the OSCE/CSA

Copyright © 1999 by *The McGraw-Hill Companies, Inc.* All rights reserved. Printed in the United States of America. Except as permitted under the United States Copyright Act of 1976, no part of this publication may be reproduced or distributed in any form or by any means, or stored in a data base or retrieval system, without the prior written permission of the publisher.

234567890 MALMAL 99

ISBN 0-07-135012-8

This book was set in New Baskerville and Fresh Script by *TopDesk Publishers' Group.* The editors were *John Dolan, Susan Noujaim,* and *Peter McCurdy;* the production supervisor was *Catherine Saggese;* the cover design was by *TopDesk Publishers' Group.* Project management was by *TopDesk Publishers' Group. Malloy Lithographing, Inc.* was printer and binder.

This book is printed on acid-free paper.

Library of Congress Cataloging-in-Publication Data

Reteguiz, Jo-Ann.
    Mastering the OSCE/CSA/Jo-Ann Reteguiz, Beverly Cornel
-Avendaño.
       p.   cm.
    Includes bibliographical references.
    ISBN 0-07-135012-8
    1. Diagnosis–Examinations, questions, etc. 2. Medical history taking–Examinations, questions, etc. 3. Physical diagnosis-
-Examinations, questions, etc. 4. Clinical competence-
-Examinations, questions, etc. I. Cornel-Avendaño, Beverly.
II. Title.
    [DNLM: 1. Clinical Competence. 2. Medical History Taking.
3. Physical Examination–examination questions. 4. Communication.
WB 18 R437m 1999]
RC71.R48   1999
616.07'5'076–dc21
DNLM/DLC
for Library of Congress   98-55698
                                       CIP

To Mom and Dad, whose love and encouragement give special meaning to every new journey; and to Christopher, whose bounding spirit, loving soul, and warm heart soar above all others.

—J.R.

To my mother, Thelma, whose unceasing love and support have made all the difference in my life. To my husband, Gary, whose lifelong love and companionship I cherish deeply. To my son, J. Andrew Philippe, who constantly opens my heart, making joy a reality.

—B.C.A.

Contents

Check out updated OSCE/CSA information at:
http://www.books.mcgraw-hill.com/medical/osce

WHO WILL FIND THIS BOOK USEFUL:

■ The U.S. medical student required to pass the clerkship OSCE when rotating through the disciplines of Internal Medicine, Family Medicine, Ob/Gyn, Pediatrics, Psychiatry, Emergency Medicine, and Surgery.

■ The U.S. medical student required to pass a senior year multidisciplinary OSCE prior to graduation.

■ The international medical graduate who must pass the CSA after completing Step 1 and Step 2 of the USMLE for ECFMG certification. This book will guide the IMG through the standardized patient examination.

HOW THIS BOOK WILL HELP YOU:

■ Mastering the OSCE/CSA focuses your interviewing and physical examination skills so you are able to finish test stations in the required time limit.

■ It explains how you can develop the secret "checklist" each standardized patient is using at every test station.

■ It sharpens your interpersonal skills to improve overall clinical performance.

■ It reveals the pitfalls of the standardized patient examination and shows how to avoid them.

■ It allows you to practice your approach to the standardized patient examination at home using "real" standardized patient cases.

■ It gives you the confidence and experience you need to do your best in any standardized patient interaction.

■ It offers great practice for physicians and students when they interact with "real life" patients in the future.

HOW TO USE THIS BOOK:

■ Read the information in the early chapters to learn how to prepare for the standardized patient examination.

■ Understand the role of the standardized patient. This lay person is often the only person evaluating your performance.

■ Learn how to develop, accurately and quickly, the checklist used by the standardized patient at each test station. The examination requires you to develop a specific strategy based on the "hidden" checklist. If you can develop the checklist mentally before the actual interaction, the test becomes easy.

- Use the 50 standardized patient cases in this book to practice and grade your checklist developing skills in the areas of:

  1. interviewing

  2. physical examination

  3. communication

- Use the 12-page supplement (inside back cover) prior to the exam as a "last minute" high-yield review.

- Review Pearls:

 OSCE Interstation Pearl

 CSA Patient Note Pearl

 History-Taking Pearl

 Physical Examination Pearl

Check out updated OSCE/CSA information at:
http://www.books.mcgraw-hill.com/medical/osce

Background

The gold standard by which physician competence is measured has eluded medical educators for over a century. Early in the history of medicine, senior physicians mentored and graded their students, but the limitations of this subjective process were obvious. Specialty boards began using the oral examination which provided more accurate information about a physician's clinical problem solving skills and fund of knowledge but these were not reliable or standardized. Excellent or poor performance on the oral examination reflected the good luck of being asked to discuss a clinical problem seen during training or the bad luck of being asked about a case one had never seen.

In the middle of the twentieth century, using multiple choice questions (MCQ) on a written examination became the method for physician evaluation and, for over four decades, medical schools and licensure bureaus relied on "the written" to assess whether a physician or student was competent. Educators soon realized that, even though MCQ examinations were standardized and reliable, they lacked validity. It was clear that an eighty percent score on the written examination did not mean that the examinee knew eighty percent of all of medicine. Was the paper and pencil examination the best way of judging competence? Could educators say that "the written" accurately simulated the tasks future physicians would be expected to perform in "real life" medicine?

In 1963, at the University of Southern California, Doctor Howard Barrows trained a healthy artist's model to portray a paralyzed patient with multiple sclerosis. Neurology students learned about the disease from a "real" patient instead of a textbook. This was the first standardized patient encounter.

In 1964, Barrows and Abrahamson suggested using standardized patients in a test format to assess student performance in medical school. Using "real" clinical situations and "real" patients, one could assess how students use their knowledge and skills when faced with realistic challenges rather than trying to infer performance from a standardized written test. This was the beginning of the standardized patient examination.

Over the last thirty years, the standardized patient examination has evolved into an important tool for the teaching and assessment of medical students and physicians. It is rapidly gaining acceptance as a requirement for licensure and medical school graduation. In a world where astronauts practice simulated space exploration before "real" flight and computers simulate everything from golf to warfare, it was only a matter of time before medicine, too, required simulated practice and assessment before allowing a physician to encounter the "real" clinical situation.

Preface

The purpose of this OSCE/CSA review book is to help medical students and physicians faced with the stress of taking a new format examination become more comfortable with the standardized patient encounter.

As the Medicine Clerkship Course Director at the University of Medicine and Dentistry of New Jersey-New Jersey Medical School, I successfully integrated an OSCE for over 500 medical students. After three years of standardized patient test writing, training, implementation, and grading, I realized that a student could perform poorly due to nervousness and inexperience with this kind of examination. Medical students seemed more concerned with the OSCE than the final written test and would approach me for advice on how to better prepare for the standardized patient examination. Recently, international medical graduates have voiced concerns regarding the new standardized patient CSA examination requirement.

The unique qualities of the standardized patient examination make it, understandably, a stressful experience. In less than fifteen minutes, a student or physician must interview and examine a patient and accurately formulate a differential diagnosis and plan. At each test station, the examinee must demonstrate excellent communication skills and remarkable composure. This is a test that relies not so much on how much one studies and what one knows but how one does things. We wrote this book for those examinees who will be competent health providers in the future but, for now, need help preparing for this new kind of test experience.

This book will walk you through the OSCE or CSA from beginning to end. The tips provided will give you the necessary guidance and direction you need to do your best. The 50 practice cases will sharpen your skills in interviewing, physical examination, and communication, preparing you for every possible interaction.

Although licensure bureaus, medical schools, and disciplines may vary in small ways, the overall structure of the standardized patient examination will be the same as in this book. So read carefully and relax on the day of the examination. Having the right preparation and confidence for the OSCE or CSA makes a challenging experience easy, educational, and fun.

Jo-Ann Reteguiz
February 1999

Acknowledgements

We wish to acknowledge the University of Medicine and Dentistry of New Jersey-New Jersey Medical School and, in particular, the Department of Medicine, for its exceptional committment to patient care and medical education.

Thank you, Dr. John Bullock—Associate Professor, Department of Pharmacology and Physiology, University of Medicine and Dentistry of New Jersey-New Jersey Medical School—for your guidance and encouragement.

REVIEWERS

Faculty Reviewers

Marilyn A. Miller, M.D.
ASSOCIATE PROFESSOR OF MEDICINE
DIRECTOR, INTERNAL MEDICINE RESIDENCY
PROGRAM
DEPARTMENT OF MEDICINE
UMDNJ-NEW JERSEY MEDICAL SCHOOL
NEWARK, NEW JERSEY

Beverly R. Delaney, M.D.
ASSISTANT PROFESSOR OF PSYCHIATRY
DIRECTOR, PSYCHIATRY RESIDENCY
PROGRAM
DEPARTMENT OF PSYCHIATRY
UMDNJ-NEW JERSEY MEDICAL SCHOOL
NEWARK, NEW JERSEY

Lawrence E. Harrison, M.D.
ASSISTANT PROFESSOR OF SURGERY
CHIEF, DIVISION OF SURGICAL ONCOLOGY
DEPARTMENT OF SURGERY
UMDNJ-NEW JERSEY MEDICAL SCHOOL
NEWARK, NEW JERSEY

Arlene Bardeguez, M.D.
ASSOCIATE PROFESSOR OF OBSTETRICS AND
GYNECOLGY
DEPARTMENT OF OBSTETRICS AND
GYNECOLOGY
UMDNJ-NEW JERSEY MEDICAL SCHOOL
NEWARK, NEW JERSEY

Norman Hymowitz, Ph.D.
PROFESSOR OF PSYCHIATRY
DEPARTMENT OF PSYCHIATRY
UMDNJ-NEW JERSEY MEDICAL SCHOOL
NEWARK, NEW JERSEY

Iris Ayala, M.D.
ASSISTANT PROFESSOR OF OBSTETRICS AND
GYNECOLOGY
DEPARTMENT OF OBSTETRICS AND
GYNECOLOGY
UMDNJ-NEW JERSEY MEDICAL SCHOOL
NEWARK, NEW JERSEY

Ruby Rivera, M.D.
ASSISTANT PROFESSOR OF PEDIATRICS
DIVISION OF PEDIATRIC EMERGENCY
MEDICINE
MONTEFIORE MEDICAL CENTER
ALBERT EINSTEIN COLLEGE OF MEDICINE
BRONX, NEW YORK

Resident and Student Reviewers

Lydia Estanislao, M.D.
RESIDENT, DEPARTMENT OF NEUROLOGY
UMDNJ-NEW JERSEY MEDICAL SCHOOL
NEWARK, NEW JERSEY

William Sanchez
CLASS OF 1999
UMDNJ-NEW JERSEY MEDICAL SCHOOL
NEWARK, NEW JERSEY

Section A: The Examination

Introduction

"Very much more time must be...given to those practical portions of the examinations which afford the only true test of...fitness to enter the profession. The day of the theoretical test is over."

SIR WILLIAM OSLER, 1885

WHAT IS THE "OSCE"?

The **Objective Structured Clinical Examination** (OSCE) has been used by medical schools and residency programs since 1975 to assess clinical skills of students and residents. You (the examinee) perform clinical tasks in a series of test stations while interacting with a trained lay person called a standardized patient (SP). This standardized patient pretends to be a patient with a real illness. You must ask appropriate questions about the illness and perform a relevant and focused physical examination in a given amount of time. You leave the room and the standardized patient assesses your performance. The "SP" uses a checklist of clinical skills being tested and gives you credit if the proper question was asked or the necessary physical examination maneuver was performed adequately. Communication skills are also evaluated and comprise an important part of the checklist. The more items marked as complete on the checklist, the higher your grade.

The OSCE consists of 5 to 15 test stations (also called interactions or encounters). A station may last from five minutes, where you are asked to interpret an electrocardiogram or identify a heart murmur, to thirty minutes where you are asked to perform a history and physical examination. Some stations are followed by an interstation (also called a tag station) where you are given an additional amount of time to compose a SOAP note or to answer detailed questions about the encounter i.e., "What bloodwork will you order?", "What is your differential diagnosis?", "What is your next step in managing this patient?" Furthermore, an interstation may provide you with additional information like laboratory data or consultation reports requiring further interpretation and assessment.

The American Association of Medical Colleges (AAMC) and the Liaison Committee on Medical Education (LCME) have directed U.S. and Canadian medical schools to incorporate the OSCE into their curricula. The OSCE is used in all four years of medical school. The clinical disciplines use this examination to teach patient-centered skills and to measure student performance. Some medical schools require senior students to pass a multi-disciplinary OSCE as a requirement for graduation. In the near future, a standardized patient examination will be a requirement for licensure by the National Board of Medical Examiners.

WHAT IS THE "CSA"?

The **Clinical Skills Assessment** (CSA) is a standardized patient examination given to International Medical Graduates after completion of the USMLE 2 (United States Medical Licensing Examination Step 2). An international graduate wishing to practice medicine in the United States is now required to take this 6-hour long examination. The test consists of ten stations each lasting fifteen minutes.

At each station, you will encounter a different standardized patient (SP) who is a lay person trained to accurately portray a "real life" patient. You must ask the SP the appropriate questions to obtain the right history of present illness and then perform the accurate and focused physical examination. Throughout the history and physical examination, you are being graded on your interpersonal skills and proficiency in communication. After the interaction with the SP, you proceed to a ten-minute interstation to compose an accurate, organized, and legible written record of the encounter called the "patient note" (PN).

As per the CSA orientation manual, history-taking and performance of physical examination is considered data gathering ability (DG) and is evaluated by the standardized patient. The DG score is combined with the patient note score (PN). The health care professional trained to read the PN is rating the note based on your legibility, organizational skills, and interpretation of the data (pertinent positives and negatives, differential diagnosis, and work-up). The PN score is automatically reduced if you suggest any dangerous action. The DG and the PN scores are averaged over 10 stations so if you perform poorly at one test station, you may be able to compensate by performing well at another station. The DG score and the PN score are combined to form the first component of the CSA final grade called ICE (Integrated Clinical Encounter).

The SP will evaluate your interpersonal skills (IPS) and spoken English language proficiency (ENG). These two scores are combined to form the Communication Skills (COM) component of the final CSA grade. The IPS score is based on your interpersonal skills in interviewing (i.e., used open-ended questions), giving information to the patient (i.e., counseling), how you interacted with the patient (rapport) and your attitude during the interaction. The four IPS skills may be rated as unsatisfactory, marginally satisfactory, good, and excellent.

The ENG score is based on your grammar, pronunciation, and how difficult it is for the SP to understand you. The four ratings used for the ENG score are low, medium, high, and very high comprehensibility. An examinee who has taken the TSE (Test of Spoken English) and scored above 35, most likely, will have no difficulty with the CSA ENG score component.

A below average score on either the COM or ICE component of the CSA will result in a failure. Your overall score (pass or fail) will be reported to you within eight weeks of your exam date. Retake examinations are allowed three months after a failure.

The CSA is a multidisciplinary examination balancing the specialties of Internal Medicine, Surgery, Pediatrics, Obstetrics and Gynecology, Psychiatry, and Family Medicine. There is a mix of subacute, acute, and chronic problems. For the time being, it is given to ten candidates daily in Philadelphia, Pennsylvania at the Educational Commission for Foreign Medical Graduates (ECFMG) Clinical Skills Assessment Center at a non-refundable cost of $1200. Once you have registered for the CSA, the ECFMG sends you a comprehensive orientation manual and videotape that provides practical and useful information about the examination.

Who Is the Standardized (Simulated) Patient?

A standardized patient (SP) is a lay person who is trained to portray a specific clinical problem. An SP may be a healthy person or someone with a stable physical finding. It is important to remember that a standardized patient is not an actor. The SP memorizes a script like an actor but his/her main task is to critique the performance of each examinee.

SPs are chosen because of their intelligence and attention to detail. They remain objective and do not volunteer any information to examinees. They do not interrupt you while you are speaking or performing the physical examination. SPs are focused on your performance from the moment you walk into the testing room until the time you leave.

The SP accurately portrays the emotional or physical symptoms required for the test station. They are chosen for a particular interaction because of their understanding of the medical or ethical problem of the case. The roles played by SPs are diverse to challenge your ability to remain nonjudgemental and sensitive regardless of a patient's gender, race, intellect, sexual orientation, or ability to pay.

Just like a "real" patient, the SP will ask you specific questions about his/her presenting problem i.e., "Tell me Doctor, does this mean I have cancer?" or "Doctor, am I having a heart attack?" The SP is challenging you with these questions and they must not be ignored or avoided. The concerns of the SP must be addressed as you would for a "real" patient. If you do not know the answer to an SP's question, simply say you don't know.

All acceptable and unacceptable standardized patient behavior and dialogue is memorized by the SP. Maneuvers necessary for an accurate physical examination, when required for a specific case, are rehearsed to perfection. You, therefore, should expect a remarkably realistic and experienced SP.

During each test station, the standardized patient is evaluating you to assess if the tasks on the checklist are being met adequately (checklists are covered in Chapter 5). Your nonverbal and verbal behavior is critically observed. Is the doctor arrogant? Is the doctor indifferent? Is the doctor interested in my problem? Does the doctor look bored? Is the doctor empathetic? Does the doctor seem aware of my modesty during the physical examination? Keep in mind that the main objective of the SP is to assess your ability to obtain a focused history and physical examination while interacting effectively with a patient.

The Day of the Test

Prior to the start of the standardized patient examination, you are given a detailed orientation, usually on videotape, sometimes lasting one hour, explaining how you go from station to station and your role at the interstations. You always have sufficient time to travel from one place to another and read the instructions for the new test station so never aggravate yourself or others by rushing.

The standardized patient encounters take place in private rooms resembling either a physician's office or a hospital room. You should wear a white coat and bring a stethoscope. The rooms are equipped with gloves and the medical instruments necessary for the specific test station. The SP will be dressed appropriately depending on the location of the encounter. Testing rooms are equipped with video cameras which are hidden so as not to detract from the realism of the interaction. Do not waste time trying to look for video cameras, just assume they exist at every test station.

In most examinations, alarms or verbal announcements are used to signal the start and the end of a test station. Extra time is not allowed and standardized patients are instructed to stop the interaction upon hearing the "end of the station" signal. A warning signal, when only a few minutes are left at a station, is used by certain test centers to help you pace yourself. Wear a watch in case warning signals are not being used in your examination so you can check your pace at each encounter. When only a few minutes are left at a station, you must:

1. Complete any remaining tasks in the history or physical examination that are considered to be critical to the test station, and

2. Begin to achieve adequate closure with the standardized patient

The grade you receive for each interaction is based on the checklist completed by the standardized patient after you leave the encounter and, when applicable, your interstation written record which is reviewed by a qualified individual. The overall grade reflects your ability to gather the appropriate data while communicating and interacting effectively with each standardized patient.

The Day of the Test

Step 1

- Read "instructions to the examinee"
- Formulate a mental checklist
- 2-minute station

Step 2

- Obtain a history
- Do a focused physical exam
- Utilize interpersonal skills
- 15-minute station

The Day of the Test

Step 3

The OSCE Interstation	The CSA Patient Note
• Pertinent history	• Pertinent history
• Key physical findings	• Key physical findings
• List differential diagnosis	• List up to five differential diagnoses
• Interpret lab data	• List five diagnostic tests/studies needed
• Order more lab tests	• 10-minute station
• Indicate therapy	
• Discuss follow up plans	
• 10-minute station	

Step 4

• Proceed to the next patient

Beginning the Standardized Patient Encounter

"A bad beginning makes a bad ending."

EURIPIDES

Instructions to the examinee are posted outside each examination room or are in the patient's chart at bedside and must be read prior to starting a test station. You must read the instructions carefully since they will reveal the type of encounter (new patient or follow-up patient) and the location of the patient (office, on the telephone, emergency room, hospital room, home visit). Important background information about the patient will be included in the instructions when relevant like age, past medical problems, and occupation.

The background information will help you prepare for performing the tasks to be evaluated at the test station. The instructions will inform you of the patient's chief complaint and reason for seeing the doctor. Vital signs will be included in the instructions if they are required for the station.

After you finish reading the instructions, you should consider the skills being tested and plan your patient interaction strategy. Entering the test station prepared to begin makes you appear confident and knowledgeable and an SP tends to remember a good first impression.

The doorway instructions will state what is required at each test station. For example, you may be told to perform a focused history and relevant physical examination within fifteen minutes. The instructions may specifically ask that you not perform a pelvic or breast examination. You may be asked to discuss the differential diagnosis and work-up with a patient. Your tasks at each station are clearly stated and you should not deviate from what is required. The identical instructions found outside the examination room are posted inside each room in case you need a reminder about the tasks, vital signs, or presenting problem. Do not be embarrassed to look at them in the room if you need a reminder.

There are certain instances, when a patient complaint has nothing to do with the "real" reason the patient has come to the hospital or office. Drug seeking patients, for example, might present to the emergency room complaining of severe migraine headaches or kidney stones. Sometimes the background information provided in the instructions to the examinee, if read carefully, will help expose these underlying problems.

Developing the Checklist

"Where observation is concerned, chance favors only the prepared mind."

LOUIS PASTEUR

Each test station has specific objectives or checklist items that reflect the skills to be critically assessed by the standardized patient. In some testing situations, there is an observer in the room with the standardized patient either in full view of you or standing behind a one way mirror. In this case, the observer, who is often a physician, will complete the checklist. This frees up the SP to concentrate fully on the scenario. If the standardized patient is alone in the room, as in the majority of test situations, the SP will complete the checklist after you leave the room.

A checklist is usually twenty-five items and is restricted to the skills being tested at each test station. The checklist is, in actuality, the test and is never revealed to you. It consists of the tasks that must be accomplished successfully by you during a standardized patient encounter. These checklist items may be in the areas of history, physical examination, or communication.

In order to perform well on the standardized patient examination, you must learn how to mentally formulate the "secret" checklist at the beginning of each test station. After obtaining the chief complaint for the encounter, you should focus on the presenting problem and mentally decide which specific parts of the history of present illness, past medical history, social history, family history, and physical examination are essential for the particular encounter.

Regardless of the task you are asked to perform at a test station, approach every standardized patient as if he or she is a "real" patient using your best bedside manner because communication skills may be the "real" task being assessed. The standardized patient's perception of you as a physician is vital to performing well at each test station.

Following is an example of a checklist for a test station:

1. The instructions given at the start of the test station reveal a chief complaint of abdominal pain with fever in a 31-year old man.

2. You are asked to obtain a history and a brief physical examination in 15 minutes.

3. Try to develop your own "mental checklist".

4. What is important to ask and do for this patient?

5. Check your "mental checklist" against the actual examination checklist.

6. Would you have passed this test station?

SP CHECKLIST FOR MR. JOHN SMITH

Responses by the imaginary standardized patient appear in parenthesis
after each checklist item.

History of Present Illness. The Examinee Asked About:

___1.　onset of pain ("4 hours ago.")

___2.　location of pain ("Right lower quadrant and around the umbilicus.")

___3.　quality of pain ("Deep and burning.")

___4.　any aggravating factors ("Deep breath, movement, food.")

___5.　any alleviating factors ("Lying still helps.")

___6.　severity of pain ("On a scale of 1 to 10 where 10 is the worst, this is a 9.")

___7.　any association with vomiting ("Two episodes at home.")

___8.　any blood in the vomitus ("No.")

___9.　any association with a change in bowel movements ("No diarrhea or constipation.")

___10.　any blood in the stools ("No.")

___11.　any urinary problems ("No.")

___12.　any past medical problems ("No.")

___13.　any medication use ("No.")

___14.　any alcohol abuse ("No.")

___15.　any allergies ("None.")

Physical Examination. The Examinee:

___16.　listened for bowel sounds over all 4 quadrants (normal bowel sounds heard).

___17.　palpated gently throughout my abdomen (no pain).

___18.　palpated deeply throughout my abdomen (pain localized to right lower side of abdomen).

___19.　elicited rebound tenderness (severe pain when letting go of right lower abdomen).

___20.　attempted to elicit a psoas or obturator sign (both are positive for appendicitis).

___21.　checked for costovertebral angle tenderness (none).

___22.　asked to do a rectal examination (after examinee asks to perform rectal exam, SP gives card revealing results of examination; card states: no masses or tenderness; fecal occult blood negative).

Communication Skills. The Examinee:

___23.　washed his/her hands before the start of the examination.

___24.　introduced self warmly as he or she came into the room.

___25.　seemed to care about my discomfort and pain.

___26.　discussed initial diagnostic impression (plausible diagnosis is appendicitis).

___27.　discussed initial diagnostic tests that would be done (bloodwork, radiographs).

___28.　discussed initial management and plan (intravenous fluids, surgery).

___29.　discussed prognosis (excellent).

___30.　addressed my concerns about surgery.

Approach to the Standardized Patient

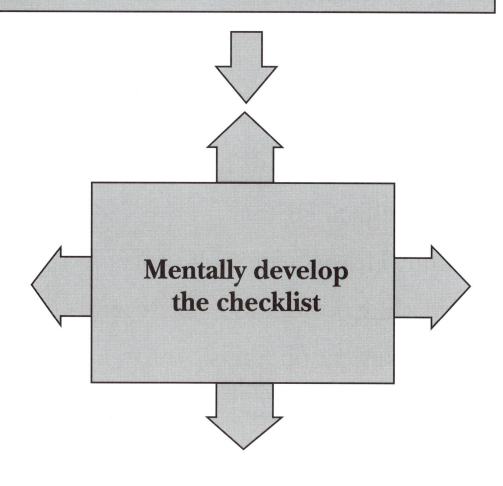

Read the
instructions to the examinee

Focus on the patient's problem

Mentally develop
the checklist

**Develop the following Checklist items
for each patient:**

- History of Present Illness (Pertinent +/-)

- Past Medical History

- Family History/Social History

- Physical Examination (Pertinent +/-)

- Communication Skills

The History

"Much unhappiness has come into the world because of bewilderment and things left unsaid."

FYODOR DOSTOYEVSKY

When you enter a test station introduce yourself to the standardized patient. Begin the interview with an open-ended question like "How can I help you today?" or "What brings you to the hospital today?" Greet the patient warmly by shaking hands and smiling.

Start building upon the chief complaint given in the examinee instructions by eliciting accurate information in a logical and systematic fashion. For example, a common standardized patient complaint is pain. An SP may have abdominal pain, chest pain, or a headache. You should ask the seven pertinent pain-related questions:

1. onset of pain
2. location of pain
3. quality of pain
4. severity of pain
5. alleviating factors
6. aggravating factors
7. associated symptoms

An examinee should probe into areas of past medical history and family history when appropriate. If social history is relevant, all habits should be investigated including the use of tobacco, alcohol, illicit drugs, and caffeine. The patient's lifestyle including exercise habits, sexual history, diet, hobbies, travel, occupation and environmental exposure to toxins (even radon) should be included if relevant to the chief complaint. Personal life problems and emotional stresses should be explored when necessary.

Try and use open-ended questions when possible and never repeat the same questions. Demonstrate appropriate listening skills like good eye contact and a leaning forward posture at eye level. Be silent when necessary and try not to interrupt the patient when he/she is speaking. Nod your head, once in a while, to let the SP know you are listening.

You will want to be as thorough as possible and obtain a complete history at each test station but you need to stay focused and within areas of appropriate questioning. Do not make a hasty diagnosis and end the interview prematurely. Consider the differential diagnosis for each presenting problem.

Make sure you address the following four questions at each test station:

1. What organ system am I dealing with?
2. What are the likely causes of the problem?
3. What risk factors could have contributed to the problem?
4. What complications of the problem exist in this patient?

At the end of the interview, you must achieve closure by summarizing the patient problem, soliciting questions or concerns and discussing the plan. Remember to say "thank-you" and "good-bye" in an appreciative manner before leaving each test station.

The History

**Make sure you address the following
four questions at each test station:**

1. What **organ system** am I dealing with?

2. What are the **likely causes** of the problem?

3. What **risk factors** could have contributed to the problem?

4. What **complications** of the problem exist in this patient?

**To be systematic and ensure all aspects of the
complaint of "pain" are covered, ask:**

The seven pain-related questions

1. onset and chronology

2. location and radiation

3. quality of pain

4. severity of pain

5. alleviating factors

6. precipitating factors

7. associated symptoms

The Physical Examination

If directed to perform a physical examination, utilize the data you have gathered from the history to keep your physical examination focused on the chief complaint. The standardized patient mentally critiques your physical examination skills and will judge whether you have performed the essential maneuvers and techniques appropriately. *This is a test not only of what you know and do but how you do it.*

Although the physical exam should be focused, you must always be thorough. For example, if an SP is portraying a college student with a sore throat and the history leads you to a diagnosis of mononucleosis, you should perform an abdominal exam, looking for hepatosplenomegaly, as well as the throat examination.

The standardized patient, in real life, may have the abnormal physical finding you elicit (i.e., a heart murmur, gallop, hepatomegaly, or splenomegaly) or simply have been trained to imitate a particular finding (Murphy's sign, Kernig's sign). Some physical findings are simulated with make-up (jaundice). In certain OSCE situations, an SP, without the physical finding, may provide you with a card or picture detailing the results of the physical examination after you have completed the exam appropriately. You should review this information carefully.

Be prepared to perform the following categories of the physical examination:

1. vital signs including orthostatic changes if necessary

2. ears, eyes, nose, mouth and neck examination including proper use of an ophthalmoscope and otoscope; proper examination of the thyroid

3. upper and lower extremity musculoskeletal examinations

4. lung examination including the use of proper sequence (inspection, fremitus, dullness, auscultation) and listening anteriorly or at the right midaxillary line to auscultate the right middle lobe

5. heart examination including palpation of the point of maximum impulse; auscultation over all valve areas and listening for radiation of murmurs when indicated; performing augmentation maneuvers including valsalva and inspiration when indicated

6. abdominal examination including the use of proper sequence (inspection, auscultation over all quadrants, percussion of the liver at the midclavicular line and midsternal line, and palpation); evaluating for splenomegaly by percussion or palpation; observing Cullen's sign or Turner's sign;

eliciting a Murphy's sign, obturator sign, or psoas sign; eliciting for costovertebral angle tenderness if appropriate

7. breast (with axillary node palpation), rectal, pelvic, or genital examinations should be requested by the OSCE examinee when appropriate to the case; the SP will tell the examinee it was completed and will present a card stating the results of the requested examination; an examinee should never hesitate to ask permission to perform these examinations when relevant (most standardized patient examinations including the CSA will not require the actual breast, pelvic, rectal, or genital examination; Ob/Gyn and Urology disciplines may utilize patient instructors who allow students to perform these actual examinations).

8. neurologic examination including cranial nerves (I-XII), motor (tone and strength), sensory (position sense, touch, and vibration) and cerebellar (finger-nose-finger, heel-shin and rapid alternating movements) examinations; assessing deep tendon reflexes; eliciting Babinski sign; testing for a Romberg sign; eliciting Kernig's sign and Brudzinski's sign for meningitis

9. mental status examination including the use of a mini-mental examination or alcohol screening instrument when appropriate

10. functional assessment of an elderly patient to document impairments such as vision loss, hearing loss, immobility, frailty, and gait disturbances

Let the patient know when you are going to begin the physical examination. Wash your hands before examining every patient. Show consideration for the patient's discomfort and pain. Do not repeat painful maneuvers unless absolutely necessary. Keep the patient draped as much as possible during the examination and ask the patient for permission prior to touching him/her or removing any clothing. Use the examination table pull-out extension if you wish the patient to recline. Tell the patient what you plan to do and explain findings when appropriate. Ask the patient to dress as soon as the physical examination is over and assist the patient off the examination table. You should not begin a discussion with the patient if he/she is partially undressed.

The Physical Examination

Vital Signs	Blood pressure, pulse rate, respiratory rate, orthostatics
HEENT Exam	Fundoscopic and otoscopic exam, thyroid palpation
Pulmonary Exam	IFDA (Inspection, Fremitus, Dullness, Auscultation)
Cardiac Exam	PMI, auscultation, augmentation maneuvers (e.g., Valsalva, inspiration)
Abdominal Exam	IAPP (Inspection, Auscultation, Percussion, Palpation), Cullen's, Turner's, Murphy's signs, obturator and psoas signs, CVA tenderness, splenomegaly
Neurological Exam	Cranial nerves, motor, sensory, cerebellar, DTRs, Babinski, Romberg, Kernig's and Brudzinski's signs
Mental Status	Mini-mental exam, CAGE screening
Geriatric Functional Assessment	ADL, IADL assessment, vision loss, hearing loss, mobility and gait disturbance, "get up and go test"

Don't repeat painful maneuvers

The Physical Examination

- Do not do a comprehensive physical exam

- Do a focused physical examination based on the presenting problem

- Perform maneuvers appropriately

- Don't repeat painful maneuvers

- Show consideration for the patient's discomfort

This is a test not only of what you know and do, but of how you do it.

CHAPTER 8

Physical Examination Findings That May Be Seen in a Standardized Patient

HEENT
Hearing loss/ visual loss
Ptosis

Cardiovascular System
Bruits (abdominal, carotid, renal, thyroid)
Chest Pain - reproducible with palpation
Hypotension/hypertension (using a fake cuff)
Tachycardia/bradycardia

Respiratory System
Airway obstruction
Cheyne-Stokes respirations
Cyanosis
Diminshed breath sounds/pneumothorax
Hemoptysis
Hoarseness
Kussmaul respirations
Shortness of breath/dyspnea/tachypnea
Wheezing/stridor

Gastrointestinal System
Abdominal tenderness/rebound/guarding
Breath odor of DKA
Caput medusae/fetor hepaticus
Costovertebral-angle tenderness
Cullen's sign/Turner's sign
Melena/hematochezia
Murphy's sign
Pregnancy
Psoas sign/obturator sign
Vomiting/hematemesis

Extremities
Casts for fractures
Deep venous thrombosis
Joint restriction/joint immobility
Joint warmth/joint erythema
Pretibial myxedema

Psychiatry
Anxiety/panic attack
Anger/hostility
Dementia/delirium/depression
Hypomania/mania
Altered mental status/confusion

Neurologic System
Dilated pupil/nonreactive pupil
Alcohol intoxication/alcohol withdrawal
Aphasia
Ataxia/incoordination
Babinski sign/extensor plantar reflex
Asterixis
Brudzinski's sign/Kernig's sign
Chorea
Coma/unresponsiveness
Decerebrate/decorticate rigidity
Dizziness/vertigo
"Doll's Eye" response
Dysarthria
Facial nerve paralysis/Bell's palsy
Gait abnormalities
Hyperactive tendon reflexes/clonus
Muscle rigidity/cogwheel rigidity
Muscle spasms/spasticity
Muscle weakness
Nuchal rigidity
Photophobia
Romberg sign
Seizures
Tinel's sign/Phalen's sign
Tremor

Skin
Anaphylaxis
Allergic reaction/hives
Bruising/ecchymosis/petechiae
Burns
Cellulitis
Diaphoresis/perspiration
Janeway lesions/Osler's nodes
Jaundice
Lyme disease rash/erythema chronicum migrans
Malar rash
Palmar erythema
Photosensitivity
Rashes
Skin track marks
Spider telangiectasia
Surgical scars
Tophi

CHAPTER 9

Five Simple Steps to Effective Communication

Expect your communication skills to be assessed *continuously* during the standardized patient examination. You should expect that certain stations will be devoted totally to communication, i.e., when you are instructed to deliver bad news to a patient at a test station. At other stations, the standardized patient will observe you throughout the performance of the history and, if required, the physical examination, then reflect upon your effectiveness in overall communication, language proficiency and use of interpersonal skills. These are essential tasks that, if not performed to the satisfaction of the standardized patient, will result in a poor outcome for the test station. You will be proficient in communicating with patients by following the five simple steps outlined below:

1. **EXPLAIN YOUR FINDINGS**   You must make an effort to educate every patient about the chief complaint by clearly explaining the features of the disease or problem. You must explain the pertinent findings on physical examination and discuss the course you expect the problem to take. Try to identify the patient's emotional response and understanding of the problem then offer your support and reassurance. Do not give the patient a premature diagnosis. If you are not sure what the diagnosis is, simply say so. Don't give the patient false information or false reassurance.

2. **DISCUSS THE PROGNOSIS**   The Prognosis should be stated clearly even if the patient fails to bring this up. Reassure the patient when and if recovery is expected. You should discuss available family and community support systems in the case of severe or terminal illness. Discuss the patient's feelings about the prognosis and help the patient cope if faced with a poor prognosis.

3. **OUTLINE THE PLAN**   You must counsel the patient regarding compliance and convince him/her to undergo the necessary care. You should clearly outline the steps of care and check to see if the patient is planning to cooperate with the plan. Discuss the patient's feelings regarding the plan. Make it clear to the patient that you will continue to participate in his/her care even when consultation is necessary.

4. **INVOLVE THE PATIENT IN THE PLAN**   You must explain how the patient can assist in his/her own care (teaching a diabetic patient to check his/her own finger-stick or teaching an asthmatic patient to follow peak flow meter readings). Lifestyle changes (safe sexual practices, diet, exercise) or risk factor reduction (tobacco cessation, limiting sun exposure) requires the patient to commit to change. You must invite the patient to actively participate in his/her own management and plan.

5. **EDUCATE THE PATIENT**   You must incorporate the principles of preventive health care and counsel the standardized patient appropriately. Examinees should demonstrate fundamental knowledge of these measures during the standardized patient examination.

Throughout the performance of the five communication tasks, you should use appropriate language and avoid medical terminology. Your approach to the patient should be organized and systematic. Because of time constraints, you must stay on track to meet all five of the communication test objectives, but transitions from one area to another should be hardly noticeable. Listen to the standardized patient carefully and allow him/her to complete statements without interruption. If you must interrupt the patient, as in the case of a manic patient or an overly talkative patient, do so tactfully.

Ralph Waldo Emerson said that "when the eyes say one thing and the tongue another, a practiced man relies on the language of the first", therefore, be flexible enough to follow upon a standardized patient's nonverbal clues by responding appropriately to the emotional situation. Do not continue to march through the communication tasks ignoring the emotional state of the standardized patient. Stopping to address the emotion may not allow you enough time to complete all the communication tasks but, in the long run, doing so, will reflect positively upon your overall performance. While exchanging information with the standardized patient always convey a sense of warmth and show empathy, concern, and consideration for the SP's feelings. Be sensitive to his/her pain and dignity.

Lack of good communication skills can be the downfall of an examinee because these skills, you should assume, are being evaluated at each test station. It is difficult to remember about good communication when you are trying to be thorough and get the job done especially with the time constraints at each test station but failure to interact appropriately with the standardized patient will have an adverse affect on your overall performance. In every encounter with a standardized patient, always remember the five simple steps to effective communication:

E - **E**xplain your findings

P - discuss **P**rognosis

P - outline the **P**lan

I - **I**nvolve the patient in the plan

E - **E**ducate the patient

Five Simple Steps
to Effective Communication

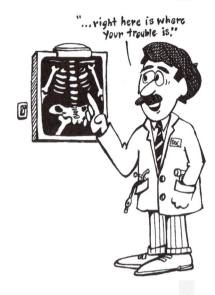

"...right here is where your trouble is."

E - **E**xplain your findings
  - Features of the disease
  - Pertinent physical exam findings
  - Don't give a premature diagnosis

P - discuss **P**rognosis
  - Prognosis should be stated clearly
  - Help the patient cope

P - outline the **P**lan
  - Counsel the patient regarding compliance
  - You and the patient are allies

I - **I**nvolve the patient in the plan
  - Lifestyle changes
  - Risk factor reduction

E - **E**ducate the patient
  - Preventive measures

"We'll work together to make you better."

"Thanks!"

Preventive Measures to Discuss with the Standardized Patient

1. Alcohol, drug, and tobacco counseling

2. Cancer screening

   • Breast self-examination, mammography, and pap smear
   • Testicular and prostate examination
   • Fecal occult blood testing (FOBT)
   • Screening sigmoidoscopy
   • Skin examination

3. Infectious disease prevention

   • Annual PPD
   • Safe sexual practices
   • Vaccinations (influenza, pneumococcal, hepatitis B, MMR, diptheria, tetanus)

4. Proper diet and exercise

   • To prevent heart disease, diabetes, cancer, hypertension, and osteoporosis

5. Methods of stress reduction (when necessary)

6. Environmental and occupational hazards (when appropriate)

7. Injury prevention

   • Wearing automobile seatbelts
   • Using bicycle helmets properly

Improving Your
Interpersonal Skills Quickly

HISTORY TAKING SKILLS:

- Use open ended questions i.e., "What is troubling you ?" "Can you tell me about your symptoms?"
- Use pauses; allow the patient time to think and react.
- Never interrupt the patient when he/she is speaking.
- Go smoothly from one area of discussion to another.
- Use listening techniques like good eye contact, an open (arms uncrossed) leaning forward posture at eye level.
- Repeat last statements made by the standardized patient so he/she will continue speaking.
- Use plain, understandable language.
- Do not be in a rush; let the patient answer a question before you ask another question.
- Be open to questions; never avoid or ignore a question.
- Show interest in the patient's story; never act bored.

PHYSICAL EXAMINATION SKILLS:

- Wash your hands in front of the patient.
- Do not examine the patient through the gown but keep the patient draped as much as possible.
- Ask the patient for permission prior to touching him/her or removing clothing.
- Tell the patient what you plan to do.
- Explain your physical examination findings.
- Be sensitive to the patient's pain, suffering and discomfort.
- Never begin a discussion with the patient partially undressed.
- Never repeat painful maneuvers.
- Help the patient on and off the exam table.

COMMUNICATION AND INTERPERSONAL SKILLS:

- Introduce yourself to the patient warmly; shake hands.
- Acknowledge the emotion the patient is showing, then discuss the emotion, i.e., "You seem sad."
- Don't give the patient more information than he/she can handle.
- Demonstrate empathy when appropriate.
- Demonstrate an attitude of confidence, reliability, and warmth.
- Seek the patient's point of view; inquire about any concerns the patient may have.
- Never be judgemental or confrontational with a difficult patient.
- Establish a partnership with the patient; i.e., "We'll work together to make you better."
- Do not give the patient false reassurance.
- Praise the patient, i.e., "You are coping very well with this illness."
- Provide the patient with closure.

Don't give the patient more
information than he can handle.

Wash your hands.

Show interest in the
patient's story. Never act bored.

Use plain, understandable language.

Never lecture the patient.

Don't rush the patient.

Introduce yourself.

Listen to the patient.

Don't embarrass
the patient.

Never give
false reassurance.

Common Communication Challenges

"It's either easy or impossible."

SALVADOR DALI

An examinee should be prepared to manage at least one difficult communication problem during a standardized patient examination. Below are the more common communication challenges encountered on a standardized patient examination.

1. **DELIVERING BAD NEWS TO A PATIENT**   This station may require you to discuss an abnormal mammogram report, an abnormal pap smear result, or inform a patient that he/she has cancer, HIV/AIDS, or Alzheimer's Disease. In these encounters, you must quickly establish good rapport and address the specific needs and emotions of the patient. Try to summarize the problem and talk about prognosis but only if you feel the patient can handle it. You must stop often and acknowledge the patient's distress. Inquire about the patient's thoughts and concerns. Talk about the patient's support system such as family or close friends. Offer to help the patient inform loved ones about the medical condition. Give a step by step follow-up plan and offer your ongoing support. If the patient is able to discuss it, talk about a living will or an advance directive. Always inquire at the end of the interview: "Is there anything we didn't cover?"

2. **THE DECISION TO FOREGO TREATMENT**   This test station may be a patient refusing a life-saving blood transfusion due to religious beliefs, a patient refusing surgery, intubation or resuscitation or a patient requesting removal of life-sustaining treatment such as a ventilator or feeding tube. At this test station you must inquire about the patient's emotional well-being to ensure the patient is not depressed, confused, or angry. You must make sure the patient understands his/her disease and the consequences of the decision (death). Inquire if family members or loved ones are aware of the decision. When there is a substitute decision-maker for the patient, make sure you are speaking to the appropriate person. Agree to honor the request and offer the patient support from a psychiatrist or person from the clergy. Let the patient know the decision may be changed in the future if the patient so desires. Ask about other life-sustaining treatments such as oxygen or antibi-

otics. Describe your intentions to the patient clearly ("I will go to the chart and write the do not resuscitate order."). This test station requires empathy and good closure.

3. **THE NEED TO TELL THE TRUTH**   This station may require triadic interviewing if a physician is asked by a standardized patient family member not to tell a patient about an illness. During this interaction, you should inquire about the reasons for the request and inform the family member that the patient has the right to know about the medical problem. Let the family member know that if the patient asks directly about his/her health, ethically, you must tell the truth. If the patient does not ask, you will not give the patient any information the family member feels the patient cannot handle. At this test station, you must never promise not to tell the patient.

4. **THE NONCOMPLIANT PATIENT**   These patients are usually misinformed about their disease and the reasons for the medications. You must make sure the patient understands the illness and why the medications are being prescribed. Discuss the reasons for noncompliance with the patient and switch to an alternate medication if side effects are responsible. You must interest the patient in his/her own condition and enter into an agreement of compliance with the patient. Schedule follow-up visits and praise the patient's progress. If a patient prefers a nontraditional therapy, such as acupuncture or hypnosis, you must counsel the patient on the need for traditional therapy along with the alternative method. Respect the patient's right to individuality.

5. **THE BATTERED PATIENT**   This standardized patient may present to the physician's office with a minor complaint. The astute examinee will obtain the history of violence during the interview or notice bruises on the patient. Regardless of the presenting complaint, if you notice bruises on any patient, ask specifically about violence in the home (spousal abuse, elder abuse or child abuse depending on the test station). Inform the patient that domestic violence is illegal and that police involvement helps prevent further abuse. Inquire about weapons in the home. In cases of spousal abuse, talk about the children and inform the patient that violence in a home affects the future behavior of children. Acknowledge to the wife that it is difficult leaving an abusive husband. Show concern for the safety of the patient and inquire about available support systems. Offer your own support,

counseling and follow-up. Be prepared to discuss domestic violence support systems in the community.

6. **THE ISSUE OF CONFIDENTIALITY** A good example of this is an adolescent requesting contraception who does not wish her parents to know. First, you must discuss the benefits and risks of contraception with the adolescent. If you feel the adolescent patient has the competency and judgment of an adult, you can prescribe contraception and not share the information with the parents. If the parents wish to know why the daughter visited the physician, you must clearly inform the parents of the daughter's right to confidentiality. Try to convince the parents to discuss the issue directly with the daughter. Offer to counsel the family together as a solution to improving communication. Keep in mind that the parent-physician relationship is as confidential as the daughter-physician relationship. You must not divulge information about the parents' visit to the daughter.

7. **THE OVERTALKATIVE PATIENT** The talkative, hypomanic or manic patient is very difficult to interrupt but you must do so tactfully without sacrificing rapport. With this kind of patient, it is often better to use the close-ended style of questioning. As difficult as it may seem, since the standardized patient will not let you get a word in edge-wise, try to remain in control of the interview. Avoid becoming frustrated, angry and impatient. Focus on obtaining an accurate history and physical examination.

8. **THE ALCOHOLIC PATIENT** You must identify this issue during a routine history and physical examination. The patient may complain of tremors, insomnia, blackouts, frequent falls, weight loss, sexual dysfunction, depression or problems with personal relationships. The patient may smell intoxicated or appear intoxicated during the interview. The spouse may accompany the patient to inform the physician of the drinking problem. You must address the alcohol abuse in a nonjudgemental and nonconfrontational manner. Inquire as to why the patient drinks. Ask about the frequency and quantity of alcohol consumed by the patient daily. Ask about a family history of alcoholism. Inquire about attempts to stop drinking in the past. Ask about stresses in the patient's life that may be contributing to the drinking and the relapses. Identify the patient in denial. When necessary, integrate the **CAGE** questionnaire into the interview ("Have you ever attempted to **C**ut down on your drinking?, Have people **A**nnoyed you by criticizing

your drinking?, Have you felt **G**uilty about your drinking?, Do you need an **E**ye-opener first thing in the morning to cure a hangover or steady your nerves?"). Tell the patient you have confidence in his/her ability to stop drinking. Ask the patient if he/she is willing to work on the problem then discuss specific treatment options (support groups, hospitalization for withdrawal, outpatient counseling, medications). Negotiate a plan and offer your continuous understanding and support.

9. **THE SUBSTANCE ADDICTED PATIENT**   In treating a drug abuser, including the drug seeking patient, you must control your own biases and remain respectful. Try to appear comfortable discussing the drug use and initiate the topic if you notice needle track marks on the standardized patient. Inquire about the pattern of use and explore the concerns the patient may have about stopping. Discuss the health risks of drug use. Inquire about the patient's support system and develop a clear plan for management of the drug problem. Offer the patient choices for detoxification (hospitalization, outpatient management) and state clearly that you will treat withdrawal symptoms. Discuss follow-up visits to assess progress and to reinforce the efforts made by the patient.

10. **THE SMOKER**   You must inquire about nicotine addiction whether it be cigarette smoking, exposure to passive smoke, or use of smokeless tobacco. On physical examination, if you observe nicotine stains on the fingernails of the standardized patient, bring up the topic of smoking cessation. Ask about the number of years the patient has been smoking and the number of cigarettes per day. Inquire as to how many times the patient attempted to quit smoking and explore the reasons for relapse. Educate the patient about nicotine as a risk factor for coronary artery disease, cancer, and lung disease. Ask the patient specifically if he/she is willing to stop. Show the patient that you have confidence in his/her ability to stop ("You can do it!"). Discuss the strategies to quit smoking (gum, patch, pills, behavioral modification). Negotiate a plan with the patient and discuss follow-up for monitoring progress. Remember to give the stop smoking message to every standardized patient who smokes.

11. **THE PATIENT WITH SPECIAL EMOTIONAL PROBLEMS**   This category is broad and diverse and includes the hostile patient ("I'm going to sue you.") and the anxious patient ("This headache is so bad, I'm sure I

have a brain tumor."). These patients still require a thorough interview and, if appropriate, a focused physical examination. These patients need a great amount of patience, empathy and reassurance. Offer understanding and do your best to address the patient's concerns.

12. **THE PATIENT NEEDING CONSENT FOR A PROCEDURE** You must obtain informed consent by explaining step by step how the procedure is performed. Explain the purpose of the procedure and the possible complications. Explain the indications, contraindications, risks and benefits of the procedure using plain and concise language. Tell the patient what his/her experience during the procedure will be and assure the patient that his/her comfort during the procedure is a priority. Respect the decision of a patient to refuse a procedure. You should be prepared to obtain informed consent for arterial line placement, arthrocentesis, autopsy, organ donation bronchoscopy, central line venous catheterization placement, flexible sigmoidoscopy, liver biopsy, lumbar puncture, paracentesis, Swan-Ganz catheter placement, and thoracentesis.

COMMON COMMUNICATION CHALLENGES

Delivering bad news to a patient	• Abnormal mammogram or pap smear • Positive HIV test • Recently diagnosed cancer or Alzheimer's disease
The patient who decides to forego treatment	• Patient refuses life-saving surgery, blood transfusion, intubation, resuscitation or feeding • Patient requests removal of life support
The patient's right to be informed	• The patient has the right to know the truth about his/her disease and its prognosis
The noncompliant patient	• Make sure the patient understands the illness and the need for medication • Interest the patient in his/her condition and discuss the reasons for non-compliance
The battered patient	• May be spousal, elder or child abuse • Carefully obtain a history of violence, note bruises, or evidence of trauma
The patient's right to confidentiality	• Respect the confidentiality of the patient-physician relationship
The over-talkative patient	• In the manic or hypomanic patient, tactfully interrupt and use close-ended style of questioning • Avoid becoming impatient or frustrated
The alcoholic patient	• Address the alcohol abuse issue in a non-judgemental and non-confrontational manner • Integrate the CAGE questionnaire into the interview
The substance addicted patient	• Offer detoxification choices • State that you will treat withdrawal symptoms • Control your own biases
The smoker	• Discuss strategies to quit smoking
The patient with special emotional problems	• The hostile or anxious patient • Address the patient's concerns
Obtaining informed consent	• Explain the indication, risks, benefits, and possible complications using plain and concise language

The Interstation or Patient Note: How to Pass the Written Part

THE OSCE INTERSTATION:

After completing an encounter with a standardized patient, you may be required to go to an interstation (also called a tag station) to compose a written record of the interaction. While at the interstation, you should recollect any "mental notes" of the standardized patient encounter and compose a concise, thorough and legible essay.

Sometimes, these interstations will ask specific questions about the encounter (i.e., differential diagnosis, tests you would order, management) or ask for interpretation of bloodwork, body fluid results, pulmonary function tests, chest radiographs, or electrocardiograms. The purpose of the interstation is to measure the fund of knowledge, clinical judgement, and reasoning skills of an examinee.

At each interstation, justify your differential diagnosis, treatment, and plan. Defend your plausible diagnosis by describing the key history and physical examination findings pertinent to your thinking. Your diagnostic evaluations should be cost effective and appropriate to the case. Formulate a therapeutic plan and explain the risks and benefits of treatment. Discuss prognosis and how the patient will be involved in the decision making process regarding therapeutic options, future management and quality of life issues.

THE CSA PATIENT NOTE (PN):

As per the CSA manual, each fifteen minute encounter with a standardized patient is followed by a ten minute patient note (PN) interstation. This note must contain the pertinent positives and negatives (relating to the presenting problem) obtained during the history-taking including relevant information about the past medical history, social history, family history, and review of systems. The pertinent positives and negatives found on physical examination must also be discussed in the PN. You are then asked to list up to five diagnostic possibilities, in order of likelihood, and up to five diagnostic studies you would order (you must also explain the rationale for test ordering). The CSA interstation does not require any further test interpretation. You are not required to discuss treatment (including consultation, hospitalization, or therapeutics). The PN should be an organized, logical, and legible note containing accurate information regarding the patient's history, physical examination, differential diagnosis, and diagnostic work-up.

OSCE INTERSTATION: BE PREPARED TO INTERPRET COMMON DIAGNOSTIC TESTS

Blood Smears	microcytosis, macrocytosis, hypersegmented neutrophils, atypical lymphocytes, rouleau formation, sickle cells, target cells, basophilic stippling, eosinophils, fragmented cells, elliptocytes, normal red blood cells, normal platelets, Howell-Jolly bodies, Heinz bodies, Auer rods, Reed-Sternberg cells, malaria parasites, plasma cells, acute lymphocytic leukemia, chronic lymphocytic leukemia, acute myelocytic leukemia, chronic myelocytic leukemia
Urine Sediments	uric acid crystals, calcium oxalate crystals, white blood cells, red blood cells, white blood cell casts, red blood cell casts, waxy casts, bacteria, dirty brown casts, oval fat bodies
Bacteriological Stains of Body Fluids	Streptococcus, Staphylococcus, *Neisseria meningitidis*, *Neisseria gonorrhoeae*, *Haemophilus influenzae*, gram-negative rods, fungi, *Mycobacterium tuberculosis*, Trichomonas, *Gardnerella vaginitis*
Chest Radiographs	normal chest radiograph, lobar pneumonia, lung abscess, tuberculosis, pleural effusion, interstitial infiltrates, hilar adenopathy, pneumothorax, solitary pulmonary nodule, metastatic disease to the lungs, congestive heart failure, cardiomegaly, pericardial effusion, mediastinal mass, mastectomy radiograph
Other Radiographs	lateral neck films for epiglottitis, KUB for kidney stones, pancreatic calcifications, sentinel loop, colon cut-off sign, subdiaphragmatic free air, esophagram, bowing of the legs (rickets)
Electrocardiograms	normal electrocardiogram, acute myocardial infarction, myocardial ischemia, left axis deviation, right axis deviation, left bundle branch block, right bundle branch block, hyperkalemia, hypocalcemia, pericarditis, pericardial tamponade (low voltage, electrical alternans), atrial flutter, atrial fibrillation, supraventricular tachycardia, Wolff-Parkinson-White syndrome, sinus tachycardia, sinus bradycardia, first- second-degree and complete heart block, premature atrial contractions, premature ventricular contractions, ventricular tachycardia
Echocardiograms	mitral valve prolapse, aortic stenosis, mitral stenosis, pericardial effusion
Mammograms	normal study, abnormal calcific densities consistent with malignancy, fibrocystic breast disease
Sonograms	cholelithiasis, intrauterine pregnancy, ectopic pregnancy
Heart Sounds	normal splitting of S2, abnormal splitting of S2, murmurs of aortic stenosis, aortic regurgitation, mitral stenosis, mitral regurgitation, S3 gallop, S4 gallop, pericardial friction rub, atrial fibrillation (irregularly irregular)

THE OSCE INTERSTATION

- Determine important features of the *history*.
- What are the key *physical findings*?
- Formulate a broad *differential* diagnosis.
- Interpret available laboratory data.
- Order *lab tests* or *diagnostic procedures*.
- Indicate *treatment* options.
- Discuss plans for *follow-up*.

THE CSA PATIENT NOTE

- Discuss the important features of the *history* most relevant to your diagnosis.
- Discuss the key *physical findings.*
- Include *pertinent positives and negatives.*
- List up to five diagnostic possibilities in order of likelihood.
- List up to five *diagnostic tests* to be ordered.

Do not obtain consults, hospitalize, or discuss therapeutic management at this station.

THE REVIEW OF SYSTEMS:
THE PERTINENT POSITIVES AND NEGATIVES

The CSA challenges an examinee's ability to obtain a thorough history and formulate a broad differential diagnosis. The review of systems is an essential component of the CSA and must be thorough and relevant. The examinee must be able to justify the differential diagnosis and list the pertinent positives and negatives for each presenting problem. A CSA examinee should memorize the ROS and practice writing the "patient note" using pertinent negatives and positives. **For the CSA, think in terms of the organ system involved, not the disease or your diagnosis.**

General	weight loss, weight gain, fatigue, chills, night sweats, overall general health
Skin	rashes, lumps, itchiness, dryness, hair changes, nail changes
Head	headaches
Eyes	double vision, blurred vision, eye redness, eye discharge, watery eyes, light bothers eyes, wear reading glasses, history of glaucoma or cataracts
Ears	hearing loss, ringing in ears, room spinning, dizziness, infections, discharge
Nose	history of allergies and hay fever, frequent colds, nasal congestion, nosebleeds, sinus problems
Mouth/Throat	hoarseness, bleeding gums, mouth sores, bad teeth, sore tongue, taste disturbance, sore throat, trouble swallowing
Neck	neck swelling (lymphadenopathy or goiter)
Breasts	nipple discharge, nipple inversion, bleeding nipple, asymmetry of the breasts, lumps, tender breasts, monthly self-examination, last mammogram
Respiratory	cough, chest pain, wheezing, shortness of breath, dyspnea on exertion, bloody cough, history of TB, pneumonia or asthma, last PPD, last CXR
Cardiac	chest pain, pressure or tightness, palpitations, wakes up short of breath (PND), number of pillows slept on (orthopnea), shortness of breath, dyspnea on exertion, fainting, dizziness, feet swelling, history of angina, MI, CHF, HTN, high cholesterol level
Gastrointestinal	abdominal pain, indigestion, loss of appetite, weight change, food intolerance, difficulty swallowing, painful swallowing, nausea, vomiting, constipation, diarrhea, blood in stools, blood in vomitus, change in bowel movements, jaundice, dark colored urine, dark-colored stools, history of gall stones, pancreatitis, hepatitis, ulcer and hemorrhoids

THE REVIEW OF SYSTEMS:
THE PERTINENT POSITIVES AND NEGATIVES

Urologic	painful urination, frequent urination, blood in urine, cloudy urine, wakes up at night to urinate (nocturia), trouble starting, holding or stopping urine, history of UTI or stones
Genital (F)	menarche, last menstrual period, number of pregnancies, miscarriages or abortions, menopause, hot flashes, vaginal discharge, vaginal itching, abnormal vaginal bleeding, menstrual cramps, change in menstrual pattern, history of sexually transmitted diseases, painful intercourse, last Pap smear
Genital (M)	discharge from penis, sores on penis, painful or swollen testicles, history of hernias, history of sexually transmitted diseases, problems with erections, impotence
Rheumatologic	back pain, joint pain, swollen joints, warm joints, joint deformities, muscle weakness, history of gout, osteoarthritis or rheumatoid arthritis
Peripheral Vascular	varicose veins, leg swelling, leg cramps, cold hands and feet, phlebitis, leg pain with walking (claudication)
Neurologic	headache, dizziness, weakness, numbness, fainting spells, problems with walking or coordination, room spinning (vertigo), tremors, problems with memory, problems with controlling urine (incontinence), history of seizures, paralysis or strokes
Psychiatric	sadness, crying, irritability, nervousness, anxiety, fearfulness, hopelessness, sexual troubles, sleep disturbances, depression, hearing voices, thoughts about suicide, history of mental illness
Hematologic	bruises, paleness, history of anemia or blood transfusions
Endocrinologic	excessive urination, hunger or thirst, tremors, weight change, fatigue, feeling hot or cold all the time (temperature intolerance), history of thyroid disease or diabetes mellitus

Medicine

Obstetrics & Gynecology

Pediatrics

Surgery

Psychiatry

Section B: The 50 Practice Cases

General Case Instructions

The cases that follow are examples of standardized patient interactions in Internal Medicine, Family Medicine, Obstetrics/Gynecology, Pediatrics, Psychiatry, and Surgery.

Read the instructions given at the beginning of each case and quickly develop your own checklist. Ask the standardized patient whatever you feel is pertinent, perform the appropriate physical examination, if required, then check your strategy and checklist developing ability against the "SP" checklist. Aim for a score of at least seventy percent on each encounter.

Review the learning objectives provided to enhance your understanding of the encounters. Pearls are included in certain cases in preparation for the OSCE interstation and the CSA patient note. History-taking and physical examination pearls are also included.

Remember, it is the SP who is grading your performance. The history you obtain, the physical examination you perform, and the way you communicate must match up with the SP's checklist for a passing grade.

To help you during the simulation, the responses of the standardized patient during the examination are in parenthesis at the end of each checklist item.

Good Luck Examinee !

PRESENTING PROBLEMS

1. 70-year old woman with forgetfulness
2. 76-year old woman complaining of fatigue and a twenty-five pound weight gain
3. 65-year old woman complaining of hearing loss
4. 20-year old woman complaining of a cough for four days
5. 25-year old man complaining of a sore throat
6. 68-year old man requesting pain medications
7. 50-year old woman requesting a blood pressure check
8. 55-year old man complaining of abdominal pain for three months
9. 48-year old man with chest pain
10. 25-year old woman with leg pain
11. 35-year old man with a chronic cough
12. 65-year old woman with arm and leg weakness
13. 25-year old female with a rash
14. 65-year old man with difficulty swallowing
15. 62-year old man with a history of frequent falls

16. 22-year old woman with a headache
17. 18-year old woman with burning on urination
18. 18-year old man with a rash
19. 20-year old woman with rectal bleeding
20. 31-year old man with blurred vision
21. 70-year old man with difficulty urinating
22. 65-year old woman who has become withdrawn
23. 40-year old man with abdominal pain
24. 30-year old man with a rash
25. 31-year old woman with a wrist injury after falling down stairs
26. 50-year old woman with hand tingling
27. 33-year old man with back pain
28. 10-year old with shortness of breath
29. 14-month old with fever
30. 4-month old for well baby visit
31. 9-year old with knee pain
32. 4-year old with respiratory distress
33. 19-month old with new seizure
34. 26-year old with lower abdominal pain
35. 50-year old woman with hot flashes
36. 22-year old woman with abdominal pain
37. 24-year old pregnant woman with vaginal bleeding
38. 30-year old woman with worsened menstrual cramps
39. 25-year old pregnant woman for prenatal visit
40. 37-year old woman with third trimester bleeding
41. 16-year old girl with weight loss
42. 45-year old man despondent since the death of his wife
43. 26-year old woman with frequent chest pain
44. a young woman emotionally drained since having a baby
45. 50-year old man with insomnia
46. 52-year old woman with abdominal pain
47. 35-year old man with left sided back pain
48. 50-year old man with abdominal pain
49. 72-year old man with abdominal pain
50. 32-year old man hit in the stomach with a baseball bat

Case 1

Case 1

Please evaluate Mrs. Doe, a 70-year old female, who is a retired schoolteacher. She is visiting her daughter who is your longtime patient. Mrs. Doe's daughter feels that her mother has become forgetful over the last two years and she wishes you to evaluate her for Alzheimer's Disease.

The nurse informs you that Mrs. Doe's heart rate, temperature, and blood pressure are normal. You have fifteen minutes to see Mrs. Doe. Perform a focused history and physical examination on this patient. Please limit yourself to the time provided.

Try and develop the checklist for this encounter based on the presenting problem. Use the next page to make your own checklist.

MY CHECKLIST

History of Present Illness. The Examinee:

1. _____
   _____
2. _____
3. _____
4. _____
5. _____
6. _____
7. _____
8. _____
9. _____
10. _____
    _____
    _____
11. _____
12. _____
    _____
    _____

Physical Examination. The Examinee:

13. _____
14. _____
15. _____
16. _____
    _____
    _____
17. _____

Communication Skills. The Examinee:

18. _____
19. _____
20. _____
21. _____
22. _____
23. _____
24. _____
25. _____

SP CHECKLIST FOR MRS. DOE

History of Present Illness. The Examinee:

___1. started with an open-ended question i.e., "What brings you in today?" ("My daughter insisted I come in but I've never felt better.")

___2. asked about past medical history i.e high blood pressure, stroke, irregular heart beat ("No.")

___3. asked about any use of medications ("None.")

___4. asked about alcohol use ("None.")

___5. asked about changes in weight ("No.")

___6. asked about any history of head trauma ("None.")

___7. asked if I was having trouble remembering things ("No.")

___8. asked about neurological symptoms i.e., weakness, dizziness, gait problems, incontinence ("No.")

___9. asked about home living arrangements ("I live with two cats.")

___10. asked about loneliness or sadness ("My husband died 10 years ago; I play bingo at the church every Tuesday; I teach reading at the community center; I visit the sick at the hospital after church on Sundays; I play bridge with my friends; I think my life is rich and full.")

___11. asked about support systems ("My daughter is always there for me and I have supportive girlfriends.")

___12. asked about at least 3 instrumental activities of daily living i.e., shopping, cooking, money management, housework, telephone use, and travel outside the home ("I did take the wrong bus a few times, my house is a mess, I let my neighbor shop for me, my phone was disconnected because I did not pay the bill, I stopped cooking when the stove caught fire and I did forget to pay my rent 3 months in a row but that's normal for people my age, isn't it?")

Physical Examination. The Examinee:

___13. listened to my heart in at least 3 places (normal examination).

___14. tested my strength in both arms and legs (normal strength in arms and legs).

___15. tested reflexes in arms and legs (normal reflexes).

___16. conducted parts of the mini-mental status examination i.e., checked for at least 3 of the following: spell world backwards, serial sevens, 3 object recall, orientation to place and time, follow 3 stage command, copy design (patient could not calculate, spell backwards, recall objects, copy design or follow 3 stage command).

___17. asked me to walk across the room to check my gait (normal gait).

Communications Skills. The Examinee:

___18. greeted me warmly.

___19. had an organized approach to gathering information.

___20. created an atmosphere that put me at ease.

___21. provided a summary of case (dementia is the most plausible diagnosis).

___22. inquired about my understanding of the problem.

___23. gave a follow-up plan (bloodwork, CT scan of the head).

___24. asked for permission to speak with my daughter to discuss the diagnosis.

___25. offered partnership and ongoing support throughout my illness.

If you performed 18 of these 25 tasks, you passed this test station.

LEARNING OBJECTIVE FOR MRS. DOE:
RECOGNIZE THE MOST LIKELY CAUSE OF DEMENTIA

This 70-year old woman has had a gradual worsening of cognitive function involving memory and judgment over the last several years. She is no longer independent in her instrumental activities of daily living and performed poorly on the mini-mental status examination (MMSE).

Mrs. Doe uses no medications or alcohol to explain her cognitive impairment. A subdural hematoma without a history of head trauma is unlikely. There is no weight gain, bradycardia, or depressive symptoms to suggest hypothyroidism. Lack of depressive symptoms makes the diagnosis of pseudo-dementia unlikely as well. Normal pressure hydrocephalus is often accompanied by gait apraxia and urinary incontinence but the patient denied these symptoms.

The normal cardiac and neurological examinations and the absence of vascular risk factors such as hypertension, heart disease, and previous history of stroke make Alzheimer's Disease the most likely etiology of dementia in this patient.

A physician should investigate the home situation and existing support system for every patient with dementia and offer interdisciplinary assistance from medical and community resources when necessary.

OSCE Interstation Pearl: Be prepared to explain the components of the Folstein mini-mental status examination and what score indicates dementia (23 or less out of a possible score of 30). Know the Katz activities of daily living or ADLs (**DEATH**=**D**ressing, **E**ating, **A**mbulating, **T**oileting, **H**ygiene) and the instrumental activities of daily living or IADLs (**SHAFT**=**S**hopping, **H**ousekeeping, **A**ccounting, **F**ood preparation, **T**ransportation). Familiarize yourself with the "get up and go" test to assess gait (the patient gets out of chair, walks 10 feet, and returns to the chair). This test should be performed by the patient in under 15 seconds.

CSA Patient Note Pearl: Differential diagnosis for dementia includes Alzheimer's Disease, multi-infarct dementia, normal pressure hydrocephalus, hypothyroidism, vitamin B12 deficiency, folic acid deficiency, depression, neurosyphillis, and subdural hematoma. The work-up for dementia includes complete blood count, electrolytes (especially calcium and renal function), liver function tests (hepatic encephalopathy), TSH level, syphilis serology, and vitamin B12 level. Certain patients may require other studies, such as HIV testing, folic acid level, erythrocyte sedimentation rate, CT scan of the head, EEG, and lumbar puncture.

Case 2

Please evaluate Ms. Olive Goode, a 76-year old female, who is complaining of fatigue and a thirty pound weight gain occurring over several months. She has been your private patient for nearly twenty years with a history significant for hypertension controlled with oral hydrochlorothiazide 50 mgs. per day.

Her blood pressure today is 130/85 mmHg and her heart rate is regular at 52 beats per minute. Please perform a focused history and brief physical examination on Ms. Goode. You have fifteen minutes for this test station. Limit yourself to the time provided.

MY CHECKLIST

History of Present Illness. The Examinee:

1. _____
_____
2. _____
3. _____
4. _____
5. _____
6. _____
7. _____
8. _____
9. _____
10. _____
_____
_____

Physical Examination. The Examinee:

11. _____
_____
12. _____
13. _____
_____
14. _____

Communication Skills. The Examinee:

15. _____
16. _____
17. _____
18. _____
19. _____
20. _____
21. _____
22. _____
23. _____

SP CHECKLIST FOR MS. GOODE

History of Present Illness. The Examinee:

___1. started with an open-ended question i.e., "What brings you in today?" ("Doctor, I have gained over 25 pounds in the last 2 months and I'm not even eating anything.")

___2. asked about depression i.e., sadness, hopelessness, no interest in activities, inability to concentrate, loss of sexual desire ("I am feeling sad and hopeless lately; I have difficulty concentrating and have no interest in activities or sex.")

___3. asked about the fatigue ("I'm tired all day; I have no energy; I really don't feel like myself.")

___4. asked about sleep habits ("I sleep 20 hours a day.")

___5. asked about constipation ("Yes, I move my bowels once a week; I was never like that.")

___6. asked about cold intolerance ("I'm wearing a sweater even in hot weather; I am always cold.")

___7. asked about voice changes ("Yes; I feel like I'm hoarse.").

___8. asked about dry skin ("Yes; my skin is flaking off because of dryness.")

___9. asked about hair falling out ("Yes, in clumps it is falling out.")

___10. asked about chest pain ("No.")

Physical Examination. The Examinee:

___11. looked in mouth for size of tongue (after examinee looks in mouth, SP should show him/her picture of thickened tongue).

___12. examined thyroid gland properly (gland diffusely enlarged but nontender).

___13. listened to heart in at least 3 places (after examinee performs this task, SP should give card with results: bradycardia; heart rate is 52 beats per minute).

___14. examined reflexes in arms and legs (delayed relaxation phase in reflexes in arms and legs).

Communication Skills. The Examinee:

___15. had an organized approach to gathering information.

___16. made good eye contact.

___17. used appropriate body posture.

___18. responded to my nonverbal clues.

___19. acknowledged my distress.

___20. explained my problem (hypothyroidism is most plausible diagnosis).

___21. provided me with a plan (bloodwork, electrocardiogram, medication).

___22. inquired about my understanding of the plan.

___23. discussed prognosis with me.

If you performed 17 of these 23 tasks, you passed this test station.

LEARNING OBJECTIVE FOR MS. GOODE:
DIAGNOSE HYPOTHYROIDISM IN AN ELDERLY PATIENT

Thyroid problems must be considered in the differential diagnosis of any patient presenting with fatigue and an unexplained weight change. Ms. Goode is a 76-year old patient who presents with three clinical features of hypothyroidism, namely, weight gain, fatigue, and bradycardia. With further questioning, the patient admits to other common features of hypothyroidism, such as, cold intolerance, dry, flaky skin, voice change, constipation, and generalized hair loss. Elderly patients with hypothyroidism may present with symptoms of depression and Ms.Goode admits to feeling sad and hopeless.

Although the patient denied the symptoms of angina often associated with hypothyroidism, a cardiac examination and electrocardiogram should be performed to verify the bradycardia and to look for signs of pericardial effusion. An examination of the mouth in a hypothyroid patient may reveal a thickened tongue. Deep tendon reflexes, especially those of the achilles tendon, should be examined for a prolongation in the relaxation phase seen in a hypothyroid patient. Proper examination of the thyroid gland may reveal a non-palpable thyroid gland or a nontender goiter.

The symptoms of hypothyroidism are insidious and erroneously attributed to normal aging. The examinee must be aware of the atypical and subtle presentation of this disease and order a serum thyroid stimulating hormone (TSH) level. Undiagnosed and untreated, hypothyroidism may progress to respiratory depression and coma.

History-Taking Pearl: Fatigue or lethargy ("feeling tired") is a common chief complaint. The possible etiologies include depression, hypothroidism, acute diseases (infectious mononucleosis) and chronic diseases, such as, congestive heart failure, anemia, HIV, cancer, tuberculosis, and chronic fatigue syndrome. Medications (beta blockers and antihistamines) may also cause fatigue.

OSCE Interstation Pearl: Be prepared to interpret thyroid function tests at this interstation. In primary hypothyroidism, the T4 may be low or even normal but the TSH will be elevated. A patient with hypothyroidism may have other laboratory abnormalities such as anemia, hypercholesterolemia, hyponatremia, and an elevated creatine phosphate kinase level (CPK). Serum T3 is a poor test for primary hypothyroidism. It is not clinically useful to distinguish between the two major causes of hypothyroidism, Hashimoto's disease and chronic autoimmune thyroiditis (both have antibodies to thyroglobin and thyroid peroxidase) and both are treated with hormone replacement therapy. Remember that amiodarone, used in treating certain cardiac arrhythmias, and lithium may cause significant hypothyroidism.

CSA Patient Note Pearl: The differential diagnosis for weight gain includes hypothyroidism, depression, obesity, Cushing's disease, and anasarca (due to cardiomyopathy, nephrotic syndrome and cirrhosis). The work-up for hypothyroidism includes a TSH, T4, CBC, electrolytes and cholesterol level.

Case 3

Case 3

A 65-year old woman, Mrs. Edna West, is concerned about her hearing and has made an appointment to see you. Lately, she finds herself asking her husband to repeat himself because she does not hear him well the first time he says things. Two days ago she went to the movies and had trouble hearing the dialogue. She wishes you to evaluate her. Her vital signs are normal.

You have fifteen minutes to perform the focused history and physical examination on Mrs. West. Please limit yourself to the time provided.

MY CHECKLIST

History of Present Illness. The Examinee:

1. _____
_____
2. _____
3. _____
_____
4. _____
5. _____
6. _____
7. _____
_____
8. _____
9. _____
10. _____

Physical Examination. The Examinee:

11. _____
_____
12. _____
_____
13. _____
14. _____
_____

Communication Skills. The Examinee:

15. _____
16. _____
17. _____
18. _____
19. _____
20. _____
21. _____

SP CHECKLIST FOR MRS. WEST

History of Present Illness. The Examinee:

___1.   asked about the onset of the hearing loss ("It started gradually 6 months ago.")

___2.   asked if one ear or both ears were affected ("It seems to be only the left ear.")

___3.   asked if hearing loss was complete in the affected ear or partial ("Oh, I do hear something but not much.")

___4.   asked about a history of vertigo ("No.")

___5.   asked about a history of tinnitus ("No.")

___6.   asked about any history of trauma to the ear ("No.")

___7.   asked about exposure to loud noises for extended periods of time i.e., in the armed forces or due to occupation ("No; I was never in the armed forces and I worked as a seamstress.")

___8.   asked about any recent infections ("None.")

___9.   asked about the use of any medications that may be ototoxic i.e., diuretics, antibiotics ("None.")

___10.   asked about family history of hearing loss ("No.")

Physical Examination. The Examinee:

___11.   tested my hearing by speaking to me with his/her back turned (SP cannot hear the examinee speaking).

___12   looked into both ears properly with otoscope (after examinee performs task, the SP should give card with results: no cerumen impaction, foreign body, infection, or tympanic membrane perforation or sclerosis).

___13.   performed the Weber test properly (SP will state the stimulus is perceived on the right side).

___14.   performed the Rinne test properly (SP will state both air and bone conduction are decreased but air conduction is still greater than bone conduction).

Communication Skills. The Examinee:

___15.   discussed the diagnosis with me (probable hearing loss from normal aging).

___16.   gently informed me I needed a full audiological evaluation.

___17.   offered to schedule the audiology appointment for me.

___18.   stated I would benefit from an amplification device (hearing aid).

___19.   did not cause me discomfort when examining me with the otoscope.

___20.   was empathetic towards me.

___21.   addressed my concerns about looking old with a hearing amplification device.

If you performed 15 of these 21 tasks, you passed this test station.

LEARNING OBJECTIVE FOR MRS. WEST:
Properly work-up hearing loss

Approximately fifty per cent of people over sixty-five years of age are hearing-impaired. A loss of hearing can occur from lesions in the external auditory canal or middle ear causing a conductive hearing loss. Examples of conductive hearing loss include impaction due to cerumen, otitis externa, foreign body in the external canal, and tympanic membrane perforation.

Lesions of the inner ear or eighth cranial nerve cause a sensorineural hearing loss. When sensory hearing loss is suspected, the examinee must inquire about a history of infection, intense exposure to noise, and ototoxic drug use. Aging (presbycusis) may also cause sensory hearing loss. Neural hearing loss is due mainly, to trauma, vascular events, an infectious process and tumors like acoustic neuroma.

The Rinne-Weber tuning fork tests are used to differentiate between conductive and sensorineural hearing losses. In conductive hearing loss, the Weber test lateralizes and perceives tone in the affected ear. A Weber test in a patient with a sensorineural hearing loss, as in the case of Mrs. West, results in the tone being perceived in the unaffected ear.

The Rinne test further helps to differentiate between a conductive and sensorineural hearing loss. In conductive hearing loss, bone conduction stimulus is perceived to be louder than air conduction stimulus while in sensorineural hearing loss, both air and bone conduction are diminished but air conduction stimuli remain greater.

Mrs. West complains of gradual deterioration of her hearing. She has no vertigo or tinnitus which are seen with tumors such as acoustic neuroma. Her otoscopic examination was unremarkable. She has no obvious risk factors to explain the hearing loss like trauma, noise exposure, infections, or medication use. She has no family history of hearing loss, therefore, pre-existing congenital abnormalities are unlikely to explain her recent deficit.

The Weber and Rinne examinations confirm a sensorineural hearing loss in this patient. An audioscope, if available, would have been the best method of accurately assessing the patient's hearing loss. Mrs.West, however, could not hear the physician speaking when his/her back was turned away from her which indicates a true hearing deficit. The patient would benefit from a full audiological evaluation followed by an amplification device.

Physical Examination Pearl: Check for hearing loss by turning your face away from patient and speaking. Practice the Rinne and Weber tests described above.

Physical Exam

CSA Patient Note Pearl: In adults, the differential diagnosis for conductive hearing loss includes cerumen impaction, otitis externa, foreign body in the external canal and TM perforation. The differential diagnosis for sensory hearing loss includes aging, infection, noise exposure, and medication use. The differential diagnosis for neural hearing loss includes infection, trauma, vascular event, and tumor.

OSCE Interstation Pearl: Hearing loss in children may appear on a multidisciplinary standardized patient examination. You should review the following differential diagnosis for hearing loss in children:

Sensorineural hearing loss may be:

congenital:
TORCH infections
chromosomal abnormalities (trisomy 18, 21)
syndromes (Alport's, Usher's)
anatomic (aplasia of the cochlea)

acquired:
bacterial infections (meningitis, otitis)
viral infections (mumps, CMV, Herpes, rubeola)
vascular insufficiency (sickle cell disease, diabetes)
trauma (noise, temporal bone fracture)
tumor (leukemia, acoustic neuroma, neurofibromatosis)
autoimmune, hypothyroidism, hypoparathyroidism

Conductive hearing loss may be due to:
impacted cerumen, a foreign body, or an otitis with an effusion

Case 4

Case 4

Ms. Hazel Harris is a 20-year old woman who presents to your office complaining of a cough. Her vital signs reveal:

Blood pressure	120/75 mm Hg
Heart rate	96 beats per minute
Respiratory rate	12 breaths per minute
Temperature	101.4° F

You have 10 minutes to evaluate Ms. Harris. Please perform an appropriate history and brief physical examination in the time provided.

MY CHECKLIST

History of Present Illness. The Examinee:

1. _____
2. _____
3. _____
4. _____
5. _____
6. _____
7. _____
8. _____
9. _____
10. _____
11. _____
12. _____
13. _____
14. _____

Physical Examination. The Examinee:

15. _____
_____

16. _____
_____

17. _____
_____

18. _____
_____

Communication Skills. The Examinee:

19. _____
20. _____
21. _____
22. _____
23. _____
24. _____

SP CHECKLIST FOR MS. HARRIS

History of Present Illness. The Examinee:

___1. asked about the onset of cough ("Started 4 days ago.")

___2. asked about production of sputum ("Small amount of thick green sputum; no blood in sputum.")

___3. asked about fever ("For the last 2 days, my temperature has been 101.5° F.")

___4. asked about shaking chills ("Yes, I did have some chills last night.")

___5. asked about pleuritic chest pain ("None.")

___6. asked about past medical history ("None.")

___7. asked about tobacco use ("I've been meaning to stop smoking; I smoke 10 cigarettes a day for 3 years.")

___8. asked about alcohol use ("None.")

___9. asked about illicit drug use ("No.")

___10. asked about contacts being ill ("Yes; everyone at work seems to have this bug, whatever it is.")

___11. asked about occupation ("I work as a cashier in a toy store.")

___12. asked about pets or animal exposure ("No.")

___13. asked about any recent travel ("No.")

___14. asked about last PPD placement ("2 months ago for employment purposes and it was negative.")

Physical Examination. The Examinee:

___15. asked me to say "99" while he/she was moving hand from side to side over my back (after examinee performs this task, SP should give card with results: increased fremitus at right base).

___16. tapped on my back from side to side (after examinee performs this task, SP should give card with results: dullness at right base).

___17. listened to front and back of my chest with a stethoscope (after examinee performs this task, SP should give card with results: crackles at right base).

___18. asked me to whisper or say the letter "e" while listening with a stethoscope (after examinee performs this task, SP should give card with results: positive "e" to "a" changes and positive whispered pectoriloquy at the right base).

Communication Skills. The Examinee:

___19. explained the results of the physical examination to me (consistent with a pneumonia).

___20. explained the work-up (chest radiograph).

___21. explained the treatment (antibiotics as an outpatient).

___22. scheduled a follow-up appointment with me.

___23. discussed tobacco cessation with me.

___24. inquired if I was going to comply with the plan.

If you performed 17 of these 24 tasks, you passed this test station.

LEARNING OBJECTIVE FOR MS. HARRIS:
DIAGNOSE COMMUNITY-ACQUIRED PNEUMONIA

Pneumonia is a common medical problem. The acute features of this disease include cough, production of purulent sputum, fever, and pleuritic chest pain. Patients usually complain of an upper respiratory tract infection prior to the onset of the more prominent features.

Streptococcus pneumoniae is the most common pathogen causing community-acquired pneumonia. Other pathogens responsible for pneumonia include viruses, Haemophilus influenzae and, less commonly, Mycobacterium tuberculosis.

"Atypical" pneumonia is due primarily to Mycoplasma pneumoniae. The presentation is one of gradual onset of symptoms, dry cough, and extrapulmonary involvement. Other causes of atypical pneumonia include Chlamydia pneumoniae and Legionella pneumophila.

When suspecting pneumonia, a physician should inquire about risk factors that predispose an individual to aspiration such as loss of consciousness from drug or alcohol use. The past medical history should document any existing comorbid conditions, such as diabetes mellitus, kidney, heart, or lung disease. A thorough social history including recent travel, hobbies, occupational history, animal exposure, and contact with ill individuals should be investigated.

On physical examination, the patient who presents with tachypnea, hypotension or tachycardia requires hospitalization. Other indications for inpatient management of community-acquired pneumonia include age over sixty-five years old, comorbid illness, leukopenia and hypoxemia.

A thorough lung examination should include an evaluation for signs of consolidation which may include increased tactile fremitus, dullness to percussion, and auscultation of crackles or bronchial breath sounds. Egophony and pectoriloquy should be performed when abnormalities are detected in any lung area.

A chest radiograph is critical to making the diagnosis of pneumonia but the pattern of infiltrate is not diagnostic for any specific organism. Bacterial pneumonia, however, is often a lobar infiltrate with air bronchograms and perhaps a pleural effusion, while viral and atypical pneumonias are usually diffuse or multilobar in distribution, rarely accompanied by an effusion.

Physicians treating an outpatient for a community-acquired pneumonia must form a partnership with the patient to ensure compliance with medications and follow-up visits. Any patient not responding appropriately to oral antibiotic therapy requires inpatient management.

Physical Examination Pearl: Know how to determine the probable location of the pneumonia by physical examination.

OSCE Interstation Pearl: You will be asked to interpret sputum gram stains and chest radiographs. The extent of the infiltrate should be identified by lobe and segment. Patients with chronic obstructive lung disease may have pulmonary function tests ($\downarrow$ FEV1/FVC and normal FVC is pure obstructive lung disease while normal FEV1/FVC and $\downarrow$ FVC is restrictive lung disease) or arterial blood gases requiring interpretation. Always choose an appropriate but cost-effective antibiotic for treatment. Be able to discuss pneumococcal vaccination in patients over the age of 65 years old and in patients at risk for pneumonia because of underlying illness or medication use (i.e., steroids).

CSA Patient Note Pearl: The differential diagnosis for cough includes pneumonia, tuberculosis, asthma, bronchitis, congestive heart failure, and drug allergy. The work-up includes a complete blood count and chest radiograph. When indicated, other tests may include measurement of peak flow, sputum for acid fast bacilli, oxygen saturation, and arterial blood gas.

Case 5

Case 5

You are about to see Mr. Donald Dearborn, a 25-year old college student, who presents to your office practice complaining of a sore throat. He has a temperature of 101.2° F. The rest of his vital signs are normal. You walk into the examination room and see a jaundiced young man in no acute distress.

You have fifteen minutes to see Mr. Dearborn. Perform the history and physical examination you feel are necessary to evaluate this patient appropriately. Please limit yourself to the time provided.

MY CHECKLIST

History of Present Illness. The Examinee:

1. _____
2. _____
3. _____
4. _____
5. _____
6. _____
7. _____
8. _____
9. _____
10. _____
    _____
11. _____
12. _____
13. _____
14. _____
15. _____
16. _____
    _____
17. _____

Physical Examination. The Examinee:

18. _____
    _____
19. _____
20. _____
21. _____
22. _____

Communication Skills. The Examinee:

23. _____
24. _____
25. _____
26. _____
27. _____
28. _____

SP CHECKLIST FOR MR. DEARBORN

History of Present Illness. The Examinee:

___1. asked about the onset or duration of sore throat ("I've had it for 7 days now.")

___2. asked about fever ("Yes but never greater than 101.5° F.")

___3. asked about cough ("No.")

___4. asked about swollen glands ("Yes. I feel my neck glands are swollen and tender.")

___5. asked about the jaundice ("I noticed it yesterday for the first time.")

___6 asked about abdominal pain ("My upper abdomen feels swollen to me; no pain felt.")

___7. asked about nausea or vomiting ("None.")

___8. asked about loss of appetite ("Definitely yes. I just don't feel like eating anything at all.")

___9. asked about change in bowel movements ("No.")

___10. asked about past medical history ("No history of jaundice, hepatitis, blood transfusions, ear piercing, or tattoos.")

___11. asked about medications ("None.")

___12. asked about illicit drug use ("No.")

___13. asked about alcohol use ("None.")

___14. asked about any risk factors for hepatitis A i.e., shellfish, overcrowding, contaminated water or food ("No.")

___15. asked about ill contacts ("My girlfriend has a sore throat, fever, swollen glands and is jaundiced too.")

___16. asked about sexual history ("I am heterosexual; one girlfriend; always use condoms now and with 2 previous partners.")

___17. asked about immunization against hepatitis B ("I did get that before starting college.")

Physical Examination. The Examinee:

___18. looked inside my mouth to examine throat (after examinee performs this task, give picture showing erythematous pharynx to the examinee).

___19. palpated my neck glands (scattered tender nodes bilaterally are palpable).

___20. tapped my liver for size (after examinee performs this task, give card with results: liver size is 20 cm by 10cm).

___21. pressed over my abdomen (SP will complain of tenderness on right upper side).

___22. pressed over spleen area (after examinee performs this task, SP should give card with results: spleen palpable 3cms. below left rib margin).

Communication Skills. The Examinee:

___23. washed hands before beginning physical examination.

___24. explained results of the physical examination (inflamed throat, swollen glands, enlarged liver and spleen).

___25. explained diagnosis (plausible diagnosis is mononucleosis).

___26. explained plan (bloodwork to check for mononucleosis and hepatitis).

___27. discussed precautions necessary so as not to infect others (virus is transmitted in saliva).

___28. stated that the girlfriend should be examined by a physician.

If you performed 20 of these 28 tasks, you passed this test station.

LEARNING OBJECTIVE FOR MR. DEARBORN:
RECOGNIZE THE VARIABLE SYMPTOMATOLOGY OF MONONUCLEOSIS

Infectious mononucleosis is an acute disease due to Ebstein-Barr virus (herpesvirus) which commonly occurs in individuals who are ten to thirty-five years of age. The symptoms of this disease are so variable that it is often difficult to form a narrow and focused differential diagnosis. Fever, anorexia, sore throat, and tender posterior cervical lymphadenopathy are the common symptoms on presentation.

Mr. Dearborn is a young man who presented with the complaints of fever, sore throat, and tender cervical lymphadenopathy. He denied cough, so respiratory infection is less likely to explain his symptoms.

The patient presented with new onset jaundice but denied the common risk factors for viral hepatitis such as past medical history of blood transfusion, illicit drug use, ear piercing, tattoos, and sexual promiscuity. He denied risk factors for hepatitis A virus. He has been vaccinated against hepatitis B. He uses no medications that may have caused hepatotoxicity. He denies alcohol abuse, therefore, alcoholic hepatitis is unlikely.

The abdominal fullness without associated gastrointestinal symptoms and the hepatosplenomegaly on physical examination may be seen with many diseases, including infectious mononucleosis. The patient may still have viral hepatitis and serology will be sent for hepatitis A, B, and C once infectious mononucleosis is ruled out.

The patient's girlfriend having similar symptomatology is significant since the mode of transmission of mononucleosis is through saliva. The doctor should recommend that the patient's girlfriend be seen by a physician and evaluated for infectious mononucleosis.

A complete blood profile on Mr. Dearborn would most likely reveal a predominance of atypical lymphocytes and a "monospot" test (IgM) would confirm the diagnosis. Even though mononucleosis has a benign course, its possible complications (mononeuritis, encephalitis, arrhythmia) and infectious precautions must be discussed with each patient.

OSCE Interstation Pearl: You should be prepared to interpret liver function tests (aminotransferases, bilirubin, and alkaline phosphatase levels) and hepatitis A (IgM means acute infection), B, and C serology. You must be able to identify atypical lymphocytes on a peripheral blood smear. Remember that atypical lymphocytes may be seen in EBV, CMV, toxoplasmosis, drug reactions, viral hepatitis, rubella, mumps, and rubeola. If monospot test is negative, you should order Cytomegalovirus titers since mononucleosis may be due to CMV infection.

CSA Patient Note Pearl: The differential diagnosis for this patient would include mononucleosis, hepatitis A, B, C, and alcoholic hepatitis. Rotor's syndrome and Dubin-Johnson syndrome cause elevations in conjugated bilirubin and may produce jaundice (Gilbert's syndrome produces elevations in unconjugated bilirubin). Jaundice may also be due to disorders of bilirubin metabolism, such as hemolytic anemia and sickle cell disease. Posthepatic causes of jaundice include gallstones, biliary stricture, and primary sclerosing cholangitis. The diagnostic work-up includes a peripheral blood smear to identify atypical lymphocytes, monospot test, bilirubin (unconjugated and conjugated levels), AST, ALT, and alkaline phosphatase level.

Case 6

Case 6

A 68-year old man named David Dubois recently moved to the small town where you are the only practicing physician. He was diagnosed with pancreatic cancer 7 months ago and knows he is dying. He wants you to be his physician for the remaining days or months of his life.

As you enter the examination room, you notice a frail and cachectic man looking much older than his 68 years of age. He is jaundiced. He is requesting a prescription for narcotics. You have 15 minutes to see Mr. Dubois. A physical examination is not required at this test station.

MY CHECKLIST

History of Present Illness. The Examinee:

1. _____
2. _____
3. _____
4. _____
   _____
5. _____
6. _____
   _____
7. _____
8. _____
9. _____

Communication Skills. The Examinee:

10. _____
11. _____
12. _____
13. _____
14. _____
15. _____
16. _____
    _____
17. _____
18. _____
19. _____
20. _____
21. _____
22. _____

SP CHECKLIST FOR MR. DUBOIS

History of Present Illness. The Examinee:

___1. started with an open-ended question i.e., What is troubling you, Mr. Dubois?.

___2. asked about appetite i.e., worsening weight loss ("I just don't have the strength to eat anything.")

___3. asked about recent fevers ("None.")

___4. asked about any pain ("This cancer causes a lot of pain in my whole body; I definitely need more pain medication.")

___5. asked about any other medical problems ("None.")

___6. asked about present medications ("I take morphine pills twice a day; they aren't strong enough though; I need a higher dose; will you give me a stronger prescription?")

___7. asked about my support system i.e., family and friends ("I really have no one; I'm all alone in this world.")

___8. asked about home situation ("I live alone.")

___9. asked if I needed help at home ("I could use a little help now and then with shopping, cooking, and cleaning.")

Communication Skills. The Examinee:

___10. greeted me warmly.

___11. introduced himself/herself to me.

___12. created an atmosphere of trust and respect.

___13. made good eye contact.

___14. used appropriate body language.

___15. adapted his/her style of speech to my needs.

___16. asked me about advance directives i.e., living will ("Yes; I want to have one of those; I wish to die at home in peace without pain.")

___17. stated he/she would increase the pain medication ("Oh, thank-you doctor.")

___18. stated he/she would help me to die at home ("Oh, thank-you, doctor.")

___19. offered hospice involvement ("Oh, thank-you, doctor.")

___20. addressed my concerns.

___21. showed interest in me as a person.

___22. offered ongoing partnership and support.

If you performed 16 of these 22 tasks, you passed this test station.

LEARNING OBJECTIVE FOR MR. DUBOIS:
DISCUSSING END OF LIFE ISSUES WITH A DYING PATIENT

Mr. Dubois has accepted his diagnosis of pancreatic cancer and wants his doctor to help him with terminal care. His wish is to die at home without pain. He seeks a physician willing to discuss advance directives and hospice care. He wants a physician who will not hesitate to increase his pain medications even if higher doses of narcotics may hasten his death. Pain is Mr. Dubois' greatest fear about dying.

During the interview, the physician should inquire about symptoms the patient may be having secondary to the malignancy. Mr. Dubois admits to anorexia and weight loss but denies fever or other signs of infection. He complains of diffuse body pain.

The physician should ask about preexisting medical problems or comorbid conditions that may require future treatment. Mr. Dubois denies any past medical history.

Social history should include a discussion about the patient's existing support system. Does the patient have friends and family? What is the home situation like for this patient? Arrange for community resources to assist a dying patient if necessary.

A physician discussing end of life decisions must allow the patient an opportunity to state concerns and ask questions. A patient's nonverbal clues should be acknowledged and addressed. There must be an atmosphere of trust and respect between the patient and physician.

The physician must state that he/she will respect the wishes of the patient. The physician should not be concerned about hastening the patient's death with narcotics. A doctor must promise to increase pain medications to relieve a patient's suffering and pain. Competent and informed patients must be given the dignity and autonomy to make end of life decisions.

History-Taking Pearl: Remember to ask the patient about a durable power of attorney for health care decisions or a health care proxy in addition to the living will.

Case 7

You are instructed to see Mrs. Dolores Darling, a 50-year old security guard. She has not seen a physician in five years. Recently, she went to a health fair and, after a free blood pressure check, was told to see a physician for possible high blood pressure. Your name was in her managed care book so she made an appointment to see you. This is her first visit.

The nurse informs you that Mrs. Darling's blood pressure today is 150/95 mm Hg in both arms and her heart rate is 80 beats per minute and regular. You enter the examination room and see an obese female (210 lbs with a height of 63 inches). She is in no distress.

You have fifteen minutes to see Mrs. Darling. Please perform a focused history and brief physical examination on this patient.

MY CHECKLIST

History of Present Illness. The Examinee:

1. _____
2. _____
3. _____
4. _____
5. _____
6. _____
7. _____
8. _____
9. _____
10. _____
    _____
11. _____
12. _____
13. _____
14. _____
15. _____
16. _____
    _____
17. _____

Physical Examination. The Examinee:

18. _____
    _____
19. _____
20. _____
21. _____
22. _____

Communication Skills. The Examinee:

23. _____
24. _____
25. _____
26. _____
27. _____

SP CHECKLIST FOR MRS. DARLING

History of Present Illness. The Examinee:

___1. asked about any symptoms i.e., headaches, blurred vision, palpitations, chest pain, dizziness ("No.")

___2. asked about past medical history ("None.")

___3. asked about medication use ("None.")

___4. asked about diet ("I eat a lot of junk food.")

___5. asked about tobacco use ("I smoke 2 packs per day for 20 years.")

___6. asked about illicit drug use ("Never.")

___7. asked about exercise ("None.")

___8. asked about stresses in life i.e., employment or family ("None.")

___9. asked about family history ("My father had a heart attack at the age of 60 and my mother suffered a stroke at the age of 65; a sister who is 50 years old has congestive heart failure and diabetes.")

___10. asked if cholesterol level is known ("At the fair, they told me my cholesterol was 300. Is that high?")

Physical Examination. The Examinee:

___11. checked my blood pressure in both arms (blood pressure in both arms is 150/95mm Hg).

___12. checked my blood pressure sitting and standing (blood pressure is 150/95mm Hg).

___13. chose the large cuff to measure my blood pressure (examination room had a small and large cuff available for the examinee to choose from).

___12. looked into eyes with ophthalmoscope (after examinee performs this task, show picture with results of opthalmoscopic examination: arteriolar narrowing, arterio-venous nicking, and exudates visible bilaterally).

___13. listened to heart in at least 3 places (normal examination).

___14. listened to lungs in at least 4 places (normal examination).

___15. listened over abdomen with stethoscope (no bruits audible).

___16. palpated sides of abdomen to determine kidney size (kidneys not enlarged).

___17. felt at least 2 of my pulses i.e., carotid, radial, posterior tibialis, dorsalis pedis (normal pulses are palpable).

Communication Skills. The Examinee:

___18. created an atmosphere that put me at ease.

___19. explained the results of the physical examination (eyes show changes of long standing high blood pressure).

___20. discussed all my medical problems (hypertension, hyperlipidemia, obesity, tobacco use).

___21. discussed diet as a treatment for hypertension, obesity and hyperlipidemia.

___22. discussed exercise as a treatment for hypertension, obesity, and hyperlipidemia.

___23. educated me regarding prognosis if problems are left untreated.

___24. discussed structured plan (bloodwork, urinalysis, electrocardiogram, exercise program, nutrition guidelines, tobacco cessation program).

___25. inquired about my understanding of the problems.

___26. inquired whether I would comply with the plan.

___27. appeared supportive and confident that I would succeed.

If you performed 19 of these 27 tasks, you passed this test station.

LEARNING OBJECTIVE FOR MRS. DARLING:
APPROACH TO THE PATIENT WITH HYPERTENSION

Even though patients with hypertension are usually asymptomatic, when a patient presents with hypertension, a physician should inquire about headaches, dizziness, blurred vision, palpitations, chest pain, and shortness of breath. If a secondary cause of hypertension is suspected, such as Cushing's disease (hirsutism, facial plethora, truncal obesity, headache, acne) or pheochromocytoma (headache, palpitations, diaphoresis), the physician should inquire about the symptoms specific to those diseases.

Risk factors that contribute to hypertension include a past medical history of hyperlipidemia or diabetes mellitus and the use of medications such as estrogen in oral contraceptives. A patient must be asked about a family history of cardiac disease or hyperlipidemia. A physician should inquire about tobacco and cocaine use. A patient's lifestyle can affect blood pressure and a physician should inquire about diet, exercise, living arrangements, and stressful employment.

Blood pressure readings should be measured twice during two separate examinations with the appropriate size cuff before making the diagnosis of hypertension. Both arms should be used to record blood pressure (one arm may be lower due to a narrow brachial/axillary artery and, in the future, the arm with the higher recording should be used). Blood pressure should be measured sitting and standing to identify patients with orthostatic hypotension.

A fundoscopic examination may reveal information about the duration of the hypertension. The heart examination may reveal a murmur, gallop, or displaced point of maximum impulse (PMI). A lung examination may reveal cardiac decompensation. The abdominal examination is required for palpation of enlarged kidneys secondary to polycystic renal disease and to auscultate for renal artery bruits. Peripheral pulses should be palpated for diminished flow secondary to atherosclerosis.

The work-up for hypertension includes a hematocrit, serum glucose level, potassium level, creatinine level, urinalysis for protein and blood, and an electrocardiogram. Special studies to screen for secondary causes of hypertension should be ordered when necessary (consider aortic coarctation, Cushing's disease, hyperaldosteronism, pheochromocytoma, hypothyroidism, renal artery stenosis, and hyperparathyroidism).

Risk factor modification and patient compliance must be addressed when treating a patient with hypertension. Mrs. Darling should be encouraged to stop smoking, increase her physical activity, and reduce her salt and fat intake in an effort to lose weight. She should be educated about the complications of untreated hypertension and the importance of compliance and follow-up.

Physical Examination Pearl: The Keith-Wagener-Barker classification for hypertensive retinopathy:
Grade 1 is arteriolar narrowing and copper wiring
Grade 2 is grade 1 changes and arterio-venous nicking
Grade 3 is grade 2 changes and hemorrhages and exudates
Grade 4 is grade 3 changes with the addition of papilledema

OSCE Interstation Pearl: You should be able to define the stages of hypertension:
Stage 1: mild hypertension (140/90-159/99mmHg).
Stage 2: moderate hypertension (160/100-179/109mmHg) and
Stage 3: severe hypertension (180/110-209/119mmHg).
Stage 4: a blood pressure reading higher than the severe range is called very severe hypertension.

Know that patients <25 or >45 years old with new hypertension should be examined closely for secondary causes of hypertension (pheochromocytoma, renal artery stenosis, hyeraldosteronism, Cushing's disease, polycystic kidney, coarctation of the aorta, hyperparathyroidism, thyroid disease, acromegaly) even though these are responsible for less than 5 % of all hypertension.

You should be able to order the appropriate daily diet for this patient (30% fat; 55% carbohydrates, 15% protein; less than 300 mg of cholesterol and less than 10% saturated fat per day). The body mass index (BMI)for this patient is presently 714 x 210 pounds/63 inches tall^2 = 37.78. Good BMI is considered to be <25.

Case 8

Case 8

Please evaluate Mr. Michael Brown, a 55-year old construction worker, with the chief complaint of abdominal pain. He has a ten year history of hypertension well controlled on an oral ACE inhibitor agent. His vital signs today are normal. He is afebrile. He has been your patient for five years.

Please see Mr. Brown and perform the relevant history and physical examination. You have fifteen minutes for this test station.

MY CHECKLIST

History of Present Illness. The Examinee:

1. _____
2. _____
3. _____
4. _____
5. _____
6. _____
7. _____
8. _____
9. _____
10. _____
11. _____
12. _____
13. _____
14. _____

Physical Examination. The Examinee:

15. _____
16. _____
17. _____
18. _____

Communication Skills. The Examinee:

19. _____
20. _____
21. _____
22. _____
23. _____
_____
24. _____

SP CHECKLIST FOR MR. BROWN

History of Present Illness. The Examinee:

___1. asked about onset of pain ("It has been about 2 months.")

___2. asked about location of pain ("In the upper part of my abdomen.")

___3. asked about the quality of the pain ("Burning and gnawing in nature")

___4. asked about radiation of pain ("None.")

___5. asked about the severity of the pain ("On a scale of 1 to 10, where 10 is the worst, the pain is a 3.")

___6. asked about any aggravating factors ("Alcohol, caffeine, smoking, stress, and not eating make it worse.")

___7. asked about any alleviating factors ("Food and antacids make it better.")

___8. asked about any association with nausea or vomiting ("None.")

___9. asked about any change in bowel movements ("No diarrhea or constipation.")

___10. asked about blood in the stools or tarry colored stools ("No.")

___11. asked about alcohol use ("Just a beer on Sundays.")

___12. asked about tobacco use ("I smoke a pack per day.")

___13. asked about frequent aspirin or nonsteroidal pain medication use ("No.")

___14. asked about weight loss ("None.")

Physical Examination. The Examinee:

___15. listened over the abdomen with a stethoscope (normal bowel sounds are heard).

___16. pressed gently on abdomen (SP will complain of mild pain in midepigastric area).

___17. pressed deeply on abdomen (SP will complain of marked pain in midepigastric area).

___18. asked to perform a rectal examination (after making this request, SP will give examinee card with results of rectal examination: brown stool which is positive for blood).

Communication Skills. The Examinee:

___19. explained the results of the physical examination (stool has some blood).

___20. discussed the plausible diagnosis (ulcer or gastritis).

___21. discussed the follow-up steps in management (bloodwork, gastroenterology consult for endoscopy).

___22. discussed treatment options (will need medications and follow-up).

___23. recommended abstinence from alcohol, tobacco, aspirin, nonsteroidal anti-inflammatory drugs, and caffeine-containing beverages.

___24. discussed prognosis with patient.

If you performed 17 of these 24 tasks, you passed this test station.

LEARNING OBJECTIVE FOR MR. BROWN:
EVALUATE CHRONIC ABDOMINAL PAIN IN A PATIENT
WITH HEME POSITIVE STOOLS

This patient presents with a two month history of epigastric discomfort relieved with food and antacids. He appears to be in no acute distress and is afebrile. His mild and infrequent abdominal pain is alleviated with antacids and food and is aggravated by stress, caffeine, tobacco, and mild alcohol use.

Mr. Brown, a 55-year old man, denies a history of weight loss or change in bowel movements, but with stools that are positive for blood, malignancy must remain a consideration. Pancreatitis is unlikely since the epigastric pain does not radiate to the back, is relieved with food and is not associated with nausea or vomiting. Peptic ulcer disease and gastritis remain plausible considerations and require further investigation in this patient.

There are 500,000 new cases of peptic ulcer in the United States per year. The disease occurs more commonly in men than women. Helicobacter pylori and use of nonsteroidal anti-inflammatory agents are the main etiologies of ulcer disease. The most common complaint in a patient with ulcer is epigastric discomfort or dyspepsia. Fecal blood testing in patients with peptic ulcer is positive in thirty percent of all patients.

A physician should evaluate Mr. Brown for chronic blood loss by ordering a hematocrit. A gastroenterology consult for endoscopy with antral biopsy to detemine if Helicobacter pylori is present would be the most accurate method to diagnose ulcer and exclude malignancy. If ulcer disease and Helicobacter pylori infection are confirmed, the patient will need antibiotics combined with acid suppression therapy. The patient should attempt to abstain from tobacco, alcohol, and caffeine-containing beverages.

OSCE Interstation Pearl: Be prepared to discuss the proper treatment (triple therapy) for Helicobacter pylori associated peptic ulcer disease. Two antibiotics for 10-14 days are required for eradication of this gram negative bacillus in addition to a proton pump inhibitor (omeprazole) for 4 weeks (if duodenal ulcer) or 8 weeks (if gastric ulcer). It is not recommended to confirm eradication of the organism after treatment is completed. Helicobacter pylori is associated with duodenal ulcer, gastric ulcer, antral gastritis, gastric carcinoma, and gastric lymphoma.

CSA Patient Note Pearl: The differential diagnosis for a patient with chronic abdominal pain includes peptic ulcer disease, nonulcer dyspepsia, gastritis, pancreatitis, and malignancy. The diagnostic work-up includes fecal occult blood test (FOBT), CBC and, possibly, amylase and lipase. Other tests to consider include an upper barium gastrointestinal study (80% accurate for gastric and duodenal ulcers) and H. pylori by urease breath test (95% sensitive) or serum antibodies (95% sensitive but not able to distinguish between past and present infection).

Case 9

Case 9

A 48-year old man named Louis Levitt is brought to the emergency room complaining of chest pain. His vital signs are recorded to be the following:

Blood pressure	140/90 mm Hg
Heart rate	100 beats per minute
Respiratory rate	14 breaths per minute
Temperature	98.6° F

You have 15 minutes to evaluate Mr. Levitt. Please perform a focused history and physical examination on this patient.

MY CHECKLIST

History of Present Illness. The Examinee:

1. _____
2. _____
3. _____
4. _____
5. _____
6. _____
7. _____
8. _____
9. _____
10. _____
11. _____
12. _____
13. _____
14. _____

Physical Examination. The Examinee:

15. _____
16. _____
    _____
17. _____
18. _____

Communication Skills. The Examinee:

19. _____
20. _____
21. _____
22. _____
23. _____
24. _____
25. _____
26. _____
    _____

SP CHECKLIST FOR MR. LEVITT

History of Present Illness. The Examinee:

___1. asked about the location of chest pain ("In the middle of my chest.")

___2. asked about quality of chest pain ("It almost feels like indigestion.")

___3. asked about onset of chest pain ("Started about 1 hour ago.")

___4. asked about severity of chest pain ("On a scale of 1 to 10 where 10 is the worst, this is a 10.")

___5. asked about radiation of the pain ("It goes to my left arm.")

___6. asked what makes the chest pain worse ("Walking makes it worse.")

___7. asked what makes the chest pain better ("Nothing really.")

___8. asked if pain was associated with nausea or vomiting ("I do feel nauseated right now.")

___9. asked about past medical history ("Never ill before; have not seen a doctor in 10 years.")

___10. asked about tobacco use ("I smoke 2 packs per day for 15 years.")

___11. asked about cocaine use ("No.")

___12. asked about diet ("I eat junk food.")

___13. asked about family history ("My brother and father died of heart attacks before the age of 60.")

___14. asked about lifestyle stresses i.e. family or occupation ("I work as a stockbroker on Wall Street; It is a stressful job.")

Physical Examination. The Examinee:

___15. palpated the precordium for point of maximal impulse or PMI (normal PMI).

___16. listened to heart in at least 3 places (after examinee performs this task, SP will give card stating that an S4 gallop was audible).

___17. listened to lungs in at least 4 places (lung examination is normal).

___18. evaluated neck veins looking for elevation of pressure (no jugular venous distension).

Communication Skills. The Examinee:

___19. made me feel at ease.

___20. conveyed confidence.

___21. alleviated my fears.

___22. explained diagnosis (probable myocardial infarction).

___23. explained work-up (electrocardiogram, bloodwork for cardiac isoenzymes, admission).

___24. explained treatment (aspirin, thrombolytics, beta blocker agents, nitrates, oxygen).

___25. discussed prognosis (very good).

___26. discussed the risk factors that contributed to the cardiac problem (smoking, family history, diet, and stress).

If you performed 19 of these 26 tasks, you passed this test station.

LEARNING OBJECTIVE FOR MR. LEVITT:
DIAGNOSE MYOCARDIAL INFARCTION

Mr. Levitt presents with typical symptoms of myocardial infarction. The severe chest pain he is experiencing feels like an indigestion that radiates to his left arm and is associated with nausea. His risk factors for coronary artery disease include age, tobacco use, family history, lack of exercise, and improper diet. The stress of his occupation may also contribute to his illness.

Other risk factors for myocardial infarction may include obesity, cocaine use, and a past medical history of diabetes mellitus, hypertension, or hyperlipidemia. Mr. Levitt does not have these risk factors.

There are 1.5 million myocardial infarctions in the United States per year. The mortality rate in patients presenting acutely is thirty percent. Patients over the age of sixty-five years old have reduced survival and may present with atypical complaints such as shortness of breath instead of chest pain.

The differential diagnosis of chest pain includes gastrointestinal problems, pericarditis, pulmonary embolus, aortic dissection, and costochondritis. Symptomatology and physical examination often help to distinguish among etiologies. A cardiac examination in myocardial infarction may reveal an S4 gallop. Complicated cases may reveal an S3 gallop or a systolic murmur consistent with mitral valve dysfunction. Lung congestion is found in cases of myocardial infarction complicated by cardiac decompensation.

Laboratory tests for diagnosis of myocardial infarction include an electrocardiogram and serum cardiac markers. Management strategies include reperfusion therapy using thrombolytic agents or primary angioplasty. Pharmacotherapy for acute infarction includes the use of aspirin, beta blockers, angiotensin converting enzyme inhibitors, nitrates, and oxygen.

The complications of myocardial infarction include cardiac arrhythmias, persistent ischemia, ventricular dysfunction, ventricular rupture, pericarditis, ventricular septal defect, papillary muscle dysfunction, and postmyocardial infarction syndrome. Patients with persistent complications after infarction are at increased risk for reinfarction and death.

Secondary prevention of myocardial infarction requires the patient to modify all risk factors for atherosclerosis. Mr. Levitt must stop smoking and begin a low fat diet. He must begin an exercise program. The occupational stress of being a Wall Street stockbroker should be reduced if possible.

OSCE Interstation Pearl: Electrocardiogram interpretation will be necessary at this interstation. ST elevation, ventricular arrhythmias, and heart blocks are common EKG findings. The area of ST elevation should be identified (leads 2, 3, and AVF for inferior wall; leads 1, AVL, and V6 for lateral wall; leads V1 and V2 for the anteroseptal wall and V3, V4, and V5 for an anterior wall infarct). Know that the left anterior descending artery supplies the anterior wall, the circumflex artery supplies the lateral wall and the right coronary artery supplies the inferior wall (in most cases). Tests ordered must include CPK-MB (which peaks in 24 hours) or troponin I or T (remains elevated > 1 week) which are sensitive and specific enzymes for detection of myocardial injury. Be prepared to discuss the risk factors for coronary artery disease and the complications of myocardial infarction.

CSA Patient Note Pearl: The differential diagnosis for chest pain includes myocardial infarction, angina, pericarditis, pulmonary embolus, costochondritis, and aortic dissection. Other etiologies may include gastroesophageal reflux disease (GERD), esophageal spasm, cholecystitis, peptic ulcer disease, and herpes zoster. The diagnostic work-up includes CBC, FOBT, electrocardiography, cardiac isoenzymes, and CXR.

Case 10

Case 10

You are about to evaluate 25-year old Ms. Julia Gordon in the emergency room. She called the ambulance because of leg pain. The paramedics inform you that her:

Blood pressure is 110/70 mm Hg
Heart rate is 80 beats per minute
Respiratory rate is 12 breaths per minute
Oxygen saturation is 100 per cent

As you enter the examination room, you notice a thin woman lying on the stretcher looking at her right lower extremity. You have fifteen minutes to see Ms. Gordon. Perform a focused history and relevant physical examination on this patient.

MY CHECKLIST

History of Present Illness. The Examinee:

1. _____
2. _____
3. _____
4. _____
5. _____
6. _____
7. _____
8. _____
9. _____
10. _____
11. _____

Physical Examination. The Examinee:

12. _____
13. _____
    _____
14. _____
15. _____

Communication Skills. The Examinee:

16. _____
17. _____
18. _____
19. _____
20. _____
21. _____
22. _____

SP CHECKLIST FOR MS. GORDON

History of Present Illness. The Examinee:

___1.   asked about onset of leg pain ("It started 2 days ago.")

___2.   asked about trauma to the leg ("No.")

___3.   asked about chest pain ("No.")

___4.   asked about shortness of breath ("No.")

___5.   asked if I could be pregnant ("Absolutely not.")

___6.   asked about past medical history ("Never ill before. I was feeling great until this happened.")

___7.   asked about medications ("Birth control pills for 7 years.")

___8.   asked about tobacco use ("I smoke 2 packs per day for 5 years.")

___9.   asked about illicit drug use ("None.")

___10.   asked about family history of blood clots ("No.")

___11.   asked about any recent periods of immobilization i.e., airplane trips ("No.")

Physical Examination. The Examinee:

___12.   listened to lungs in at least 4 places (normal breath sounds are heard).

___13.   checked leg for tenderness (right leg will be erythematous and warm to simulate either a deep venous thrombosis or a cellulitis, if leg is touched by examinee, SP complains of severe pain).

___14.   checked pulses of right foot to confirm good arterial circulation (normal pulse).

___15.   checked for a Homan's sign (positive calf pain with passive dorsiflexion of right foot).

Communication Skills. The Examinee:

___16.   acknowledged my discomfort.

___17.   discussed diagnosis in terms I could understand (plausible diagnosis is deep venous thrombosis).

___18.   discussed risk factors of tobacco and oral contraceptives for deep venous thrombosis.

___19.   checked my understanding of the problem.

___20.   discussed plan (bloodwork, venous ultrasonography of leg, admission to hospital).

___21.   discussed treatment with me (anticoagulation with heparin).

___22.   discussed prognosis (excellent).

If you performed 16 of these 22 tasks, you passed this test station.

LEARNING OBJECTIVE FOR MS. GORDON:
DIAGNOSE DEEP VENOUS THROMBOSIS

Ms. Gordon presents with an erythematous, warm and tender right lower extremity which suggests a deep venous thrombosis (DVT). She has no complaints or symptoms that suggest a pulmonary embolus.

Her risk factors for deep venous thrombosis include smoking and oral contraceptive use. Other risk factors for deep venous thrombosis including a previous history of a DVT, trauma, recent surgery, or a history to suggest malignancy were denied by the patient. There is no family history of hypercoagulable problems to suggest protein c resistance (factor V Leiden abnormality), homocystinuria, antiphospholipid antibody syndrome, or deficiencies in protein c, protein s, or antithrombin III. She is not an obese woman and she denies pregnancy. There is no history of prolonged immobilization (airplane trip).

The differential diagnosis of deep venous thrombosis includes cellulitis, ruptured popliteal cyst, and arterial insufficiency. Work-up includes a leukocyte count to determine an infectious process and duplex venous ultrasonography to image the deep veins of the leg. Treatment with anticoagulants is required to prevent the complication of pulmonary embolus.

When a patient presents with deep venous thrombosis, the responsible risk factors should be modified when possible to prevent recurrence of clot formation. Ms. Gordon should practice another method of contraception and stop smoking. Every patient with a DVT who complains of chest pain or shortness of breath or who presents with tachypnea, tachycardia, or hypoxemia should be urgently investigated for pulmonary embolus.

CSA Patient Note Pearl: The differential diagnosis for this patient includes deep venous thrombosis, cellulitis, muscle rupture, lymphedema, ruptured popliteal cyst, and arterial insufficiency. The diagnostic work-up would include venous ultrasonography of the right lower extremity, CBC with platelet count, PT, PTT, and INR.

Case 11

Mr. Thomas Green is a 35-year old paramedic. His wife has been your patient for fifteen years. She has forced her husband to make an appointment to see you because of his nagging cough. His temperature today is 100.5° F. The rest of his vital signs are normal.

Upon entering the examination room, you see a thin man coughing continuously in no respiratory distress. Please obtain a history and a do a focused physical examination on Mr. Green. You have ten minutes for this test station.

MY CHECKLIST

History of Present Illness. The Examinee:

1. _____
2. _____
3. _____
4. _____
5. _____
6. _____
7. _____
8. _____
9. _____
10. _____
11. _____

Physical Examination. The Examinee:

12. _____
13. _____
14. _____
15. _____

Communication Skills. The Examinee:

16. _____
17. _____
18. _____
19. _____
20. _____
21. _____
22. _____

SP CHECKLIST FOR MR. GREEN

History of Present Illness. The Examinee:

____1.   asked about the onset of cough ("It started about 3 months ago.")

____2.   asked about a history of lung problems ("None; no history of asthma, tuberculosis, or pneumonia.")

____3.   asked about blood in the sputum ("Well, I noticed a teaspoon amount of blood yesterday.")

____4.   asked about any fever ("Lately, my temperature has been 101° F almost every day.")

____5.   asked about night sweats ("Yes; I have to change my pajamas because I sweat so much at night.")

____6.   asked about weight loss ("Yes. I've lost 20 pounds in 2 months.")

____7.   asked about alcohol use ("No.")

____8.   asked about illicit drug use ("No way; are you joking?")

____9.   asked about other risk factors for HIV i.e., promiscuity ("I'm heterosexual and monogamous for 10 years.")

___10.   asked about last PPD ("8 months ago and it was negative.")

___11.   asked about TB exposure ("I know there are many patients I transport in the ambulance with TB.")

Physical Examination. The Examinee:

___12.   checked my neck for swollen lymph glands (none are palpable).

___13.   tapped on my back (normal results on percussion of lungs).

___14.   listened to my lungs in the front (normal lung sounds are audible).

___15.   listened to my lungs in the back (normal lung sounds are audible).

Communication Skills. The Examinee:

___16.   shook my hand and introduced himself/herself to me.

___17.   explained the working diagnosis (tuberculosis or pneumonia; malignancy less likely).

___18.   explained the plan (bloodwork looking for infection, chest radiograph, sputum collection).

___19.   asked me to put on a mask as a precaution and explained reason for this to me in a calm manner.

___20.   explained that a new PPD would need to be placed now.

___21.   explained that, if tuberculosis was diagnosed, close contacts would need to have PPD placement.

___22.   offered ongoing support.

If you performed 16 of these 22 tasks, you passed this test station.

LEARNING OBJECTIVE FOR MR. GREEN:
RECOGNIZE TUBERCULOSIS

Worldwide, there are nearly four million new cases of tuberculosis each year. HIV infection, drug use, alcoholism, and poverty have contributed to this large number. Even though his tuberculin skin test was negative in the past, Mr. Green's occupation makes him at risk for continuous exposure to tuberculosis.

Although a patient with tuberculosis may be asymptomatic, the thirty-five year old Mr. Green has symptoms often seen with tuberculosis. He complains of chronic cough with production of bloody sputum, fever, weight loss, and night sweats.

The physical examination of a patient with tuberculosis may be unremarkable. Lymphadenopathy may be absent and auscultation of the lungs may be normal. The chest radiograph may show apical involvement but, in reality, any radiographic abnormality can be seen with tuberculosis.

Mr. Green will need a PPD (purified protein derivative) and a chest radiograph. Sputum samples will be collected for AFB (acid fast bacilli) smears and culture. The patient needs to wear a mask (or, at least, cover his mouth when coughing) to prevent transmission pending the result of the smears. He does not, however, require hospitalization. If tuberculosis is diagnosed, Mr. Green's wife and other close contacts will need a PPD placement and a physician evaluation. This compliant patient can remain at home and be managed as an outpatient.

OSCE Interstation Pearl: Be prepared to interpret a chest radiograph and acid fast stain at this interstation. You must know the recommended treatment for tuberculosis (four drugs for six months is the easiest regimen to remember) and know that directly observed therapy (DOT) improves success rates. Be able to discuss when chemoprophylaxis is needed for a positive PPD of ≥ 5 mm (HIV infection, close contacts, chest radiograph with healed tuberculosis) and ≥ 10 mm (persons from countries with a high incidence of tuberculosis, intravenous drug abusers, medically underserved populations, residents of institutions, and persons with an underlying illness or taking immunosuppresive therapy). All other persons receive prophylaxis for a PPD ≥ 15mm.

CSA Patient Note Pearl: The differential diagnosis for persistent cough includes tuberculosis, pneumonia, malignancy, asthma, postnasal drip, GERD, chronic obstructive lung disease, bronchiectasis, and certain medications. The diagnostic work-up may include CXR, PPD placement, sputum for acid fast bacilli, and pulmonary function tests.

Case 12

You are working in the emergency room when the paramedics rush a 65-year old woman named Eva Divine to the critical care area of the emergency room. The woman called 911 because of difficulty moving her left arm and leg. Her blood pressure is 170/110 mm Hg and her heart rate is irregularly irregular at a rate of 86 beats per minute. She is afebrile and breathing normally.

When you enter the examination room, you see an anxious, tearful patient lying on a stretcher wearing a nasal cannula. She is attached to an EKG monitor showing atrial fibrillation at a rate of 86 beats per minute and a blood pressure monitor showing a reading of 170/110 mm Hg. Her oxygen saturation is 99%. She has an inch of nitroglycerin paste applied to her chest wall.

You have a very crowded emergency room and have only fifteen minutes to see Ms. Divine. Perform the focused history and physical examination within this time frame.

MY CHECKLIST

History of Present Illness. The Examinee:

1. _____
2. _____
3. _____
4. _____
   _____
5. _____
   _____
6. _____
7. _____
8. _____

Physical Examination. The Examinee:

9. _____
10. _____
    _____
11. _____
12. _____
13. _____
14. _____
15. _____
16. _____
17. _____
18. _____
19. _____
20. _____
21. _____

Communication Skills. The Examinee:

22. _____
23. _____
24. _____
25. _____
26. _____
27. _____
28. _____
29. _____

SP CHECKLIST FOR MRS. EVA DIVINE

History of Present Illness. The Examinee:

___1.   asked about the onset of arm and leg weakness ("It started about 45 minutes ago.")

___2.   asked about sensory changes in arm and leg ("Yes; the entire arm and leg feel numb.")

___3.   asked if my speech was affected ("No.")

___4.   asked about any cardiac symptoms i.e., palpitations, irregular heart beat, chest pain, dizziness, syncope ("No.")

___5.   asked about my past medical history ("I was told by my doctor that I had borderline high blood pressure but that diet and exercise would help. He told me that I did not need medications.")

___6.   asked about history of frequent falls ("No.")

___7.   asked about tobacco abuse ("No.")

___8.   asked about alcohol use ("No.")

Physical Examination. The Examinee:

___9.   looked in my eyes with a flashlight to check pupil size (normal and reactive pupils).

___10. tested the strength in my face i.e., stick out tongue, grin, squeeze eyes shut (SP will be weak on left side of face when smiling).

___11. asked me to stick out my tongue (SP will deviate tongue to the left side).

___12. tested the strength in my arms (SP will have a weak left arm).

___13. tested the strength in my legs (SP will have a weak left leg).

___14. tested sensation in my arms i.e., sharp or dull (SP will have decreased sensation in left arm).

___15. tested sensation in my legs i.e., sharp or dull (SP will have decreased sensation in left leg).

___16. tested reflexes in my arms (SP will have decreased reflexes in left arm).

___17. tested reflexes in my legs (SP will have decreased reflexes in left leg).

___18. tested my Babinski reflex by scratching soles of my feet (SP will have upgoing left toe and downgoing right toe).

___19. listened to my heart in at least 3 places (after examinee performs this task, SP will give examinee card with results: irregularly irregular rhythm at a rate of 86 beats per minute).

___20. listened to my lungs in at least 4 places (normal lung examination).

___21. listened over my neck for carotid bruits (none heard).

Communication Skills. The Examinee:

___22. made empathetic statements.

___23. explained the plausible diagnosis (stroke).

___24. explained about atrial fibrillation as a risk factor for embolic stroke.

___25. explained about hypertension as a risk factor for stroke.

___26. explained the plan (bloodwork, electrocardiogram, CT scan of the head, neurology consult, echocardiogram).

___27. explained the treatment (admission to hospital, fibrinolytics, blood pressure control).

___28. inquired about any family members that should be notified.

___29. offered reassurance.

LEARNING OBJECTIVE FOR MRS. DIVINE:
RECOGNIZE ATRIAL FIBRILLATION AS A RISK FACTOR FOR EMBOLIC STROKE

Risk factors for thrombotic stroke include hypertension, tobacco use, drug use, excessive alcohol use, diabetes mellitus, and hyperlipidemia. Atrial fibrillation and valvular heart disease are risk factors for embolic stroke. Mrs. Divine presents with a neurological deficit and is hypertensive. Her heart rate is irregularly irregular which is consistent on the cardiac monitor with atrial fibrillation. She has no cardiac complaints on arrival to the emergency room.

A history of frequent falls from either alcohol use or aging is denied by Mrs. Divine. She has no history of recent head trauma.

The physical examination on Mrs. Divine reveals no evidence of congestive heart failure. Her neurological examination reveals normal sized, reactive pupils and a weak left upper and lower extremity. She has a hemisensory loss and is hyporeflexic with a positive Babinski reflex on the affected extremity. There is facial asymmetry (shallow left nasolabial fold) and left facial weakness but her speech is fluent. The tongue deviates to the left side. Auscultation of the carotid arteries reveals no audible bruit. The presentation is consistent with a right (nondominant) acute hemispheric stroke.

The work-up for Mrs. Divine requires a cardiac and neurological evaluation. Thrombolytic agents will be considered for her stroke if hemorrhage is ruled out by CT scan of the head and blood pressure is controlled. Atrial fibrillation predisposes Mrs. Divine to future embolic stroke, therefore, she will be considered for lifelong anticoagulation.

OSCE Interstation Pearl: Occlusion of the anterior cerebral artery causes weakness and sensory loss of the contralateral leg and mild weakness of the contralateral arm. Middle cerebral artery occlusion causes contralateral hemiplegia, sensory loss, homonymous hemianopsia, and, if the dominant hemisphere is involved, a global aphasia. The eyes may deviate to the side of the lesion. Posterior cerebral artery occlusion (if dominant hemisphere is involved) causes a homonymous visual field defect and a Wernicke's aphasia (receptive).

CSA Patient Note Pearl: The differential diagnosis for this patient with left sided weakness includes stroke (thrombotic or embolic), hemorrhage, subdural hematoma, intracranial mass, and hypoglycemia. The diagnostic work-up for this patient would include serum glucose level, a CT scan of the head, electrocardiogram, echocardiogram (looking for thrombus formation), and carotid doppler studies.

Case 13

Your golfing buddy, a dermatologist, asks you to consult on a 25-year old female law student named Judy Justice. She originally presented to the dermatology practice 2 weeks ago complaining of a rash on her leg which your friend immediately biopsied. The skin biopsy revealed discoid lupus.

Upon entering the examination room, you notice a smiling young woman dressed in a tee-shirt and shorts wearing a scarf on her head. Please obtain the appropriate history from Ms. Justice and then perform a brief physical examination. You have 15 minutes to complete this test station.

MY CHECKLIST

History of Present Illness. The Examinee:

1. _____
2. _____
3. _____
4. _____
5. _____
6. _____
   _____
7. _____
8. _____
9. _____
10. _____
11. _____
    _____
12. _____
13. _____
14. _____

Physical Examination. The Examinee:

15. _____
    _____
16. _____
17. _____
18. _____
19. _____

Communication Skills. The Examinee:

20. _____
21. _____
22. _____
23. _____
24. _____
25. _____
26. _____
27. _____
28. _____

SP CHECKLIST ON MS. JUSTICE

History of Present Illness. The Examinee:

___1. asked about any hair loss ("It comes out in chunks in the shower.")

___2. asked about any joint pain ("My wrists and fingers are always painful and stiff.")

___3. asked about photosensitivity i.e., if sun causes skin color changes ("Yes.")

___4. asked about other rashes ("Yes. Once I had a facial rash; it was in a butterfly pattern.")

___5. asked about oral ulcers (Yes. My roommate thought they were from stress.")

___6. asked about generalized symptoms i.e., fever, malaise, weight loss ("Yes, I have lost 8 pounds and I often have a temperature of 100.4° F and I am always tired.")

___7. asked about heart symptoms i.e., chest pain, palpitations ("No.")

___8. asked about pulmonary complaints i.e., shortness of breath, cough ("No.")

___9. asked about neurological complaints i.e., seizures, weakness, numbness ("No.")

___10. asked about urinary problems i.e., hematuria, foamy urine ("No.")

___11. asked about cold temperature causing problems with my fingers i.e., Raynaud's phenomenon ("Sometimes my fingers become pale then blue when I go outside in the cold weather.")

___12. asked about a history of pregnancy i.e., miscarriages ("No.")

___13. asked about medications ("None.")

___14. asked about a family history of collagen vascular disease ("I had a cousin who died from lupus.")

Physical Examination. The Examinee:

___15. asked me to remove my scarf to examine my scalp for alopecia i.e., hair loss (SP has numerous bald spots when scarf is removed).

___16. looked in my mouth for ulcers (after examinee performs this task, SP will show picture of mouth ulcers).

___17. checked at least 3 joints for any abnormalities (no joint tenderness or warmth; no nodules).

___18. listened to my heart (normal examination; no audible rub).

___19. listened to my lungs (normal examination).

Communication Skills. The Examinee:

___20. greeted me warmly.

___21. introduced himself/herself to me.

___22. put me at ease.

___23. gave me information about the diagnosis (systemic lupus erythematosus or other collagen vascular disease).

___24. talked about the plan in an organized fashion (bloodwork, urinalysis, immunologic markers).

___25. checked my understanding of the problem.

___26. offered me continuous and ongoing support.

___27. discussed a follow-up appointment with me.

___28. stated I could still be a lawyer when I expressed concern about my career choice.

If you performed 20 of these 28 tasks, you passed this test station.

LEARNING OBJECTIVE ON MS. JUSTICE:
DIAGNOSING SYSTEMIC LUPUS ERYTHEMATOSUS (SLE)

Ms. Judy Justice has recently been diagnosed with discoid lupus. The dermatologist has now referred the patient to you for further investigation of her symptoms.

Initially, Ms. Justice tells you she has no complaints. The plaque on her leg which was biopsied has resolved with the steroid cream prescribed by the dermatologist. As the physician begins to investigate systemic involvement in this patient, it becomes plausible that Ms. Justice may have systemic lupus erythematosus.

The risk factors for SLE include genetic predisposition and Ms. Justice admits that a cousin died of lupus. Most cases of the disease occur in women during their child-bearing years and Ms. Justice is 25 years old. Drugs may induce lupus but the patient does not take any medications such as isoniazid, hydralazine, or procainamide. The incidence of SLE appears to be higher in African-Americans and Hispanics.

Ms. Justice admits to several symptoms of SLE including joint pain, Raynaud's phenomenon, hair loss, malar rash, oral ulcers, and photosensitivity. She also complains of weight loss, fever, and generalized malaise. She has no heart, lung, kidney, or central nervous system complaints. She has no previous history of miscarriages which may be seen in SLE patients with anti-phospholipid antibodies.

On physical examination, heart and lung examinations reveal no evidence of pericarditis or pleuritis. Ulcers are present in the mouth but joints are normal. Alopecia is evident after the patient is asked to remove her scarf and the scalp is examined.

The differential diagnosis for Ms. Justice should include autoimmune diseases such as systemic lupus erythematosus, rheumatoid arthritis, and progressive systemic sclerosis. Further evaluation looking for hematologic abnormalities (thrombocytopenia, anemia, leukopenia), renal dysfunction (hematuria and proteinuria), and immunological markers is required. Ms. Justice requires reassurance that the outlook for this disease has improved significantly and, with proper treatment, she can continue her studies and become a lawyer.

OSCE Interstation Pearl: Be prepared to discuss the immunologic tests for SLE. Antinuclear antibody is a very sensitive screening test but antibodies to native or double-stranded DNA are more specific for the diagnosis of SLE. Complement levels become depressed during active disease but return to normal levels during remissions. The most common manifestation of SLE is arthritis. The most common cause of death is infection not renal disease.

CSA Patient Note Pearl: The differential diagnosis for this patient may include SLE, discoid lupus, progressive systemic sclerosis, and rhematoid arthritis. The diagnostic work-up may include CBC with platelet count, electrolytes, urinalysis, ANA, and antibodies to double stranded DNA.

Case 14

Case 14

A 65-year old man named Charlie Champion presents to your office complaining of difficulty swallowing. His vital signs are normal. Please interview Mr. Champion and perform a brief physical examination on this patient. You have fifteen minutes.

MY CHECKLIST

History of Present Illness. The Examinee:

1. _____
2. _____
   _____
3. _____
4. _____
   _____
5. _____
6. _____
7. _____
   _____
8. _____
9. _____
10. _____
11. _____

Physical Examination. The Examinee:

12. _____
13. _____
14. _____
   _____

Communication Skills. The Examinee:

15. _____
16. _____
17. _____
   _____
18. _____
19. _____
20. _____
21. _____
22. _____
23. _____
24. _____

SP CHECKLIST FOR MR. CHAMPION

History of Present Illness. The Examinee:

___1. asked if there was "real dysphagia" i.e., a feeling of food sticking in the chest ("Yes, that describes what I'm feeling.")

___2. asked about the onset of dysphagia ("It started about 2 months ago.")

___3. asked specifically about difficulty swallowing solid foods (" I definitely can't swallow anything solid.")

___4. asked specifically about difficulty swallowing liquids ("Not in the beginning but now it's getting to the point where swallowing water is becoming a problem.")

___5. asked about painful swallowing i.e., odynophagia ("No.")

___6. asked about weight loss ("Yes. I've lost 20 pounds in the last month.")

___7. asked about alcohol use ("I used to be a heavy drinker; a pint of whiskey a day for 25 years; I stopped drinking 2 months ago when this problem started.")

___8. asked about tobacco use ("Yes. I still smoke 2 packs of cigarettes per day for over 25 years.")

___9. asked about a previous history of gastrointestinal problems i.e. reflux ("No")

___10. asked about a history of lye ingestion ("No.")

___11. asked about any hoarseness ("No.")

Physical Examination. The Examinee:

___12. looked inside my mouth for obstructive lesions (normal mouth and pharynx).

___13. checked my neck for an enlarged thyroid gland or other obstructive masses (none evident).

___14. checked for either axillary or supraclavicular nodes (after the examinee performs this task, SP should give card with results: 3cm. fixed left supraclavicular node is palpable).

Communication Skills. The Examinee:

___15. explained the possible diagnosis (esophageal carcinoma, achalasia, stricture).

___16. explained that risk factors for the disease include tobacco and alcohol use.

___17. explained the next step in the work-up (bloodwork to check for dehydration, esophagram, gastroenterology consult for possible endoscopy).

___18. explained that the supraclavicular node was probably due to the cancer.

___19. stated that I would need nutritional support either in the hospital or at home.

___20. inquired about my support system ("I have a wife at home; no children.")

___21. offered to help me tell my wife ("Oh, that would be a big help, Doctor.")

___22. demonstrated empathy for my situation.

___23. discussed prognosis (this is a serious problem).

___24. asked me if there was anything not covered in the discussion.

If you performed 17 of these 24 tasks, you passed this test station.

LEARNING OBJECTIVE FOR MR. CHAMPION:
RECOGNIZE DYSPHAGIA SECONDARY TO ESOPHAGEAL CARCINOMA

Mr. Champion presents with the chief complaint of dysphagia, initially to solids then progressing to liquids(progressive dysphagia), accompanied by anorexia and rapid weight loss. It is important to inquire about the dysphagia symptoms (food sticking implies "real" dysphagia). Dysphagia accompanied by odynophagia (painful swallowing) may indicate mediastinal invasion by the tumor. Other symptoms of esophageal cancer may include cough, hoarseness, choking, fever, and aspiration pnemonitis. The patient has a long history of alcohol and tobacco abuse which predisposes him to developing esophageal carcinoma. Other risk factors for esophageal cancer include chronic gastric reflux causing a Barrett's esophagus, achalasia, and lye ingestion. The differential diagnosis for dysphagia in this patient would include a stricture and achalasia.

On physical examination, Mr. Champion has a normal sounding voice. Tumor involvement of the recurrent laryngeal nerve would cause hoarseness. The mouth and neck examinations reveal no obstructive lesions responsible for the dysphagia. A careful search for metastatic lymphadenopathy reveals a fixed node in the left supraclavicular area. In most cases, the physical examination in patients with esophageal carcinoma is unremarkable.

The work-up for Mr. Champion includes admission to the hospital for nutritional support and to prevent further weight loss. A barium esophagram is the first step in the work-up of any patient with dysphagia. If a lesion is seen radiographically, further evaluation with endoscopy, biopsy, and histological assessment is warranted to confirm the diagnosis.

The treatment for esophageal carcinoma is palliative when the disease is metastatic. The goal of therapy is to relieve dysphagia if possible and maximize quality of life for each patient.

OSCE Interstation Pearl: Squamous cell carcinoma is the more common histology in African-Americans while adenocarcinoma is more common in white patients with esophageal cancer. A chest radiograph at this interstation may reveal lung or bony metastases. The first step in the work-up for dysphagia is an esophagram not endoscopy.

CSA Patient Note Pearl: The differential diagnosis for esophageal dysphagia is:

Solid food dysphagia (mechanical problem)
       Intermittent: lower esophagus (Schatzki's ring)
       Progressive: stricture (has heartburn)
                      cancer

Solid or liquid dysphagia (neuromuscular problem)
       Intermittent: diffuse esophageal spasm (has chest pain)
       Progressive: scleroderma (has heartburn)
                      achalasia (may have respiratory symptoms)

Case 15

A 62-year old man, named Mr. Samuel Samson, has an appointment to see you. His neighbor has scheduled the appointment for Mr. Samson because he feels that his friend frequently trips and falls at home. The neighbor feels that, one day, Mr. Samson will fall and really hurt himself. Vital signs for Mr. Samson reveal:

Blood pressure	160/80 mm Hg
Heart rate	80 beats per minute and regular
Respiratory rate	12 breaths per minute
Temperature	98.6° F

There are no orthostatic changes in this patient. Upon entering the examination room, you notice a man looking older than his stated age. He has noticeable tremors of his right hand. You have 15 minutes to perform a focused and appropriate history and physical examination on Mr. Samson. Please limit yourself to the time provided.

MY CHECKLIST

History of Present Illness. The Examinee:

1. _____
2. _____
3. _____
4. _____
5. _____
6. _____
7. _____
   _____
   _____
   _____
   _____
8. _____
   _____
   _____

Physical Examination. The Examinee:

9. _____
10. _____
    _____
    _____
11. _____
    _____
12. _____
    _____

Communication Skills. The Examinee:

13. _____
14. _____
15. _____
16. _____
17. _____
18. _____
19. _____
    _____
20. _____
21. _____
22. _____

SP CHECKLIST FOR MR. SAMSON

History of Present Illness. The Examinee:

___1.   asked about the onset of the frequent falls ("It started about 3 months ago.")

___2.   asked about the last time I fell ("This morning. It was more like a tripping than a falling.")

___3.   asked about dizziness or vertigo with the falls ("No.")

___4.   asked about any loss of consciousness during falls i.e., syncope ("No.")

___5.   asked about the onset of tremors at rest ("Oh, these started maybe a year ago.")

___6.   asked about a family history of tremors ("No one in my family has these tremors.")

___7.   asked about the performance of other activities of daily living (ADLs) besides walking i.e., bathing, feeding, toileting, dressing, transferring in and out of chairs and bed ("I sometimes have a little trouble getting out of chairs, I have a little trouble with buttons and zippers when I get dressed and sometimes I don't make it to the bathroom; lately I've been wearing a diaper when I go out.")

___8.   asked about the performance of instrumental activities of daily living (IADLs) i.e., shopping, traveling, cooking, managing money, using the telephone, and cleaning the house ("My good neighbor helps me with the bills, shopping, and cooking. The house is usually a mess and I don't own a phone anymore.")

Physical Examination. The Examinee:

___9.   checked the patient for cogwheel rigidity (SP will have cogwheel rigidity).

___10. asked the patient to try and get out of a chair, walk across the room, turn around, and return to the chair (SP will have difficulty getting out of chair, gait will be shuffling, posture will be flexed and leaning forward, small steps will be taken by the patient with difficulty initiating and stopping ambulation; SP will turn-en-bloc; decreased arm swing when walking).

___11. asked the patient to perform a task to verify that tremor disappears with intention (SP will stop tremors with movement; tremors will be at rest only).

___12. performed part of the mini-mental status examination e.g., calculation, 3 object recall, spell backwards, orientation (SP will perform well).

Communication Skills. The Examinee:

___13. greeted me warmly.

___14. explained my physical findings to me (tremors, gait, cogwheel rigidity).

___15. discussed the problem with me (plausible diagnosis is Parkinson's disease).

___16. explained that the frequent falls and other difficulties were due to Parkinson's disease.

___17. discussed treatment (medications).

___18. discussed prognosis (some of the symptoms may improve with medications).

___19. asked about support systems ("No family. Only my neighbor who I can count on to help. He's like a son to me.")

___20. discussed community resources that exist to help me remain at home.

___21. offered ongoing support and help.

___22. scheduled follow-up appointment with me.

If you performed 16 of these 22 tasks, you passed this test station.

LEARNING OBJECTIVE FOR MR. SAMSON:
FUNCTIONAL ASSESSMENT OF GAIT IN A PATIENT WITH PARKINSON'S DISEASE

This patient presents with resting tremors, bradykinesia, and a history of frequent falls. Mr. Samson's posture is flexed and he has difficulty getting out of chairs due to his rigidity. He rarely blinks, has few facial movements, and he walks without swinging his arms because of the paucity of his movements. His gait is shuffling and consists of small steps. It is difficult for him to initiate and stop ambulation. For Mr. Samson, turning around when walking requires time and effort because of the many steps involved in this process. All of these symptoms are consistent with the diagnosis of Parkinson's disease.

On physical examination, Mr. Samson has cogwheel rigidity. His right hand pill-rolling tremors seem to worsen with stress and disappear with movement (if tested, he would also demonstrate micrographia). The mini-mental status examination is consistent with mild cognitive impairment. An assessment of his gait confirms that he is at risk for frequent falls due to the parkinsonian symptoms.

With appropriate medications, such as anticholinergics or dopaminergic agents, Mr. Samson's symptoms may improve to the point where he can take better care of himself. For the time being, however, it is clear that the patient needs assistance at home. Mr. Samson has no family support system but a caring neighbor seems to be interested in helping the patient. The neighbor along with resources in the community should be utilized to improve the quality of life which now exists for this patient. Careful follow-up of this patient would include home visits by a physician, nurse, and social worker.

History-Taking Pearl: Elderly patients should be screened for frequent falls regardless of the presenting problem. Simply ask the patient if he/she has fallen all the way to the ground over the last 12 months. Measures to prevent falls include proper patient footware and improved lighting in the home. Medications that contribute to falls in the elderly include sedatives, diuretics, and antidepressant agents.

Physical Examination Pearl: The "get up and go" test may be discussed at this interstation. The patient must get out of a chair, walk 10 feet, turn around, and walk back to the chair under 15 seconds. Gait abnormalities and risk for falling can be assessed with this test. Individuals who perform poorly may benefit from physical therapy.

OSCE Interstation Pearl: Be prepared to discuss the patient's ability to live alone by inquiring about the activities of daily living (DEATH = dressing, eating, ambulating, toileting, hygiene) and instrumental activities of daily living or IADLs (SHAFT = shopping, housekeeping, accounting, food preparation, transportation).

CSA Patient Note Pearl: The differential diagnosis for this patient is Parkinson's disease, dementia, hypothyroidism, depression, essential familial (benign) tremor, and parkinsonism due to postencephalitic illness, carbon monoxide poisoning, drugs (MPTP-meperidine analogue used as an illicit drug, reserpine, metoclopramide, and neuroleptics), brain tumor, Huntington's chorea, and Wilson's disease. The diagnosis of Parkinson's disease is made by physical examination and the patient's good response to levodopa. Laboratory tests may include copper, ceruloplasmin, and TSH levels. An MRI is not helpful in diagnosing Parkinson's disease and, as of yet, no biologic marker exists to confirm the diagnosis.

Case 16

Case 16

An 18-year old high school senior named Bruce Berger has made an urgent appointment to see you because of a headache which developed during football practice. He had to leave practice because of the severe pain.

Upon entering the room, you see a young man with eyes closed tightly holding the left side of his head. His blood pressure is 110/75 mm Hg. The rest of his vital signs are within normal limits. Please evaluate Mr. Berger in ten minutes. Perform a focused history and physical examination on this patient.

MY CHECKLIST

History of Present Illness. The Examinee:

1. _____
2. _____
3. _____
4. _____
5. _____
6. _____
7. _____
8. _____
9. _____
10. _____
11. _____
12. _____
    _____
13. _____
14. _____
15. _____
16. _____
17. _____

Physical Examination. The Examinee:

18. _____
19. _____
20. _____
21. _____
22. _____

Communication Skills. The Examinee:

23. _____
24. _____
25. _____
26. _____
27. _____
    _____
28. _____

SP CHECKLIST FOR MR. BERGER

History of Present Illness. The Examinee:

____1.   asked about the onset of the headache ("It started 3 hours ago after football practice.")

____2.   asked about the quality of the headache ("Pounding and throbbing.")

____3.   asked about progression of the headache ("It seems to be getting worse. It seems to be building up.")

____4.   asked about the location of the headache ("The entire left side of my head.")

____5.   asked about the intensity of the headache ("On a scale of 1 to 10, this is a 10.")

____6.   asked about alleviating factors ("Closing my eyes and staying very still help.")

____7.   asked about aggravating factors ("Movement, light, and noise make it worse.")

____8.   asked about any association with nausea or vomiting ("I vomited once and I still feel nauseated.")

____9.   asked about neurologic deficits i.e., weakness, sensory changes, speech difficulties ("No.")

____10. asked about an aura preceding headache ("Lights were flashing for about 20 minutes before it started.")

____11. asked about recent fever ('No.")

____12. asked about a previous history of headaches ("I suffer with bad headaches but they usually go away in 2 hours. I've had headaches for 10 years.")

____13. asked what precipitates the headaches ("The stress of exams or important football games.")

____14. asked about a family history of headache ("My mother and sister have migraines.")

____15. asked about a history of head trauma during football practice ('No.")

____16. asked about illicit drug use ("No.")

____17. asked about alcohol use ("No.")

Physical Examination. The Examinee:

____18. evaluated pupillary response to light with a flashlight (normal examination of pupils).

____19. looked into my eyes with an ophthalmoscope (normal fundoscopic examination).

____20. evaluated my neck for stiffness (no nuchal rigidity).

____21. tested the reflexes in my arms or legs (normal reflexes).

____22. tested the muscle strength in my arms or legs (normal strength).

Communication Skills. The Examinee:

____23. discussed the initial impression with me (plausible diagnosis is migraine headaches).

____24. discussed the plan with me (medication).

____25. discussed how the stress of football practice may have precipitated the headache.

____26. explained that my family history of migraine headaches made me at risk for headaches.

____27. discussed other precipitating factors for migraine headaches (alcohol use, chocolate, monosodium glutamate, hunger, lack of sleep).

____28. acknowledged my distress and discomfort.

If you performed 20 of these 28 tasks, you passed this test station.

LEARNING OBJECTIVE FOR MR. BRUCE BERGER:
DIAGNOSE AND TREAT MIGRAINE HEADACHE

Mr. Bruce Berger has a presentation consistent with "classic" migraine headaches. He has a severe, throbbing, left sided headache associated with vomiting and aggravated by bright light or noise. A twenty minute aura of flashing lights preceded the headache. He had to interrupt his activities because of the intensity of the headache. He has a ten year history of headaches (migraines may start around the time of puberty) and a family history remarkable for migraines. He feels that this headache was precipitated by the stress of the big football game scheduled for the weekend.

Mr. Berger denies recent fever or illness that might suggest an infectious etiology for his headaches (sinusitis or meningitis). Subarachnoid hemorrhage must be considered in the differential diagnosis for this patient but he has a long history of similar headaches and has no changes in his neurologic status. The patient denies risk factors for stroke such as cocaine use. Subdural hematoma (especially since the headache started during football practice) is unlikely without a history of head trauma. Temporal arteritis is uncommon in a twenty-two year old man. Tension headaches are usually described as being band-like and occipital in location. Cluster headaches are brief frontal headaches often associated with tearing and nasal stuffiness.

Migraine headaches may be precipitated by diet (cheese, chocolate, processed meats), stress, menses, lack of sleep, exercise, sexual intercourse, hunger, and alcoholic beverages (the patient denies alcohol use). "Common" migraine (without aura) lacks neurologic symptoms while "classic" (with aura) and "complicated" migraines may present with focal neurologic deficits. Common migraines are five times more common than classic migraines. Serotonin agonists and ergotamine agents act by vasoconstricting cranial blood vessels and are used to treat acute episodes of migraine. Patients who have frequent migraine attacks require prophylactic therapy.

History-Taking Pearl: Remember the POUNDing headaches mnemonic for migraine: **P** = **p**ulsating; **O** = last **o**ne day; **U** = **u**nilateral; **N** = associated with **n**ausea; **D** = **d**isturbance in daily activities; if the patient answers yes to 4 of these questions, it is most likely a migraine headache.

CSA Patient Note Pearl: The differential diagnosis for headache includes migraine headache, tension headache, cluster headache, subdural hematoma, sinus headache, meningitis, depression, subarachnoid hemorrhage, hypertension, intracranial mass, and temporal arteritis. The work-up may include a CT scan of the head or an MRI when clinically indicated.

Case 17

An 18-year old college freshman named Suzy Sunshine presents to the campus health center complaining of burning on urination. Her temperature is 101.2° F but the rest of her vital signs are normal.

You have ten minutes to perform a focused history and physical examination on Ms. Sunshine. Please limit yourself to the time provided.

MY CHECKLIST

History of Present Illness. The Examinee:

1. _____
2. _____
3. _____
4. _____
5. _____
6. _____
7. _____
8. _____
9. _____
10. _____
11. _____
12. _____
13. _____

Physical Examination. The Examinee:

14. _____
15. _____
16. _____
17. _____
18. _____

Communication Skills. The Examinee:

19. _____
20. _____
21. _____
22. _____
23. _____
24. _____
25. _____

SP CHECKLIST FOR MS. SUNSHINE

History of Present Illness. The Examinee:

____1.   asked about the onset of dysuria ("It started 2 days ago.")

____2.   asked about frequency of urination ("Yes, I urinate maybe 20 times a day.")

____3.   asked about hematuria ("No.")

____4.   asked about fever at home ("I was 101.5° F last night.")

____5.   asked about shaking chills ("No.")

____6.   asked about abdominal pain ("Yes, the lower part of my abdomen hurts.")

____7.   asked about back pain ("Yes; the left side of my back hurts me.")

____8.   asked about nausea or vomiting ("No.")

____9.   asked about diarrhea ("No.")

____10.   asked about a history of urinary tract problems i.e., stones, recurrent infections ("No.")

____11.   asked about my last menstrual flow ("5 days ago; no problems.")

____12.   asked about the possibility of pregnancy ("No. I use condoms with one partner.")

____13.   asked about a history of sexually transmitted diseases ("Never.")

Physical Examination. The Examinee:

____14.   listened to my abdomen with a stethoscope (normal bowel sounds appreciated).

____15.   pressed throughout my abdomen gently (no tenderness with mild palpation).

____16.   pressed deeply throughout the abdomen (positive suprapubic tenderness with deep palpation).

____17.   tapped on my back to elicit costovertebral angle tenderness (positive left CVA tenderness).

____18.   asked to perform a pelvic examination (after examinee asks to perform this task, SP should give card with results: no adnexal or cervical motion tenderness; no vaginal discharge).

Communication Skills. The Examinee:

____19.   washed hands before starting the physical examination.

____20.   cared about my embarrassment during the physical examination.

____21.   allowed me to fully dress before beginning discussion of my problem.

____22.   discussed the diagnosis with me (pyelonephritis is the plausible diagnosis).

____23.   discussed the work-up in terms I could understand (urinalysis, urine culture, bloodwork).

____24.   discussed the treatment with me (hydration, antibiotics).

____25.   discussed the importance of close follow-up.

If you performed 18 of these 25 tasks, you passed this test station.

LEARNING OBJECTIVE FOR MS. SUZY SUNSHINE:
DIAGNOSE PYELONEPHRITIS

Ms. Suzy Sunshine presents complaining of fever, back pain, dysuria and frequency. She denies hematuria. She has no gynecologic or gastrointestinal complaints. She has no previous history of urinary tract infection. She is not pregnant and has no history of previous sexually transmitted disease.

On physical examination, the patient has suprapubic tenderness with palpation and has left costovertebral angle tenderness. Her pelvic examination is normal. There are no findings in the history or physical examination that suggest pelvic inflammatory disease.

The most likely diagnosis in this patient is pyelonephritis. The symptoms may include fever, abdominal pain, back or flank pain, nausea, vomiting, and diarrhea. Blood analysis will reveal a leukocytosis and urinalysis will be positive for nitrites, leukocytes, and bacteria.

Although most cases of pyelonephritis require hospitalization, this patient could probably be treated and managed as an outpatient. She is able to tolerate oral hydration and medications and will be compliant with a fourteen-day treatment regimen. She appears well and has no predisposing risk factor for infection (stones). Ms. Sunshine will be closely followed by her physician.

OSCE Interstation Pearl: You may be asked to interpret a urine sediment with leukocytes or leukocyte casts. A urine gram stain is often found at this interstation.

CSA Patient Note Pearl: The differential diagnosis for this patient includes pyelonephritis and pelvic inflammatory disease. In any patient presenting with flank pain and fever, other etiologies should be considered, such as, a kidney stone, pneumonia, appendicitis, cholecystitis, pancreatitis, and diverticulitis. In this patient, these seem unlikely. The work-up for this patient should include a pelvic examination, complete blood count, urinalysis and urine culture. Males with dysuria should be investigated for prostatitis and epididymitis.

Case 18

Eighteen-year old Morgan Montgomery presents with the chief complaint of a rash on his right thigh. His vital signs are normal.

Upon entering the examination room, you notice a young man in boxer shorts with a circular lesion 15 cms. in diameter located on his right lateral thigh. The rash has a thin, red border with central clearing.

You have fifteen minutes to perform a history and physical examination on Mr. Montgomery. Limit yourself to the time provided.

MY CHECKLIST

History of Present Illness. The Examinee:

1. _____
2. _____
3. _____
4. _____
5. _____
6. _____
7. _____
8. _____
9. _____
10. _____
11. _____
12. _____
13. _____
    _____
14. _____

Physical Examination. The Examinee:

15. _____
16. _____
    _____
    _____
    _____
17. _____
18. _____
19. _____
20. _____

Communication Skills. The Examinee:

21. _____
22. _____
23. _____
24. _____
25. _____
26. _____

SP CHECKLIST FOR MR. MONTGOMERY

History of Present Illness. The Examinee:

___1.   asked about the onset of the rash ("It started about 2 weeks ago; I thought it would go away.")

___2.   asked if the rash was progressing ("Yes, it's getting wider.")

___3.   asked if the rash was pruritic ("No.")

___4.   asked about recent insect bites ("None that I can remember.")

___5.   asked about outdoor activity i.e., camping or hiking ("No.")

___6.   asked about occupation ("I'm a landscaper.")

___7.   asked about fever ("Sometimes my temperature is 101° F.")

___8.   asked about shaking chills ("Yes.")

___9.   asked about muscle aches ("Yes.")

___10. asked about fatigue ("I have no energy; I am not feeling well. I'm tired all the time.")

___11. asked about headache ("Definitely. Intermittent, occipital, and relieved with Tylenol.")

___12. asked about any cardiac symptoms i.e., palpitations, shortness of breath, chest pain ("No.")

___13. asked about any neurologic problems i.e., stiff neck, numbness, vision changes, problems with gait or coordination ("No.")

___14. asked about joint pain ("No.")

Physical Examination. The Examinee:

___15. examined the rash closely (rash is warm and nontender).

___16. checked for lymphadenopathy i.e., neck, axillary, inguinal (after examinee asks to perform this task, SP should give card with results: few, scattered, nontender, freely moveable nodes are palpable in cervical, axillary, and inguinal area).

___17. listened to my heart in at least 3 places (normal examination).

___18. checked at least 2 joints for abnormalities (normal joint examination).

___19. checked the movement of my eye muscles (normal extraocular muscle movement).

___20. checked sensation in my legs i.e., sharp and dull, vibration (normal sensation).

Communication Skills. The Examinee:

___21. explained the initial impression (plausible diagnosis is Lyme disease).

___22. explained that a tick bite from my occupational exposure caused the rash.

___23. discussed the work-up (bloodwork, electrocardiogram, frequent follow-up).

___24. explained that antibiotics would be needed.

___25. explained that my stage of disease was early and would most likely not progress.

___26. answered all my questions in a manner I could understand.

If you performed 19 of these 26 tasks, you passed this test station.

LEARNING OBJECTIVE FOR MR. MONTGOMERY:
RECOGNIZE LYME DISEASE

Mr. Montgomery works as a landscaper and is at risk for tick-borne illness. He presents with erythema migrans (EM) which is the rash characteristic of Lyme disease. Lyme disease occurs mostly in the summer months and is caused by the spirochete, Borrelia burgdorferi. It is important to obtain the appropriate history and physical examination to determine the extent and stage of disease (localized or disseminated).

On questioning, Mr. Montgomery admits to a headache, fever, chills, myalgias, and fatigue (this is often referred to as the pentad of Lyme disease). He denies cardiac, neurologic, and rheumatologic complaints. On physical examination, his heart examination reveals no evidence of pericarditis or left ventricular dysfunction (an electrocardiogram will be needed to exclude atrioventricular heart block). His rheumatologic examination reveals no joint warmth or erythema. On neurologic examination, cranial nerves and sensation are intact. There is no evidence of neuropathy or neuritis.

Lyme disease is a three stage disease. *Stage One* disease (up to 20 days after the tick bite) consists of the classic erythema migrans lesion (occurs in 70% of patients) and flu-like symptoms. *Stage Two* disease (up to 3 months after the tick bite) is accompanied by fever, neck stiffness, headache, lethargy, arthralgias, sore throat, generalized lymphadenopathy, splenomegaly, mononeuritis multiplex (i.e., Bell's palsy), neuropathy, encephalitis, and cardiac complications such as pericarditis and heart block.

Stage Three disease occurs months to years later in untreated patients and consists of arthritis and central nervous system manifestations such as memory loss and mood disorders.

Mr. Montgomery has early disseminated Lyme disease (EM with systemic symptoms like headache, malaise, fatigue, and arthralgias). Serologic studies will be ordered and the patient will be treated with oral antibiotic therapy. Most patients recover without residual deficits.

Physical Examination Pearl: Patients who present with Bell's palsy should be screened for Lyme disease, however, the most common cause of bilateral Bell's palsy is Guillain-Barré syndrome.

OSCE Interstation Pearl: An electrocardiogram with first, second, or third degree heart block may be found at this interstation. You may need to counsel patients at high risk for tick bites. Advise them to use long-sleeved shirts, long pants tucked into socks, and repellent sprays. Routine antibiotic prophylaxis for all tick bites is not indicated.

CSA Patient Note Pearl: EM (erythema migrans) is due to the Ixodes dammini tick bite (causative agent is Borrelia burgdorferi) that causes Lyme disease. In the absence of this rash, Lyme disease may be confused with other diseases, such as, chronic fatigue sydrome or fibromyalgia (these have no joint involvement and tend to be more debilitating). The diagnostic work-up for Lyme disease should include laboratory confirmation by either indirect immunofluorescence assay (IFA) or the more sensitive and specific ELISA (enzyme-linked immunosorbent assay). A Western blot test is sent to confirm the positive ELISA. If the Western blot is negative (for IgM and IgG) in the first four weeks of the infection, convalescent titers should be sent since some patients may be antibody negative during the early weeks of illness.

Case 19

Case 19

The gynecologist in your office building asks you to evaluate a 20-year old college student with hematochezia. Her vital signs are normal and there are no orthostatic changes.

The gynecologist has faxed you her laboratory results which include a complete blood count and electrolyte profile. All laboratory data are normal except for a mild anemia. Please perform a history and focused physical examination on Ms. Kandi Kane in 15 minutes.

MY CHECKLIST

History of Present Illness. The Examinee:

1. _____
2. _____
3. _____
4. _____
5. _____
6. _____
7. _____
8. _____
9. _____
10. _____
11. _____
12. _____
13. _____

Physical Examination. The Examinee:

14. _____
15. _____
16. _____
17. _____
18. _____

Communication Skills. The Examinee:

19. _____
20. _____
21. _____
22. _____
23. _____
24. _____
25. _____

SP CHECKLIST FOR MS. KANDIE KANE

History of Present Illness. The Examinee:

___1. asked about the onset of rectal bleeding ("It started 3 months ago. It comes and goes.")

___2. asked about the frequency of the hematochezia ("It happens once a day.")

___3. asked about diarrhea ("Yes; I move my bowels 5 times a day everyday.")

___4. asked about abdominal pain ("Sometimes crampy pain in my lower abdomen but not very often.")

___5. asked about nausea or vomiting ("No.")

___6. asked about fecal urgency ("Yes; I have to run out of class sometimes to use the ladies room.")

___7. asked about tenesmus ("I sit on the toilet an hour sometimes; I feel like I need to go.")

___8. asked about mucus in stools ("Yes")

___9. asked about fever ("No.")

___10. asked about weight loss ("Maybe 5 or 6 pounds in the last month.")

___11. asked about recent antibiotic use ("None.")

___12. asked about risk factors for infectious etiology for diarrhea i.e., recent travel, ill contacts ("None.")

___13. asked about a family history of gastrointestinal problems ("None.")

Physical Examination. The Examinee:

___14. listened to my abdomen with a stethoscope (normal bowel sounds auscultated).

___15. tapped over my liver area (no hepatomegaly).

___16. pressed gently throughout my abdomen (no abdominal tenderness).

___17. pressed deeply throughout my abdomen (mild left lower quadrant tenderness with deep palpation).

___18. asked to perform a rectal examination (after examinee asks to perform this task, SP should give card with results: brown stool; bright red blood on glove; mucus evident; no masses or hemorrhoids).

Communication Skills. The Examinee:

___19. explained the initial impression (plausible diagnosis is inflammatory bowel disease).

___20. explained the next steps in the work-up (sigmoidoscopy, biopsy).

___21. explained that medications were available for this problem.

___22. explained the prognosis (can stabilize this chronic problem).

___23. asked about family support system ("My parents are always there for me.").

___24. offered to help tell my parents ("Great. Thank-you very much.").

___25. offered continuous support.

If you performed 17 of these 25 tasks, you passed this test station.

LEARNING OBJECTIVE FOR MS. KANDIE KANE:
RECOGNIZE INFLAMMATORY BOWEL DISEASE (IBD)

Ms. Kandie Kane is a premed student who recently developed hematochezia accompanied by crampy abdominal pain. The pain is relieved after she has a bowel movement. She also complains of urgency and tenesmus. Her stool is bloody and contains mucus. Since this problem began, she has lost five pounds and developed a mild anemia.

On physical examination, the patient has normal bowel sounds and mild tenderness with palpation. Her rectal examination is remarkable for a small amount of bright red blood.

The presentation is most consistent with inflammatory bowel disease (it is unclear at this time if the patient has Crohn's disease or ulcerative colitis). IBD is more prevalent in whites, particularly Ashkenazi Jews. The sexes are equally affected. There is a higher incidence of IBD in patients with a positive family history but the patient denies this risk factor. Infectious diarrhea may present with hematochezia and the stools of this patient need to be evaluated for various bacteria, ova, and parasites. Pseudomembranous colitis from Clostridium difficile is unlikely in a patient with no history of antibiotic use. Ischemic colitis is uncommon in a young woman without a predisposing risk factor.

Ms. Kandie Kane will need sigmoidoscopy with biopsy for a definitive diagnosis. The sigmoisoscopy will reveal a uniformly friable and ulcerated colonic mucosa. Biopsy will demonstrate the inflammatory reaction consistent with ulcerative colitits.

The patient will receive medication in an attempt to diminish symptoms and improve her quality of life. The patient must be informed about the possible systemic complications of inflammatory bowel disease including liver, eye, and skin involvement. The higher incidence of colonic carcinoma in patients with IBD requires an honest and frank discussion with the patient. Close follow-up and surveillance is required for any patient with IBD. The physician must offer Ms. Kane partnership, reassurance, and ongoing support.

CSA Patient Note Pearl: The differential diagnosis for hematochezia in this patient includes ulcerative colitis, Crohn's disease, hemorrhoids, and infectious diarrhea. Patients with pseudomembranous colitis, ischemic colitis, colon polyps, angiodysplasia, diverticulosis, and malignancy may also present with rectal bleeding. The diagnostic work-up for the patient should include complete blood count to evaluate for anemia or infection, electrolytes to check for abnormalities due to diarrhea, and flexible sigmoidoscopy with possible biopsy. Stools for ova, parasites, and culture may be sent but an infectious etiology is less likely.

Case 20

A 31-year old executive presents to your office with the chief complaint of blurred vision. He went to the optometrist in the shopping mall who found nothing wrong with his eyesight. The optometrist suggested a check-up from a primary care physician. The patient has not seen a doctor in over 10 years.

The nurse in your practice tells you that the fasting fingerstick glucose level this morning for Mr. David Dunn was 210 mgs/dl. His vital signs are normal and he has no orthostatic changes.

Upon entering the examination room, you see an overweight man in no acute distress. His weight is approximately 190 pounds and he is 5 feet, 8 inches tall.

You have 15 minutes to evaluate Mr. Dunn and perform an appropriate history and physical examination. Please limit yourself to the time provided.

MY CHECKLIST

History of Present Illness. The Examinee:

1. _____
2. _____
3. _____
4. _____
5. _____
6. _____
7. _____
8. _____
9. _____
10. _____
11. _____

Physical Examination. The Examinee:

12. _____
    _____
13. _____
14. _____
    _____
15. _____
16. _____
17. _____
18. _____
19. _____

Communication Skills. The Examinee:

20. _____
21. _____
22. _____
23. _____
    _____
24. _____
25. _____
26. _____
27. _____
28. _____
29. _____

SP CHECKLIST FOR MR. DAVID DUNN

History of Present Illness. The Examinee:

___1.   asked about the onset of the blurred vision ("It started maybe 2 months ago.")

___2.   asked about excessive thirst ("Yes; I have been drinking lots of water lately.")

___3.   asked about excessive urination ("Yes; I seem to pass a great amount of urine.")

___4.   asked about my appetite ("I eat like a horse.")

___5.   asked about weight loss ("I have lost about 10 pounds the last several months.")

___6.   asked about autonomic problems i.e., impotence, incontinence, dizziness on standing, early satiety from gastroparesis ("I am having problems recently regarding impotence.")

___7.   asked about claudication i.e., pain in the back of my leg when walking ("No.")

___8.   asked about numbness and tingling of my feet ("Yes, that happens all the time now.")

___9.   asked about a family history of diabetes ("My mother uses pills for diabetes.")

___10.   asked about tobacco use ("I do smoke a pack per day for 15 years.")

___11.   asked about alcohol use ("None.")

Physical Examination. The Examinee:

___12.   looked in my eyes with an ophthalmoscope (after examinee performs this task, SP should give picture showing fundi with hard exudates).

___13.   listened over my neck for carotid bruits (no bruits audible).

___14.   felt for point of maximum impulse (PMI) over heart (after examinee performs this task, SP should give card with results: PMI at sixth intercostal space displaced 2 cms. from the midclavicular line).

___15.   listened to my heart in at least 3 places (SP will have an S4 gallop audible).

___16.   listened to my lungs in at least 4 places (normal lung auscultation).

___17.   felt my pulses in both feet (strong pulses palpable bilaterally).

___18.   tested sensation in my legs i.e., sharp or dull, and vibration (decreased sensation in a stocking-like distribution bilaterally).

___19.   used the filament test to screen for loss of pressure sensation (SP cannot feel the filament on either plantar surface).

Communication Skills. The Examinee:

___20.   discussed the diagnosis with patient (diabetes mellitus).

___21.   explained that my mother having diabetes puts me at risk for the disease.

___22.   explained the physical findings to me (eye grounds, peripheral neuropathy, and enlarged heart).

___23.   discussed the work-up with me (bloodwork including repeat fasting blood sugar, lipid profile and renal function, urinalysis, electrocardiogram).

___24.   explained the importance of a diabetic diet.

___25.   discussed smoking cessation with me.

___26.   explained how I may need medication if diet failed.

___27.   discussed the complications of diabetes (if left untreated).

___28.   explained I would need to check feet often, avoid foot trauma and choose properly fitting shoes.

___29.   told me I would learn how to check my own sugar with a glucometer.

If you performed 21 of these 27 tasks, you passed this test station.

LEARNING OBJECTIVE FOR MR. DAVID DUNN:
PROVIDING APPROPRIATE CARE TO THE NEW DIABETIC PATIENT

Mr. David Dunn has been complaining of blurred vision, polyuria, polydipsia, polyphagia, and weight loss. He has recently developed impotence. He has a family history of diabetes and a fasting finger-stick in your office reveals a glucose level of 210 mg/dl (fasting blood glucose of >126 on 2 occasions would meet the diagnostic criteria).

On physical examination, Mr. Dunn has fundoscopic changes consistent with diabetic retinopathy. His heart reveals a displaced point of maximum impulse (PMI) and an S4 gallop. His lungs are clear and there are no signs of cardiac decompensation. Neurologic evaluation reveals a peripheral neuropathy. He has no carotid bruits or evidence of peripheral vascular disease.

The patient has several complications of diabetes mellitus. He has retinopathy and neuropathy (both peripheral and autonomic) and needs further evaluation for cardiac dysfunction and microalbumin-uria (30–300 mg of albumin/24 hours).

The patient requires intensive teaching regarding his diabetes. He must learn how to monitor his own glucose level. He must be instruct-ed about proper diet and tobacco cessation. The patient must under-stand that regular foot care and eye examinations are needed to pre-vent infections and blindness.

Mr. Dunn should be aware that diabetes is a chronic disease requir-ing ongoing evaluation and treatment to prevent the life altering complications of the disease, such as renal failure, amputation, stroke, blindness, and cardiomyopathy. The patient must be involved in his own management and enter into a partnership with the physi-cian in an effort to enhance his quality of life. The goals of treatment include a hemoglobin A1c of less than 7% and a blood glucose level of 80–120 mg/dL.

Physical Examination Pearls: Be prepared to identify retinal manifes-tations of diabetic retinopathy from photographs. The identification of proliferative changes (neovascularization) requires emergent referral and treatment. Know the screening test for loss of sensation on the plantar surface of the foot. A 10g nylon filament is used for this test. If the patient cannot feel this filament, there is loss of pres-sure sensation and the patient is at risk for foot ulcers (the examinee should remove the shoes and socks of every diabetic patient and examine the feet carefully).

Physical
Exam

OSCE Interstation Pearl: You should be able to discuss an appropriate diabetic diet for this patient (36 kcal/kg in men and 34 kcal/kg in women). Know that less than 30% of his diet should be fat with less than 300 mg of cholesterol per day. Protein intake should be no more than 0.8 g/kg per day. Be prepared to calculate the patient's body mass index or BMI (weight in kgs/height in meters squared or 714 x weight in pounds/ height in inches 2). A BMI less than 25 kg/m^2 is considered a good weight for a patient. A BMI greater than 30 kg/m2 is consistent with obesity.

CSA Patient Note Pearl: The differential diagnosis for blurred vision, other than diabetes mellitus, includes hypertension, cataracts, macular degeneration and open angle glaucoma.

Case 21

Case 21

A 70-year old man presents to your office with the chief complaint of difficulty urinating. His vital signs reveal a normal blood pressure, heart rate, and respiratory rate. He is afebrile.

You have fifteen minutes to obtain the appropriate history and perform the focused physical examination on Mr. Linus Lawton. Please limit yourself to the time provided.

MY CHECKLIST

History of Present Illness. The Examinee:

1. _____
2. _____
3. _____
4. _____
5. _____
6. _____
   _____
7. _____
8. _____
9. _____
10. _____
11. _____
12. _____

Physical Examination. The Examinee:

13. _____
14. _____
15. _____
    _____
16. _____

Communication Skills. The Examinee:

17. _____
18. _____
19. _____
20. _____
21. _____
22. _____

SP CHECKLIST FOR MR. LINUS LAWTON

History of Present Illness. The Examinee:

___1. asked about the onset of difficulty urinating ("It started maybe a month ago.")

___2. asked about burning on urination ("No. Not really.")

___3. asked about frequency of urination ("I do have to urinate every 3 hours.")

___4. asked about nocturia ("I have to get up every night about 3 times.")

___5. asked about urgency i.e., feel like I will not make it to the bathroom on time ("That only happened once.")

___6. asked if I felt like I did not completely empty my bladder after urination ("Yes; that's why I think I need to go many times during the day and night; my bladder does not empty.")

___7. asked if I needed to strain to urinate ("Yes; I have to push it out sometimes.")

___8. asked about any dribbling or a weak stream when urinating ("Yes, that happens sometimes.")

___9. asked about hematuria ("No.")

___10. asked about past medical history i.e., kidney stones, neurologic disease, renal disease ("None.")

___11. asked about any medications i.e., decongestants ("None.")

___12. asked about any fever ("No.")

Physical Examination. The Examinee:

___13. palpated my abdomen (mild suprapubic tenderness).

___14. tapped on my back to elicit costovertebral angle tenderness (no CVA tenderness).

___15. asked to perform a rectal examination (after examinee asks to perform this task, SP should give card with results: prostate diffusely enlarged with no palpable areas of induration; normal sphincter tone; fecal blood test is negative).

___16. checked for neurologic deficits in my legs, i.e., sensation, strength, reflexes (normal neurologic exam).

Communication Skills. The Examinee:

___17. explained the results of the physical examination (prostate is enlarged).

___18. explained that my urinary problems are due to the enlarged prostate.

___19. explained the work-up needed (bloodwork for renal function and urinalysis).

___20. explained that medications exist that may help my problem.

___21. established good rapport with me.

___22. was sensitive to my embarrassment.

If you performed 16 of these 22 tasks, you passed this test station.

LEARNING OBJECTIVE FOR MR. LINUS LAWTON:
DIAGNOSE AND APPROPRIATELY TREAT BENIGN PROSTATIC HYPERTROPHY

Mr. Linus Lawton presents with the urinary complaints of frequency, nocturia, urgency, and dribbling. He denies hematuria. The differential diagnosis for these complaints includes infection, neurologic disease, outlet obstruction from benign prostatic hypertrophy, stricture, stones, and malignancy.

On examination, the patient has suprapubic tenderness and uniform enlargement of the prostate. There are no areas of prostate induration consistent with prostate cancer. There is no costovertebral angle tenderness and the patient is afebrile making infection unlikely. A neurologic examination is normal.

The work-up for this patient includes an evaluation of his renal function since obstruction may cause hydronephrosis and renal impairment. A prostatic specific antigen test (PSA) may be ordered but a great amount of overlap in levels exists between benign and malignant conditions. A urinalysis will be sent to exclude any infection or hematuria.

The patient may benefit from a six month trial of an alpha adrenergic blocker agent which inhibits prostatic smooth muscle contraction. Finasteride is another class of medication used for BPH which lowers prostatic dihydrotestosterone levels and reduces prostate size. If medical therapy fails, the patient requires urologic evaluation for possible balloon dilatation or surgery. Indications for immediate surgery include renal dysfunction, recurrent stones, hematuria, and persistent urinary retention.

Mr. Lawton should be told to avoid medications such as decongestants that may worsen the obstruction.

CSA Patient Note Pearl: The differential diagnosis for this patient includes infection, benign prostatic hypertrophy, neurologic disease, malignancy, stricture, and stones. The diagnostic work-up includes CBC looking for infection, electrolytes to evaluate his renal function, urinalysis and, possibly, a PSA level.

Case 22

You are the consulting physician for the senior citizen community center and are asked by the social worker to evaluate Mrs. Mildred MacDonald who is 63 years old. The social worker feels that Mrs. MacDonald has become withdrawn and quiet. In the past, Mrs. MacDonald was extremely social and extroverted.

The other senior citizens at the center have noticed the difference and are concerned about the change in their friend as well. Please interview Mrs. MacDonald in fifteen minutes. A physical examination is not required at this test station.

MY CHECKLIST

History of Present Illness. The Examinee:

1. _____
_____

2. _____

3. _____

4. _____
_____

5. _____

6. _____
_____

7. _____

8. _____

9. _____
_____

10. _____
_____

11. _____
_____

12. _____
_____

13. _____
_____

14. _____

15. _____

16. _____
_____

17. _____

Communication Skills. The Examinee:

18. _____

19. _____

20. _____

21. _____

22. _____
_____

23. _____

SP CHECKLIST FOR MRS. MILDRED MACDONALD

History of Present Illness. The Examinee:

___1.   asked why I stopped participating in activities ("I don't have the energy anymore; I'm tired of those people in the center; I would rather stay in bed.")

___2.   asked how long I've had a lack of energy (Oh, I don't know; for a while now, I guess.")

___3.   asked about weight loss ("Oh, I'm the same weight as always I guess; I really don't know.")

___4.   asked about loss of appetite ("Yes; I guess so; I really don't know; I don't feel much like cooking or eating.")

___5.   asked about difficulty sleeping ("I'm in bed all day; I sleep all day. If I could, I would be in bed right now.")

___6.   asked about difficulty concentrating ("I can't even concentrate on reading a newspaper or watching a television show.")

___7.   asked if I was feeling sad ("Well, I've been happier. I guess I'm sad.")

___8.   asked if I felt like I was worthless ("Oh, I don't know; I guess I am worthless.")

___9.   asked if I had feelings of hopelessness ("I am a hopeless case, I guess that would be a good way of putting it.") (SP becomes very tearful at this time.)

___10. asked if anything recently brought on these feelings of sadness ("My husband of 35 years walked out on me 2 months ago; he fell in love with another woman; he has filed for divorce.")

___11. asked if I felt guilty or shameful about the divorce ("I should have been a better wife, I suppose. I guess it was all my fault. I should have been a better wife. I don't want anyone to know.")

___12. asked about any other support system like children ("We don't have any children; we had a son who drowned when he was 3 years old but that was a very long time ago.")

___13. asked about a previous history of mood disorder i.e., psychiatric history ("I needed to be hospitalized for a week or so when my baby drowned but that was over 30 years ago.")

___14. asked about any alcohol use ("None.")

___15. asked about any thoughts of suicide ("Oh, I don't know; I just don't know.")

___16. asked about previous attempts at suicide ("Well; when my baby drowned I did take some pills but I don't think I really meant to kill myself at that time.")

___17. asked if I had a plan for suicide now ("Oh, I don't know. Well I do have an old bottle of sleeping pills.")

Communication Skills. The Examinee:

___18. discussed initial impression with me (plausible diagnosis is depression).

___19. discussed the plan with me (bloodwork, hospitalization, medications).

___20. was able to draw out the information from me effectively.

___21. responded to my nonverbal clues (tearfulness).

___22. inquired about my feelings regarding the hospitalization ("I really don't care anymore. Do whatever you want, Doctor.").

___23. did not become impatient or frustrated with my paucity of speech.

If you performed 17 of these 23 tasks, you passed this test station.

LEARNING OBJECTIVE FOR MRS. MACDONALD:
DIAGNOSE DEPRESSION AND SCREEN FOR SUICIDAL IDEATION

Mrs. MacDonald had a previous psychiatric hospital admission significant for a suicide attempt and depression after the drowning death of her infant son over thirty years ago. Now, the patient is expressing feelings of sadness, worthlessness, and hopelessness since her husband of thirty-five years left her for another woman and filed for divorce.

Mrs. MacDonald feels a great deal of shame and guilt about the divorce and feels somewhat responsible for her husband's actions. Feelings of shame and guilt often accompany depression.

The patient is fatigued and is staying in bed most of the day. She has withdrawn from activities with her friends at the community center. She is anorexic and lacks the concentration to watch a television show or read a newspaper. When she responds to questions, she is irritable and indifferent. The astute physician will realize that Mrs. MacDonald is, most likely, experiencing a major depressive episode.

The patient with depression may present to the physician's office with a vague complaint such as headache or with severe vegetative signs. Anxiety is present in most depressive disorders. It is not uncommon to observe psychomotor agitation or retardation. Past psychiatric history may reveal a previous history of a depressive episode.

The physician must screen every depressed patient for suicidal ideation by inquiring about thoughts and plans for suicide. Alcohol use, drug use, male gender, an older age group, a complete lack of interest in life, or a previous history of a suicide attempt are a few of the factors which make a patient a high risk for suicide. Although Mrs. MacDonald does not drink alcohol, she has several other identifiable factors for suicide and should be hospitalized for inpatient management of her depression. She will benefit from anti-depressant medications and psychotherapy. A thorough discussion regarding the side effects of medication use and the length of treatment should take place before Mrs. MacDonald is discharged from the hospital.

History-Taking Pearl: An easy mnemonic used to screen for depression is "**SIG E CAPS**":

S	=	sleep problems
I	=	interest in life
G	=	guilt feelings
E	=	energy level
C	=	concentration
A	=	appetite
P	=	psychomotor retardation or agitation, and
S	=	suicide.

Case 23

Mr. Jenkins is a 40-year old man who presents to the emergency room complaining of abdominal pain. His vital signs reveal the following:

Blood pressure	90/60 mm Hg with orthostatic changes
Heart rate	110 beats per minute
Respiratory rate	23 breaths per minute
Temperature	102.5° F

Upon entering the examination room, you notice a well-developed man in a hospital gown lying still on a stretcher in the fetal position. Please evaluate Mr. Jenkins in fifteen minutes. Do a focused history and physical examination. Please limit yourself to the time provided.

MY CHECKLIST

History of Present Illness. The Examinee:

1. _____
2. _____
3. _____
4. _____
5. _____
6. _____
7. _____
8. _____
9. _____
10. _____
11. _____
12. _____
13. _____

Physical Examination. The Examinee:

14. _____
15. _____
_____
16. _____
17. _____
18. _____
_____
19. _____
_____

Communication Skills. The Examinee:

20. _____
21. _____
22. _____
23. _____
24. _____
25. _____
26. _____
_____
27. _____

SP CHECKLIST FOR MR. JENKINS

History of Present Illness. The Examinee:

___1. asked about the onset of symptoms ("This has been going on for 2 days.")

___2. asked about the location of my pain ("It hurts in the middle of my abdomen.")

___3. asked about the quality of my pain ("It's sharp like a knife going through me.")

___4. asked about the radiation of the pain ("It goes all the way through to my back.")

___5. asked about the severity of the pain ("On a scale of 1 to 10 where 10 is the worst, it is a 10.")

___6. asked about any association with nausea or vomiting ("I cannot stop vomiting.")

___7. asked about a change in bowel movements ("No diarrhea or constipation.")

___8. asked about any blood in my stools i.e., tarry stools or bright red blood ("None.")

___9. asked about any alleviating factors ("Lying on my side helps a little.")

___10. asked about any aggravating factors ("Anything I try to eat or drink will worsen the pain.")

___11. asked about alcohol use ("Yes, I drink 10 beers every day.")

___12. asked about previous medical problems ("I had an attack of pancreatitis from drinking 2 years ago.")

___13 asked about any medication use ("None.")

Physical Examination. The Examinee:

___14. asked about the onset of the area of periumbilical ecchymosis i.e., Cullen's sign ("I woke up with it this morning.")

___15. listened with a stethoscope in at least 3 places over my abdomen (after examinee performs this task, SP should give the card with results: bowel sounds decreased throughout the abdomen).

___16. palpated gently throughout my abdomen (SP will complain of mild midepigastric pain).

___17. palpated deeply throughout the abdomen (SP will complain of severe midepigastric pain).

___18. elicited rebound tenderness by pressing my abdomen then letting go (SP will complain of severe rebound tenderness).

___19. asked to perform a rectal examination (after examinee asks to perform this task, SP should give a card with results: brown stool, fecal blood negative, no masses, no tenderness).

Communication Skills. The Examinee:

___20. seemed to care about my discomfort and pain.

___21. was gentle in eliciting rebound tenderness and during palpation of my abdomen.

___22. kept me draped as much as possible during the examination.

___23. explained the physical findings to me.

___24. explained the diagnosis to me (necrotizing pancreatitis, complicated pancreatitis).

___25. explained that the alcohol use was a risk factor for the disease.

___26. explained the work-up for the problem (admission to hospital, bloodwork, radiographic studies, surgical consult).

___27. explained prognosis (this is a serious condition).

If you performed 19 of these 27 tasks, you passed this test station.

LEARNING OBJECTIVE FOR MR. JENKINS:
DIAGNOSE NECROTIZING PANCREATITIS AS A COMPLICATION OF ACUTE PANCREATITIS

Mr. Jenkins is an alcoholic patient with a past medical history significant for acute pancreatitis. He presents with severe abdominal pain that radiates to his back and is associated with vomiting. His temperature on arrival to the emergency room is elevated and he is in severe abdominal distress. He seems to have some relief when lying in the fetal position. The patient is hypotensive, tachypneic, and tachycardic with orthostatic changes.

The differential diagnosis in this patient includes acute pancreatitis, acute cholecystitis, and perforated viscus. Pancreatitis is the most plausible diagnosis since the patient still drinks alcohol and has a history of a previous episode of pancreatitis causing similar symptoms.

Risk factors for pancreatitis, other than alcoholism, include medication use, trauma, hyperlipidemia, penetrating ulcer, and biliary disease such as gallstones. These etiologies are less likely but should still be considered in this patient.

When the patient is undraped for the physical examination, periumbilical discoloration (Cullen's sign) can be seen. There is no flank discoloration or Turner's sign. These findings suggest hemoperitoneum. The patient has rebound tenderness and severe epigastric tenderness with palpation. These physical findings, along with the history, are consistent with the diagnosis of necrotizing pancreatitis.

The patient will require bloodwork for hematologic studies, electrolyte abnormalities, amylase, and lipase. These studies will identify other complications of pancreatitis that may exist in this patient, namely infection, hypocalcemia, acidosis, and renal dysfunction. Chest and abdominal radiographs may identify a pleural effusion, ascites, or free peritoneal air. Computed tomography may be ordered to evaluate the extent of pancreatic necrosis. Vigorous hydration, antibiotics, and other supportive measures are necessary in this patient. The surgical service should be consulted for possible removal of necrotic tissue.

Mr. Jenkins should be informed that he has a life-threatening complication of pancreatitis. The patient will require a great deal of empathy, support, and reassurance.

OSCE Interstation Pearls: You should be familiar with Ranson's criteria. Prognosis in pancreatitis is worse in patients older than 55 years old and in patients with elevations in leukocyte count, glucose, blood urea nitrogen, LDH, and AST. Fluid sequestration, acidemia, hypoxemia, hypocalcemia, and decreased hematocrit also worsen mortality.

You may see a chest radiograph with a pleural effusion, atelectasis, or with free air under the diaphragm. Abdominal radiographs may show free air, a sentinel loop (air-filled small intestine in the left upper quadrant), colon cut-off sign (transverse colon with air), or the calcifications of chronic pancreatitis.

CSA Patient Note Pearl: The differential diagnosis for this patient includes acute pancreatitis, perforated viscus, and cholecystitis. The diagnostic work-up may include CBC, electrolytes, amylase, lipase, CXR, KUB, and CT scan of the abdomen.

Case 24

Case 24

Thirty-year old Jack Miller presents to the emergency room complaining of a rash. He was at a restaurant eating a shrimp salad sandwich when he suddenly became red and itchy. Vital signs for this patient are the following:

Blood pressure:	110/70 mmHg
Heart rate:	110 beats/minute
Respirations:	26 breaths/minute
Temperature:	100.0° F

As you enter the room, you notice a patient scratching his neck, arms, and legs. The patient's skin is flushed and hives are noticeable. Please evaluate Mr. Miller in ten minutes. Perform a focused history and physical examination in the time provided.

MY CHECKLIST

History of Present Illness. The Examinee:

1. _____
2. _____
3. _____
4. _____
5. _____
6. _____
7. _____
8. _____
9. _____

Physical Examination. The Examinee:

10. _____
_____
11. _____
_____
12. _____
_____
13. _____
_____

Communication Skills. The Examinee:

14. _____
15. _____
16. _____
_____
17. _____
18. _____
19. _____
20. _____
21. _____
22. _____

SP CHECKLIST FOR MR. JACK MILLER

History of Present Illness. The Examinee:

___1.   asked when the rash started ("It started about 20 minutes ago.")

___2.   asked about any difficulty breathing ("Yes, I am feeling very short of breath.")

___3.   asked about any chest pain ("My chest does feel tight.")

___4.   asked about any abdominal distress i.e., nausea or vomiting ("I do feel nauseated.")

___5.   asked about a history of allergies in the past i.e., food or medications ("Never.")

___6.   asked specifically about allergy to shellfish in the past ("No. I always ate shellfish without any problems.")

___7.   asked about a history of asthma ("No.")

___8.   asked about a family history of allergies ("No.")

___9.   asked about medications I take i.e., ACE inhibitors, beta blockers ("No.")

Physical Examination. The Examinee:

___10.   asked me to remove my shirt to look at the rash more carefully (SP will have erythematous rash through-out trunk, neck, arms, and legs with scattered scratch marks).

___11.   looked inside my mouth (after examinee asks to perform this task, SP will give a card with results: tongue and uvula enlarged to 3 times normal size).

___12.   listened to my lungs in at least 4 places (after examinee performs this task, SP will give a card with results: bilateral inspiratory and expiratory wheezes audible; air entry is good).

___13.   listened to my heart in at least 3 places (after examinee performs this task, SP will give card with the results: tachycardia at a rate of 110 beats/minute).

Communication Skills. The Examinee:

___14.   explained the diagnosis to me (angioedema or anaphylaxis).

___15.   explained the allergy was most likely due to shellfish.

___16.   explained the treatment to me (injection of epinephrine, beta agonist agent via nebulizer, oxygen, antihistamines, H2 blockers, steroids, intravenous fluids).

___17.   told me I would need to stay in the hospital for observation and further treatment.

___18.   explained that he/she would arrange for me to be seen by an allergist.

___19.   told me that in the future I would need to wear a medical alert bracelet.

___20.   told me that in the future I would need to carry a pen with medication to start self-treatment if needed.

___21.   conveyed a sense of confidence.

___22.   made me feel at ease.

If you performed 16 of these 22 tasks, you passed this test station.

LEARNING OBJECTIVE FOR MR. JACK MILLER:
RECOGNIZE AND PROPERLY TREAT ANGIOEDEMA
DUE TO SHELLFISH INGESTION

Mr. Jack Miller has no previous history of allergies or allergic reactions and has eaten shellfish in the past without problem. He presents to the emergency room with pruritus, flushing, chest pain, nausea, and difficulty breathing after eating a shrimp salad sandwich. On physical examination, his skin reveals the raised lesions of urticaria and his lung findings are significant for bilateral inspiratory and expiratory wheezes. Even though his eyes, lips and face appear normal, on inspection of the oral cavity, it is clear that Mr. Miller has a swollen tongue and uvula consistent with angioedema.

Angioedema is a medical emergency because, if left untreated, it may lead to airway obstruction. The patient needs immediate treatment with 1:1000 subcutaneous epinephrine, H1 (diphenhydramine) and H2 blockers, steroids, oxygen, and intravenous hydration. The patient needs to remain in the hospital for treatment and observation, usually in the intensive care unit, to monitor for possible airway obstruction.

Anaphylaxis is an IgE (found on mast cells) mediated reaction. These reactions are most commonly due to medications, such as, penicillin and cephalosporins, foods, insect bites, and latex. Anaphylaxis presents with chest pain, wheezing, urticaria, or angioedema. The patient may be hypotensive and tachycardic.

Angioedema and urticaria are cutaneous forms of anaphylaxis. Angioedema, unlike urticaria, occurs in the deeper subcutaneous tissues. It may be acquired (ACE inhibitor use is often a cause) or due to an autosomal dominant congenital (C1 INH or C1 esterase inhibitor) deficiency. Angioedema has been associated with malignant diseases such as lymphoma, leukemia, and adenocarcinoma.

OSCE Interstation Pearl: Know the difference between anaphylactic reactions and anaphylactoid reactions. Anaphylactoid reactions are mast cell degranulations without proven IgE antibodies (probably due to complement activation). Reactions to radiocontrast dye (occurs in 2% of patients receiving contrast) and aspirin are examples of anaphylactoid reactions.

Beta blocker agents are contraindicated in patients with a history of anaphylaxis since they make future anaphylactic reactions resistant to epinephrine treatment.

Tryptase (found with mast cell activation) may be sent to confirm anaphylactic reactions.

Case 25

A 31-year old woman named Wendy Walker presents to your office complaining of wrist pain. She states that a fall down the stairs caused the injury. She is concerned that the wrist may be fractured. Her vital signs are normal.

Upon entering the examination room, you notice a somewhat nervous woman pacing back and forth in the room. She appears older than her stated age. Sitting nearby is a man who the patient immediately introduces to you as her husband, Mr. Warren Walker. The husband is caring and loving towards his wife and appears concerned about her wrist injury.

You have 15 minutes to perform a history and physical examination on this patient. Please limit yourself to the time provided.

MY CHECKLIST

History of Present Illness. The Examinee:

1. _____
2. _____
3. _____
4. _____
5. _____
6. _____
   _____
7. _____
8. _____
   _____
9. _____
10. _____
11. _____
    _____
12. _____
13. _____
14. _____
15. _____

Physical Examination. The Examinee:

16. _____

Communication Skills. The Examinee:

17. _____
18. _____
19. _____
20. _____
21. _____
22. _____
23. _____
24. _____
25. _____

SP CHECKLIST FOR MRS. WENDY WALKER

History of Present Illness. The Examinee:

___1.   asked how the wrist injury happened ("I fell down a flight of stairs; it was an accident")

___2.   asked when the accident happened ("About one hour ago.")

___3.   asked about any other injuries ("Maybe a few bruises but nothing major.")

___4.   asked about any other medical problems ("None.")

___5.   asked about any medication use ("No.")

___6.   asked about the bruises on my arms (SP has many bruises painted on her arms; some appear old) ("I guess I got them from falling down the flight of stairs today.")

___7.   asked my husband to leave the room so he/she can talk to me alone

___8.   asked whether my husband was physically abusive ("He hits me sometimes; that's what happened today; it only happens when he drinks.")

___9.   asked about my children ("Yes, we have 2 children ages 5 and 7 years old.")

___10. asked if my husband ever abused the children ("No. Never.")

___11. asked me if I felt safe at home ("Not really; I never know when my husband is going to become angry with me; he drinks almost every day now.")

___12. asked me if I was afraid at home ("Sometimes.")

___13. asked if any family or close friends knew about the abuse ("He would kill me if I told anyone.")

___14. asked me if there were any guns at home ("He has a gun collection; he likes to hunt.")

___15. asked me if I had any emergency plan of where to go if I needed to leave my husband ("I guess I would go to a shelter with the children; I don't know.")

Physical Examination. The Examinee:

___16. checked for full range of motion at the wrist (normal wrist examination except for bruises).

Communication Skills. The Examinee:

___17. informed me that spousal abuse was illegal.

___18. told me that involving the police helps prevent further abuse.

___19. told me that I did not deserve to be abused.

___20. informed me that violence in the home affects the future behavior of children.

___21. acknowledged that leaving an abusive husband is very difficult to do.

___22. showed concern for my safety.

___23. offered ongoing support, guidance, and counseling.

___24. discussed available support groups in the community (emergency telephone numbers and shelters).

___25. discussed safety and exit plans.

If you performed 17 of these 25 tasks, you passed this test station.

LEARNING OBJECTIVE FOR MRS. WENDY WALKER:
Identify and help the victim of domestic violence

Patients who are victims of domestic violence may present to a physician's office with a poorly explained injury, especially to the face. An abuse victim may present with an obvious laceration, bruise, or fracture or with a subtle pain-related complaint such as recurrent headache, chest pain, or abdominal pain (irritable bowel). Physicians should routinely screen for domestic violence not only in the emergency room but in the office setting as well (1 in 5 patients who present to a primary care practice are involved in a relationship where abuse exists).

Mrs. Walker presents with a bruise to her wrist and has evidence of older bruises. She poorly explains these injuries by stating she fell down a flight of stairs. The physician must ask the husband (even if he appears to be loving and caring) to leave the examination room. Once the environment is made more comfortable and less threatening for the patient, she admits that her husband drinks and physically abuses her. The history of her husband's alcoholism is important to obtain since one half of all domestic violence cases are associated with alcohol or drug abuse.

The physician should inquire about the safety of the children and the presence of firearms in the home. Spousal abuse is repetitive and may lead to murder of the spouse and abuse of the children. The victim should be informed that spousal abuse is illegal and that informing the police of the situation may help prevent further abuse.

It is often difficult for women to leave the abuser and the physician should acknowledge this. Finances (fear of not being able to adequately support the children) and fear of suffering more abuse (escalating abuse) because of leaving are the reasons victims remain in abusive relationships.

The physician should, first, tell the patient that she does not deserve to be abused. The doctor should present the options to Mrs. Walker and offer to contact a support group where women with similar situations will be able to help her. The wife and children may be able to move to a "safe house" where the patient can review her options carefully without the threat of violence. The wife should never be told by the physician to leave the husband immediately. The patient should be allowed to make her own decisions since this is an important step in the treatment and recovery of the abused patient. The physician should, however, offer continuous support and be available for future guidance and counseling.

History-Taking Pearl: Remember the **SAFE** questionnaire for domestic violence screening:

S   =   Do you feel **s**afe or **s**tressed in relationships?
A   =   Have you ever been **a**bused or **a**fraid in a relationship?
F   =   Are your **f**riends and **f**amily aware of your relationship problem?
E   =   Do you have an **e**mergency plan if needed?

OSCE Interstation Pearl: You should help the patient develop a safety plan: a suitcase left with a friend or relative with essential clothing for the patient and children, necessary medications, car keys, driver's license, money, checkbook, social security numbers, savings account book, birth certificates, and special toys or books for the children.

Case 26

Case 26

A 50-year old secretary, named Mildred Payne, is in your office complaining of left hand tingling. She feels this is an early sign of a stroke and requests to be seen immediately. Her usual physician is your partner who has the day off to testify at a malpractice hearing. The patient has no appointment scheduled but is making such a scene in your waiting room that you decide to see her.

The nurse tells you that the vital signs for this patient are normal. Please perform the appropriate history and physical examination on Mrs. Payne in ten minutes.

MY CHECKLIST

History of Present Illness. The Examinee:

1. _____
2. _____
3. _____
4. _____
5. _____
6. _____
7. _____
8. _____
9. _____

Physical Examination. The Examinee:

10. _____
11. _____
12. _____
13. _____
14. _____
    _____
15. _____

Communication Skills. The Examinee:

16. _____
17. _____
18. _____
19. _____
20. _____
21. _____
22. _____
23. _____

SP CHECKLIST FOR MRS. PAYNE

History of Present Illness. The Examinee:

___1. asked about the onset of hand tingling ("It started last night before I went to bed and now it's worse.")

___2. asked about weakness of the hand ("I think my thumb is a little weak.")

___3. asked about the distribution of the tingling ("It is worse in my middle and index fingers.")

___4. asked about radiation of the tingling to the arm or neck ("No.")

___5. asked about any aggravating factors ("Sleeping and driving.")

___6. asked about any alleviating factors ("Shaking my hand makes it go away a little.")

___7. asked about signs of a stroke i.e., speech difficulty, face, arm, or leg numbness or weakness ("No.")

___8. asked about repetitive movement at work ("Yes. I do typing on a keyboard.")

___9. asked about handedness ("I am left-handed.")

Physical Examination. The Examinee:

___10. tested muscle strength in my upper arm (normal strength).

___11. tested muscle strength in my left lower arm (normal strength).

___12. tested biceps or triceps reflex of my left arm (normal).

___13. tested muscle strength of the fingers in my left hand (thumb flexion is weak).

___14. tested sensation by pinprick in my left hand (decreased sensation over the palmar aspect of left thumb, index, and middle fingers).

___15. tapped over my left wrist (SP will complain of severe tingling of the left hand; positive Tinel's sign).

Communication Skills. The Examinee:

___16. acknowledged my distress.

___17. showed empathy.

___18. did not become impatient or frustrated with me.

___19. discussed the diagnosis with me (the plausible diagnosis is carpal tunnel syndrome).

___20. talked about the plan (electromyography and splinting of the hand).

___21. talked about prognosis (good).

___22. checked my understanding of the problem.

___23. reassured me that I was not having a stroke.

If you performed 17 of these 23 tasks, you passed this test station.

LEARNING OBJECTIVE FOR MRS. PAYNE:
RECOGNIZE CARPAL TUNNEL SYNDROME

Mrs. Payne complains of left hand tingling which is worse when driving and sleeping and improves with hand shaking. She denies radiation of her symptoms and has no stroke related complaints. The tingling is confined to her first, second, and third digits. On further questioning, the patient complains of mild weakness of her left thumb. These complaints localize the problem to the median nerve distribution.

Carpal tunnel syndrome (CTS) occurs when there is compression or entrapment of the median nerve underneath the flexor retinaculum due to injury from overuse, obesity, pregnancy, or systemic diseases such as diabetes mellitus, acromegaly, amyloidosis, hypothyroidism, gout, and rheumatoid arthritis. The repetitive movements performed by Mrs. Payne in her job as a secretary may have caused her problem.

On physical examination, Mrs. Payne has normal arm strength and reflexes. There is weakness in flexion of the first digit and sensory loss, elicited by pinprick, is found in the distribution of the median nerve. When tapping the median nerve at the wrist (Tinel's sign) tingling of the hand occurs. Phalen's sign or tingling from wrist flexion could also be positive in carpal tunnel syndrome.

Electromyography is the best method to diagnose carpal tunnel syndrome. Treatment includes splinting of the hand, anti-inflammatory agents, elevation, and steroid injection directly into the median nerve. Further trauma or injury to the hand should be avoided. The patient requires reassurance that the symptoms she is experiencing are unrelated to a stroke.

Physical Examination Pearl: Normal limb compartment tissue pressure is 8mm Hg. In CTS, the pressure may be 30mm Hg at rest and may go as high as 90mm Hg with flexion (Phalen's sign is more sensitive sign than Tinel's sign).

OSCE Interstation Pearl: 50% of patients who present with unilateral carpal tunnel syndrome actually have bilateral disease.

CSA Patient Note Pearl: The differential diagnosis for this patient's presentation includes carpal tunnel syndrome, transient ischemic attack, cervical radiculopathy (pain would radiate proximally to the shoulder), ulnar neuropathy (5th digit and medial hand numbness), and thoracic outlet syndrome (sensory loss over the ulnar side of the hand and forearm and weakness of all the hand muscles). The gold standard for diagnosis of CTS is electromyography.

Case 27

Case 27

Daniel Doolittle is a 33-year old salesman who makes an appointment to see you because of a backache. He is asking your office manager to schedule him for an MRI (magnetic resonance imaging) study to evaluate his back problem. Mr. Doolittle stated that his friend had a similar backache and he needed an MRI so why not just order one for him too.

Mr. Doolittle had his annual physical examination three months ago and it was normal. He has no medical problems and takes no medications. His vital signs are normal.

You have 15 minutes to evaluate Mr. Doolittle. Please do a focused history and physical examination on this patient.

MY CHECKLIST

History of Present Illness. The Examinee:

1. _____
   _____
2. _____
3. _____
4. _____
5. _____
6. _____
7. _____
8. _____
9. _____
10. _____
11. _____

Physical Examination. The Examinee:

12. _____
13. _____
14. _____
15. _____
16. _____
17. _____
18. _____

Communication Skills. The Examinee:

19. _____
20. _____
21. _____
22. _____
23. _____
24. _____

CHECKLIST FOR MR. DOOLITTLE

History of Present Illness. The Examinee:

___1. asked about the location of my backpain ("It is in the middle of my lower back.") (SP points to L4 and L5 vertebral body areas.)

___2. asked about the onset of my back pain ("It started yesterday.")

___3. asked about the quality of my pain ("It is like a dull throbbing pain.")

___4. asked about the frequency of the pain ("It is continuous.")

___5. asked about any alleviating factors ("Lying still in bed helps a little.")

___6. asked about any aggravating factors ("Bending, standing, walking, and sitting make it worse.")

___7. asked about any precipitating event ("It started when I moved my computer monitor to my new office.")

___8. asked about any leg weakness ("No.")

___9. asked about any sensory changes in my back or legs ("No.")

___10. asked about any bowel and bladder incontinence ("None.")

___11. asked about any history of back problems in the past ("No.")

Physical Examination. The Examinee:

___12. tested muscle strength in both my legs (normal strength).

___13. tested sensation in both my legs (normal sensation).

___14. tested reflexes in both my legs (normal reflexes).

___15. checked my plantar reflex or Babinski by scratching the soles of my feet (toes are downgoing bilaterally).

___16. performed straight leg raising in both legs (no pain with straight leg raising).

___17. evaluated my spine for range of motion in all directions (SP complains of some pain when bending forward).

___18. assessed my gait by asking me to walk (normal gait).

Communication Skills. The Examinee:

___19. acknowledged my discomfort.

___20. discussed the problem with me (most likely back sprain, herniated disc and sciatica less likely).

___21. discussed treatment (bedrest for 3 days, mobilization as tolerated, nonsteroidal anti-inflammatory agents).

___22. gave clear reasons why the MRI was not needed.

___23. did not belittle or ignore my request for an MRI.

___24. scheduled a follow-up appointment to see me.

If you performed 17 of these 24 tasks, you passed this test station.

LEARNING OBJECTIVE FOR MR. DOOLITTLE:
EVALUATE BACK PAIN

The differential diagnosis for back pain includes sprain, arthritis, spinal stenosis, herniated disk, tumor, infection such as osteomyelitis, sciatic nerve irritation, and ankylosing spondylitis. Mr. Doolittle complains of low back pain which occurred after lifting a heavy computer monitor. The pain does not radiate to the lower extremities and is not accompanied by neurological symptoms such as incontinence or sensory deficit. Bladder and bowel dysfunction (cauda equina syndrome) and sensory abnormalities may be seen with disk herniation.

The pain experienced by Mr. Doolittle does not improve with activity. The back pain of ankylosing spondylitis usually lessens as activity increases. Mr. Doolittle had a normal physical examination three months ago which makes tumor and chronic infection less likely. Disk pain worsens with coughing, bending, and sitting but improves with standing (decreases disk pressure). Mr. Doolittle's back pain worsens with standing.

The physical examination performed on Mr. Doolittle reveals no sensory or motor deficits and reflexes are normal. His gait is assessed as normal and he has minimal lumbar pain with forward flexion of the spine.

Straight leg raising often helps to differentiate between sciatic nerve irritation, where symptoms of back pain worsen with elevation of the involved extremity, and disk herniation, where pain is elicited with minimum leg elevation bilaterally. Herniation may also produce a positive "crossed" straight leg raising test. Mr. Doolittle has no worsened symptoms with straight leg raising.

The most likely diagnosis in this patient is back sprain and the optimal treatment would be minimal bedrest with mobilization as tolerated. Nonsteroidal anti-inflammatory agents for pain relief should be prescribed. The physician must explain the diagnosis to Mr. Doolittle and reassure him that radiographic studies, including magnetic resonance imaging, are not appropriate at this time.

History-Taking Pearl: Pseudoclaudication with low back pain may indicate spinal stenosis. The back pain of spinal stenosis is relieved by leaning forward (flexion) and by squatting.

Physical Examination Pearl: Palpation of the spine for point tenderness is not a good diagnostic test and it yields little information. Point tenderness, if present, may indicate osteomyelitis.

The Schober test helps diagnose ankylosing spondylitis. A measuring tape is placed 10 cm above and 5 cm below the S1 area. The patient is asked to flex as far down as possible. The tape should distract 5cm or more for normal lumbar motion.

CSA Patient Note Pearl: The differential diagnosis for this patient includes back sprain, sciatic nerve irritation, arthritis, and herniated disk. The patient does not require a diagnostic work-up at this time.

Case 28

Case 28

A 10-year old girl named Jane Jett is brought to the emergency room by the school nurse with the chief complaint of shortness of breath. The vital signs are as follows:

Temperature	98.6° F
Blood pressure	100/70 mm Hg
Respiratory rate	28 breaths per minute
Heart rate	100 beats per minute
Oxygen saturation	99%

Upon entering the examination room, you observe a patient who is in mild to moderate respiratory distress. She seems to be frightened and concerned. She is looking at the peak flow meter and appears to be confused and perplexed. You have 15 minutes to perform a focused history on this patient.

MY CHECKLIST

History of Present Illness. The Examinee:

1. _____
2. _____
3. _____
   _____
4. _____
5. _____
6. _____
7. _____
8. _____
9. _____
10. _____
11. _____

Physical Examination. The Examinee:

12. _____
    _____
13. _____

Communication Skills. The Examinee:

14. _____
15. _____
16. _____
17. _____
18. _____
19. _____
20. _____
21. _____
22. _____
23. _____
24. _____
25. _____

SP CHECKLIST FOR JANE JETT

History of Present Illness. The Examinee:

___1. asked about the onset of the shortness of breath ("It started 4 hours ago.")

___2. asked what I was doing at the time the shortness of breath started ("Running in gym class.")

___3. asked about problems with shortness of breath and exercise before ("Something like this happened last year while playing soccer in camp but it went away by itself in an hour.")

___4. asked about chest tightness ("I do feel like my chest is a little tight.")

___5. asked about cough ("No.")

___6. asked about any recent upper respiratory tract infections ("None.")

___7. asked about past medical history ("I've never been sick before.")

___8. asked about any medications ("Just vitamins.")

___9. asked about any history of allergies ("None.")

___10. asked about a history of rashes ("No.")

___11. asked about a family history of asthma ("No.")

Physical Examination. The Examinee:

___12. listened to my lungs in at least 4 places (after examinee performs this task, SP should give card with results: mild bilateral expiratory wheezes audible).

___13. listened to my heart in at least 3 places (normal heart examination).

Communication Skills. The Examinee:

___14. explained asthma in words that a 10-year old could understand.

___15. explained every step of the physical examination as it was being done.

___16. explained about the treatment needed in the emergency room (nebulizer, oxygen).

___17. began treating me for the breathing difficulty at the start of the test station.

___18. explained the purpose of the peak flow meter.

___19. explained that I would stay in the emergency room a short time then be able to go home.

___20. told me my mother was on her way to the emergency room.

___21. explained that I would learn how to treat my asthma at home with medication pumps.

___22. relieved my anxiety about not being able to play sports or participating in gym class again.

___24. did not give me more information than I could handle.

___25. put me at ease.

If you performed 18 of these 25 tasks, you passed this test station.

LEARNING OBJECTIVE FOR JANE JETT:
MANAGE ASTHMA IN A 10-YEAR OLD CHILD

Jane Jett presents to the emergency room with her first asthmatic episode. The breathing difficulty and chest tightness are frightening symptoms for this child. Her mother is on the way to the emergency room to comfort and support her during this ordeal but, for the time being, Jane Jett feels alone.

The physician taking care of Jane must be aware of the child's fear and quickly try to put her at ease. Good rapport between child and physician is vital to obtaining an accurate history. Every step of the physical examination should be explained to the child to alleviate her fear and embarrassment. All equipment and monitoring devices, including the purpose of the peak flow meter, should be explained to the child in terms that are reassuring and understandable.

During the interview, Jane Jett recalls a previous episode of short-ness of breath with exercise which, in retrospect, was her first exacerbation of asthma. The present episode occurred with exertion as well. Exercise is the most likely trigger for Jane Jett's two asthmatic attacks (EIA or exercise-induced asthma).

The patient has no family history of asthma and takes no medications that may have caused asthma. She has no history of medical problems i.e., cystic fibrosis. A history of allergies and rashes is denied by the patient so an atopic condition is unlikely. She denies cough and is afebrile so it is doubtful that respiratory infection is responsible for her symptoms.

On physical examination, the patient has bilateral scattered expiratory wheezes and is in mild respiratory distress. The heart examination reveals no abnormalities consistent with congestive heart failure. There is no accessory muscle use and there is no nasal flaring. The patient is able to speak in full sentences without difficulty. She is experiencing a mild asthmatic episode.

After a single inhaled treatment of a beta-adrenergic agonist medication, Ms. Jett becomes asymptomatic and her lungs on re-examination become clear to auscultation. While speaking to the patient and obtaining the history, the physician should have treated the acute exacerbation of asthma (all of the necessary items were in the examination room) to relieve the patient's symptoms and distress.

Upon discharge from the emergency room, the patient will need instruction on using the medication pumps and the peak flow meter at home. Educating Jane Jett and her family about her disease and the triggers which may cause exacerbations requires continuous education and follow-up as an outpatient. The child should be told to breathe through her nose when exercising which will humidify and filter the air. The young patient will be able to remain active using a cromolyn inhaler (70% will respond to this alone) as prophylaxis before gym class.

OSCE Interstation Pearl: Be prepared to demonstrate how to use a metered dose inhaler. The canister must be shaken prior to use and one puff should be given at a time. The inhaler should be held 4 cm from the mouth and each inhaled breath of medication must last 5 seconds. Once the medication is inhaled, the patient should hold his/her breath for 10 seconds.

CSA Patient Note Pearl: The differential diagnosis for shortness of breath in a child includes asthma, pneumonia, upper airway obstruction, cystic fibrosis, congestive heart failure, bronchiolitis, pulmonary embolus, and pneumothorax. The diagnostic work-up may include pulmonary function tests ($FEV1$ will $\downarrow$ with exercise) and oxygen saturation. CBC, CXR, and an ABG should be ordered if infection or hypoxemia is suspected.

Case 29

Case 29

The mother of a 14-month old child, named Jenny Jones, has made an urgent appointment to see you because the child has a fever. Jenny's usual family practitioner is on vacation and you are the covering physician. The vital signs in your office reveal:

Respiratory rate	32 breaths per minute
Temperature	101.6° F rectally
Heart rate	140 beats per minute

Upon entering the examination room, you observe a nervous young mother holding a child who is quietly drinking milk.

You have fifteen minutes to speak to the mother and evaluate the child. Please limit yourself to the time provided.

MY CHECKLIST

History of Present Illness. The Examinee:

1. _____
2. _____
3. _____
4. _____
5. _____
6. _____
7. _____
8. _____
9. _____
10. _____
11. _____
12. _____
13. _____
14. _____
15. _____

Physical Examination. The Examinee:

16. _____
_____
17. _____
_____
18. _____
_____
19. _____
20. _____
21. _____

Communication Skills. The Examinee:

22. _____
23. _____
24. _____
25. _____
26. _____
27. _____

CHECKLIST FOR JENNY JONES

History of Present Illness. The Examinee:

___1. asked about the onset of fever ("It started 2 days ago.")

___2. asked about maximum temperature elevation ("It was 102.5° F rectally this morning.")

___3. asked if the child had a cough ("None.")

___4. asked if the child had cold symptoms ("Yes. She has had a runny nose for a week.")

___5. asked if the child was vomiting ("No.")

___6. asked if the child had diarrhea ("No.)

___7. asked about malodorous urine ("No.")

___8. asked if the child had any rashes ("No.")

___9. asked if the child was lethargic or drowsy ("Just more quiet than usual.")

___10. asked if the child was playful ("Yes.")

___11. asked if the child was taking juice or water ("Yes, she seems to be drinking 8 ounces every 4 hours.")

___12. asked about previous illnesses in the child ("No. She has never been ill before.")

___13. asked about any allergies the child may have ("None known.")

___14. asked about ill contacts ("None.")

___15. asked if immunizations were up to date ("Yes.")

Physical Examination. The Examinee:

___16. looked in the child's throat (after examinee performs this task, SP should give card with results: mild erythema of pharynx).

___17. looked in the child's ears with an otoscope (after examinee performs this task, SP should give card with results: erythema and bulging of the right tympanic membrane).

___18. performed insuffllation through the otoscope (after examinee performs this task, SP should give card with results: no movement of tympanic membrane with insufflation).

___19. checked the child's neck for stiffness (none).

___20. listened to the child's lungs in at least 4 places (normal examination).

___21. palpated gently on the child's abdomen (no pain with palpation).

Communication Skills. The Examinee:

___22. explained that my child's fever was due to an ear infection (plausible diagnosis is right otitis media).

___23. discussed management with me (antibiotics, antipyretics).

___24. explained the side effects of antibiotics.

___25. advised me to increase child's fluid intake during the illness.

___26. advised me to call for any new problem or worsening symptoms.

___27. told me I should follow-up with private doctor.

If you performed 19 of these 27 tasks, you passed this test station.

LEARNING OBJECTIVE FOR JENNY JONES:
EVALUATE A CHILD WITH FEVER

Fourteen-month old Jenny Jones presents to your family medicine practice with a two day history of fever. It is mandatory to perform a thorough history and physical examination on any child with fever and attempt to identify the cause of the illness. It is also important to determine whether the child has a change in personality or behavior (Jenny Jones is quiet but playful and smiling) and if hydration is adequate (oral intake should be quantified if possible).

The mother denies any infectious etiology for the fever except for a mild upper respiratory tract infection of one week's duration. The child has no vomiting or diarrhea. The urine is not malodorous and the child has no cough. There is no history of viral exanthems or rashes (especially petechiae and purpura for meningococcemia) and the mother is diligent about immunizations. Meningitis is unlikely with no history of lethargy, focal neurologic deficits, or exposure to ill contacts.

The child has no past medical history. Noninfectious etiologies which may cause fever include tumor and collagen vascular disease but these are unlikely in this patient.

On physical examination, there is mild evidence of pharyngitis but lung examination is unremarkable for pneumonia. Meningitis is unlikely since there is no neck stiffness or neurologic deficit (Kernig's and Brudzinski's sign may not be evident in children under eighteen months of age). Abdominal examination including suprapubic palpation for bladder infection is unremarkable.

On examination of the middle ear, it becomes clear that the child has a right otitis media. The tympanic membrane is erythematous and bulging. When insufflation is attempted, the membrane is immobile due to the collection of fluid.

The most common complication of an upper respiratory tract infection in children is otitis media. Allergies also predispose children to ear infections. The most common pathogens responsible for otitis media are Streptococcus pneumoniae, non-typeable Haemophilus influenzae, and Moraxella catarrhalis. Antibiotics are often prescribed for the infection. Children, however, may improve without the use of medications. Parents should be advised to increase the child's fluid intake during the febrile illness.

Complications of otitis media include hearing loss, perforation, mastoiditis, facial palsy, meningitis, and bacteremia. The infant with bacteremia will be lethargic and irritable and will require hospital admission for further work-up and treatment. All children treated for otitis media require follow-up to document improvement and identify any complications.

Physical Examination Pearl: Try to examine a child while he/she is sitting on the parent's lap face to face hugging the parent, legs around the parent's waist. The parent can then hold the child's head with one hand while the doctor examines the ear.

CSA Patient Note Pearl: Ear pain in children may be due to infection (otitis media, otitis externa, sinusitis, mastoiditis, lymphadenitis, dental abscess, and peritonsillar abscess), trauma (instrumentation and foreign body), serous otitis media, and temperomandibular joint dysfunction.

Case 30

Case 30

A mother has brought in her four-month old infant for a scheduled check-up. Please perform a health maintenance visit on infant Johnny Wilson in fifteen minutes. This is his first visit to your office.

MY CHECKLIST

History of Present Illness. The Examinee:

1. _____

2. _____
_____

3. _____

4. _____

5. _____

6. _____

7. _____

8. _____

9. _____

Physical Examination. The Examinee:

10. _____

11. _____

12. _____

13. _____

14. _____

15. _____

16. _____

17. _____

18. _____

19. _____

Communication Skills. The Examinee:

20. _____

21. _____

22. _____

23. _____

24. _____

25. _____

26. _____

27. _____

28. _____

29. _____

SP CHECKLIST FOR JOHNNY WILSON

History of Present Illness. The Examinee:

___1.   started with an open-ended question i.e., "How is everything going?" ("No problems, Doctor.")

___2.   asked about the birth history of the baby i.e., prenatal infections, method of delivery, birth weight, birth complications ("None.")

___3.   asked about any recent illnesses ("None, thank goodness.")

___4.   asked about the infant's eating habits ("Seems to be hungry all the time; I'm breastfeeding.")

___5.   asked about the infant's sleeping habits ("Wakes up once a night to feed.")

___6.   asked about the infant's hearing ("He seems to turn when he hears me speaking to him.")

___7.   asked about the infant's vision ("He follows me around with his eyes.")

___8.   checked on the infant's language development ("Infant coos and laughs.")

___9.   asked about immunizations ("I took him for immunizations at 2 months.")

Physical Examination. The Examinee:

___10.   weighed the infant on a scale (scale is in the examination room).

___11.   measured the height of the infant.

___12.   measured the circumference of the infant's head.

___13.   examined the fontanelles (posterior closed).

___14.   examined the eyes (no evidence of conjunctivitis; positive red reflex bilaterally).

___15.   examined the ears with an otoscope (no evidence of otitis media).

___16.   listened to the heart in the front and in the back (no murmurs audible).

___17.   listened to the lungs in the front and in the back (normal to auscultation).

___18.   palpated the abdomen (no masses palpable).

___19.   examined the extremities for full range of motion (normal examination).

Communication Skills. The Examinee:

___20.   explained the physical examination to me as it was being done.

___21.   allowed me to hold the infant during the examination.

___22.   stated immunization would be needed for diphtheria, tetanus, and pertussis (DTP).

___23.   stated immunization would be needed for oral polio vaccine (OPV).

___24.   stated immunization would be needed for Haemophilus influenzae type b (Hib).

___25.   discussed injury prevention with me i.e., falls, choking, appropriate car seat use.

___26.   discussed diet (breastfeeding should continue until the infant is one year old).

___27.   reinforced the positive things I was doing i.e., "You really seem to be doing great."

___28.   solicited my concerns and questions.

___29.   scheduled the 6 month visit.

If you performed 21 of these 29 tasks, you passed this test station.

LEARNING OBJECTIVE FOR JOHNNY WILSON:
Monitor growth and development in a child

Health maintenance visits for children are scheduled at regular intervals. In the first 2 years of life, the child should be seen by the pediatrician at 1, 2, 4, 6, 12, 15, 18, and 24 months of age. Laboratory testing and immunizations are performed at the appropriate intervals. Growth and development is followed at each visit by checking the child's weight, height, and head circumference. The physician should inquire about the child's pattern of sleep and diet (solid food may be started at 6 months of age). Monitoring the developmental progress of the child includes a careful assessment of the child's behavior, language, and motor skills.

The physical examination during health maintenance visits should be thorough and complete. Heart rate and blood pressure should be taken and the skin examined for lesions. Examination of the fontanelles should reveal closure by 18 months of age (the posterior fontanelle is usually closed by 8 weeks of age). The eyes should be examined for cataracts or infection. The ears should be investigated for otitis media. Anterior and posterior auscultation of the heart and lungs is necessary to elicit murmurs and assess for bilateral breath sounds. The abdomen should be palpated for masses and organomegaly. An examination of the extremities, with special attention to the hips, and a neurologic assessment, including the examination of cranial nerves, reflexes, motor and sensory systems are included in every health maintenance visit.

Health maintenance visits give the parents and physician a chance to develop a relationship which will be helpful and educational to the parents (anticipatory guidance) and rewarding to the physician. The pediatrician should solicit questions and concerns from the parents and offer positive reinforcement, support, and reassurance when appropriate. A physician should assist parents with providing a safe and comfortable environment for children. Discussions about nutrition, exercise, dental care, and discipline should be part of the routine health maintenance visit.

History-Taking Pearl: Know the landmarks for normal development:

1 month: smiles, turns head, watches a person, holds chin up
2 months: recognizes parents, smiles on social contact, listens to voice, coos
3 months: laughs, listens to music, recognizes objects, reaches for objects and brings them to mouth
5 months: babbles, rolls over, prefers mother, lifts head
8 months: single words
10 months: sits up alone, plays peek-a-boo, waves bye-bye, grasps

objects with thumb and forefinger, will point to a desired object

12 months: 2 word sentences, walks with one hand held, releases object to other person on request, plays simple ball game

17 months: conversational

OSCE Interstation Pearl: Be prepared to discuss the schedule for immunization:

At birth: HBV (if mother's HBs Ag status is positive or unknown)

1 month: HBV

2 months: DTP, HbCV (Haemophilus influenzae b Conjugate Vaccine), and OPV

4 months: DTP, HbCV, and OPV

6 months: DTP, HBV, and HbCV

15 months: MMR, HbCV, DTP, and OPV

4 years old: DTP, OPV, and MMR

11 years old: MMR

14 years old: Td

HBV schedule varies depending on HBsAg status of mother; if mother's status is negative then vaccination of HBV may be given: at birth–3 months followed by second HBV: 1 month after the first and third HBV vaccine: anytime between 6 months and 18 months of age.

Case 31

Case 31

A nine-year old named Kenneth Smith presents to the emergency room complaining of knee pain. He was at camp when the pain began. The camp counselor checked Kenneth's medical record then called the ambulance as well as the child's mother. The mother is on her way to the emergency room.

Upon entering the examination room, you observe a child who appears underdeveloped for a nine-year old. The child is pale and jaundiced. Vital signs are normal in this patient. You have ten minutes to evaluate Kenneth Smith. Perform a focused history and physical examination on this patient.

MY CHECKLIST

History of Present Illness. The Examinee:

1. _____
2. _____
3. _____
4. _____
5. _____
6. _____
7. _____
8. _____
9. _____
10. _____
11. _____
12. _____
13. _____

Physical Examination. The Examinee:

14. _____
15. _____
16. _____

Communication Skills. The Examinee:

17. _____
18. _____
19. _____
20. _____
21. _____

SP CHECKLIST FOR KENNETH SMITH

History of Present Illness. The Examinee:

___1. asked about the onset of the knee pain ("It started about 4 hours ago.")

___2. asked about the quality of the pain ("Sharp and stabbing.")

___3. asked about any aggravating factors ("Walking makes it worse.")

___4. asked about any alleviating factors ("Nothing; maybe you can give me pain medication.")

___5. asked about any trauma to the knee ("No.")

___6. asked about any past medical history ("I have sickle cell disease.")

___7. asked about any medications ("I take a vitamin pill and an antibiotic every day.")

___8. asked about the frequency of sickle cell crises ("Maybe 3 times a year I have to go to the hospital.")

___9. asked about what may have precipitated the crisis ("I think it was all the exercise at camp.")

___10. asked about recent illnesses that could have caused the crisis i.e., a cold, vomiting ("None.")

___11. asked about pain anywhere else i.e., chest pain or abdominal pain ("Just my knees")

___12. asked if this was my usual sickle cell crisis ("Yes, it is always in my knees.")

___13. asked what has been the management in the past for my crises ("I take pain pills and drink a lot of water.")

Physical Examination. The Examinee:

___14. listened to my lungs in at least 4 places (normal examination).

___15. pressed on my abdomen (no tenderness on palpation).

___16. examined my knees (no deformities or effusion; no erythema or warmth; full range of motion bilaterally).

Communication Skills. The Examinee:

___17. told me that my knees, on examination, appeared normal.

___18. discussed treatment with me (intravenous hydration, oxygen, analgesics).

___19. informed me that my mother was on her way to the hospital.

___20. established good rapport with me.

___21. used terms that I could understand.

If you performed 15 of these 21 tasks, you passed this test station.

LEARNING OBJECTIVE FOR KENNETH SMITH:
TREAT SICKLE CELL CRISIS IN A CHILD

Nine-year old Kenneth Smith presents complaining of bilateral knee pain that started four hours before arriving at the emergency room. Even though the pain began while he was playing at camp, the patient denies a history of trauma. It is only when you ask about past medical history that you learn from the patient that he has sickle cell disease and presents to the hospital with vascular occlusive crises three times a year.

This episode of sickle cell crisis was, most likely, precipitated by exertion and exercise in the camp setting. The patient denies any history of recent infection or illness that could have caused the crisis.

Since sickle cell disease is a systemic problem, Kenny should be examined appropriately for other complications of the disease. On inspection, he appears jaundiced and underdeveloped for his age. His lungs are clear on auscultation. There are no signs of pneumonia or an acute chest syndrome. Abdominal examination reveals no tenderness to indicate gall bladder disease or other gastrointestinal process. There is no palpable spleen. Careful examination of the knees reveals no warmth or erythema, therefore, infection is unlikely. The rest of the musculoskeletal examination is normal. There is no evidence of a stroke on gross neurologic examination.

The treatment of sickle cell crisis is hydration, oxygen, and pain management. Telling the child that his mother is on her way to the hospital will ease his discomfort and fear. The physician should explain findings to the child and involve him in the plan even though the patient seems familiar with his disease and the emergency room surroundings.

Physical Examination Pearl: Dactylitis (hand and foot syndrome) is a warm, tender, nonpitting edema of the hands and feet seen in children younger than 4 years old with sickle cell disease. It is often the physical finding that alerts physicians to the possibility that the child may have Sickle Cell Disease (SCD).

OSCE Interstation Pearl: Be prepared to identify the crescent-shaped sickle cells and the Howell-Jolly bodies (small, round, blue inclusion bodies due to nuclear debris seen in the hyposplenic patient) on peripheral smears at this interstation. Sickledex or the solubility test does not differentiate between sickle cell trait and sickle cell disease. Hemoglobin electrophoresis must always be ordered.

Case 32

The paramedics rush a four-year old boy to the emergency room because of respiratory distress. You have 15 minutes to speak to the mother and perform a focused physical examination on Billy Walker. The vital signs are as follows:

Blood pressure	90/60 mm Hg
Heart rate	136 beats per minute
Respiratory rate	30 breaths per minute
Temperature	103.8° F
Pulse oximeter	97 %

Upon entering the examination room, you observe a child in moderate distress. He is sitting still with his neck extended. You notice the child is drooling. The mother is attempting to comfort the child but she is obviously distraught. You hear stridor as you approach the child.

MY CHECKLIST

History of Present Illness. The Examinee:

1. _____
2. _____
3. _____
4. _____
5. _____
6. _____
7. _____
8. _____
9. _____
10. _____

Physical Examination. The Examinee:

11. _____
12. _____
13. _____

Communication Skills. The Examinee:

14. _____
15. _____
16. _____
17. _____
18. _____
19. _____
20. _____
21. _____
22. _____
23. _____

SP CHECKLIST FOR BILLY WALKER

History of Present Illness. The Examinee:

___1. asked about the onset of the breathing difficulty ("It started about 30 minutes ago.")

___2. asked if the child could have choked on food or a toy ("No.")

___3. asked how long the child had fever ("Since yesterday.")

___4. asked about any cough ("No.")

___5. asked about any voice change ("Yes; this morning he woke up hoarse.")

___6. asked about any sore throat ("Yes; he complained of sore throat yesterday.")

___7. asked about any difficulty swallowing ("Yes; he could not eat yesterday.")

___8. asked about any past medical history ("Never ill before.")

___9. asked about a history of allergies ("No.")

___10. asked about immunization against Haemophilus influenzae type b ("No.")

Physical Examination. The Examinee:

___11. did not attempt to look in the mouth with a tongue depressor.

___12. examined the neck externally for any obstructive lesions (none palpable).

___13. listened to the lungs in at least 4 places (normal breath sounds).

Communication Skills. The Examinee:

___14. explained the initial impression to me (plausible diagnosis is epiglottitis).

___15. explained the next step in the plan (intravenous antibiotics, admission to the intensive care unit).

___16. explained that the child would need examination of the airway in the operating room to make the diagnosis.

___17. explained the complications of epiglottitis (airway obstruction).

___18. explained that the child would require intubation for a short time.

___19. discussed the prognosis with me.

___20. used terms that were understandable to me.

___21. acknowledged my distress.

___22. addressed my concerns.

___23. put me at ease.

If you performed 17 of these 23 tasks, you passed this test station.

LEARNING OBJECTIVE FOR BILLY WALKER:
DIAGNOSE EPIGLOTTITIS IN A CHILD

Epiglottitis is a pediatric emergency. With widespread immunization against Haemophilus influenzae type b, the disease is being seen less frequently (other pathogens include Streptococcus pneumoniae, Staphylococcus aureus, and Groups A and C beta-hemolytic Streptococcus). The constellation of symptoms including voice change, dysphagia, difficulty breathing, drooling, sore throat, and high fever must be addressed emergently. The child is leaning forward with his head extended ("sniffing position") in an attempt to alleviate the airway obstruction. If stridor is audible, airway obstruction and respiratory arrest is imminent.

The differential diagnosis of epiglottitis includes other infectious problems such as pneumonia or croup. The patient did not have a cough and lung examination was normal. Obstruction by foreign body aspiration may lead to stridor but the mother denies an antecedent choking incident and the child's high fever is more consistent with an infectious process. In noncritical situations, neck radiologic studies are diagnostic for epiglottitis and will reveal the classic "thumbprint" sign of the inflamed epiglottis.

Billy Walker presents with the symptoms of severe epiglottitis and requires immediate intubation for airway protection. No further manipulation of the airway should be attempted. The patient should be left in the position of most comfort (usually sitting on the mother's lap). An attempt to lie the child down may cause a gravity-induced change in epiglottis position and sudden airway obstruction.

Airway protection is best accomplished by an anesthesiologist in the controlled environment of an operating room. There should be no attempt to examine the throat with a tongue depressor since this manipulation may induce laryngospasm. During intubation, the epiglottis is visualized to be enlarged and erythematous and the diagnosis is confirmed. Parents should be reassured that intubation and admission to the intensive care unit is short term until the inflammation of epiglottitis subsides with several days of antibiotic therapy.

OSCE Interstation Pearl: Be prepared to see the lateral neck radiograph demonstrating the classic "thumbprint" sign of epiglottitis.

CSA Patient Note Pearl: The differential diagnosis for stridor includes epiglottitis, croup, angioedema, and foreign body aspiration. The diagnostic work-up may include a CBC (for leukocytosis) and an oxygen saturation. If the child is stable, lateral neck radiographs may be ordered. Direct laryngoscopy with possible intubation is the safest method for evaluation of the airway.

Case 33

Case 33

Nineteen-month old Baby Jane is brought to the emergency room by her nervous parents. The baby was in the playpen when she had a seizure which lasted approximately 5 minutes. The parents immediately rushed the child to the emergency room. They are concerned that the baby may have meningitis.

Vital signs reveal a temperature of 103.7° F, rectally. Heart rate is 146 beats per minute. The blood pressure and respiratory rate are normal. You have 15 minutes to examine the child and speak to the parents.

MY CHECKLIST

History of Present Illness. The Examinee:

1. _____
2. _____
3. _____
   _____
4. _____
   _____
5. _____
6. _____
7. _____
8. _____
9. _____
10. _____
11. _____
12. _____
13. _____
14. _____
15. _____
16. _____

Physical Examination. The Examinee:

17. _____
18. _____
19. _____
20. _____
21. _____
22. _____

Communication Skills. The Examinee:

23. _____
24. _____
25. _____
26. _____
27. _____
28. _____
29. _____
30. _____

SP CHECKLIST FOR BABY JANE

History of Present Illness. The Examinee:

___1. asked me to describe the seizure ("The entire body was shaking for 5 minutes.")

___2. asked about incontinence of the bladder or bowel ("Yes, she wet herself during the seizure.")

___3. asked what the baby was doing before the seizure i.e., choking risks like eating, playing with a toy ("The baby was sleeping.')

___4. asked if the baby was acting unusual after the seizure i.e., postictal ("She seemed very different after the seizure; she seemed confused and agitated.")

___5. asked if the baby has a past medical history i.e., retardation, neurologic problems, cerebral palsy ("No.")

___6. asked about any fever ("I didn't know she had a fever until now.")

___7. asked about any recent cough ("No.")

___8. asked about any gastrointestinal symptoms i.e., vomiting or diarrhea ("No.")

___9. asked about any malodorous urine ("No.")

___10. asked about any recent rashes ("None.")

___11. asked if the baby had been irritable lately ("A little cranky for the last two days.")

___12. asked about the baby's appetite ("Not really eating very much lately.")

___13. asked about any recent immunization ("Immunizations are up to date; none recently.")

___14. asked about a family history of seizures ("No.")

___15. asked about ill contacts ("My other daughter had a cold recently but she is better now.")

___16. asked about any recent history of trauma, falls, or ingestions ("No.")

Physical Examination. The Examinee:

___17. looked in the baby's ears with an otoscope (normal examination).

___18. looked inside the baby's mouth (no evidence of pharyngitis).

___19. checked the neck for range of motion and stiffness (normal examination).

___20. listened to the lungs in 4 places (normal examination).

___21. pressed gently on the baby's abdomen (no pain on palpation).

___22. examined reflexes in the arms and legs (normal reflexes).

Communication Skills. The Examinee:

___23. made sure the baby was comfortable during the examination.

___24. discussed the diagnosis (most likely febrile seizure which is common in childhood).

___25. explained that seizure may recur.

___26. explained that this was not epilepsy.

___27. discussed the work-up (bloodwork, urinalysis, observation).

___28. discussed the prognosis (very good).

___29. explained etiology is most likely viral or an early bacterial infection.

___30. addressed our emotional concerns.

If you performed 21 of these 30 tasks, you passed this test station.

LEARNING OBJECTIVE FOR BABY JANE:
EVALUATE A CHILD WITH A FEBRILE SEIZURE

Baby Jane presents to the emergency room after experiencing a single tonic clonic seizure lasting five minutes while sleeping in her playpen. The parents' description of the episode (including the incontinence) and subsequent postictal period confirm the seizure diagnosis. Disorders that mimic seizures include breath-holding, narcolepsy, syncope, and shaking chills. "Simple" febrile seizures usually last less than ten minutes and are followed by a postictal period. These seizures should be distinguished from complex febrile seizures which reoccur over several hours or days and are focal and prolonged in duration.

There is no previous history of seizure in this child and the family history is unremarkable for seizures. The child has no existing predisposing condition for seizure such as cerebral palsy, neurofibromatosis, or brain tumor. The incident was not preceded by cyanosis or choking. The family denies trauma or accidental ingestion.

The temperature of 103.7° F, rectally, and the change in the child's personality (irritable with loss of appetite) should concern the pediatrician. A source for the fever and possible bacteremia requires a thorough interview and physical examination.

The family denies any localizing symptoms to explain the fever like cough, vomiting or diarrhea. There are no rashes or skin lesions consistent with a bacterial infection, viral exanthem, or other disease such as neurofibromatosis (cafe-au-lait spots). There are no recent immunizations which could have caused the fever. A sibling recently recovered from a viral upper respiratory tract infection and should be considered an ill contact.

There are no signs of pharyngitis or otitis media and the abdominal examination is benign. Meningitis is less likely without irritability, neck stiffness, or neurologic deficit.

The child requires observation and antipyretics. Routine CT scan of the head is not indicated. Lumbar puncture is indicated in children with signs of meningitis or who present with complex febrile seizures but an LP has a low yield (<1%) in children with no signs of meningitis who present with simple febrile seizures.

The parents should be reassured by the physician that the fever causing the seizure is either viral in origin or an early sign of a bacterial infection such as a pharyngitis or otitis media. The work-up for this patient includes leukocyte count and blood and urine cultures to search for occult bacteremia.

Inform the parents that febrile seizures are common in childhood and rarely lead to epilepsy (less than 1% lead to epilepsy which is the same as the general population). The parents should be aware that seizures may recur in up to one third of children usually within 2 years of the first episode. Anticonvulsants are not appropriate in uncomplicated febrile seizures.

CSA Patient Note Pearl: The differential diagnosis for seizure in a child includes febrile seizure, infection (meningitis, encephalitis), electrolyte imbalance (hyponatremia), metabolic disorder (hypoglycemia), cyanosis from choking, heavy metal poisoning (lead), accidental ingestion of medication (theophylline, antihistamines, phenothiazines), other accidental ingestions, head trauma, and tumor. Seizure must be differentiated from shaking chills, breath-holding, syncope, and narcolepsy. The diagnostic work-up may include CBC, electrolytes, serum glucose level, and, in selected patients, blood cultures, CT scan of the head, and lumbar puncture.

Case 34

Case 34

A 26-year old graduate student has made an urgent appointment to see you because of severe lower abdominal pain. Her temperature is 102.8° F. The remaining vital signs are normal. Please evaluate Ms. Hillary Hanson in fifteen minutes. Perform a focused history and physical examination on this patient.

MY CHECKLIST

History of Present Illness. The Examinee:

1. _____
2. _____
3. _____
4. _____
5. _____
6. _____
7. _____
8. _____
9. _____
10. _____
11. _____
12. _____
13. _____
14. _____

Physical Examination. The Examinee:

15. _____
    _____
16. _____
    _____
17. _____
18. _____
19. _____
20. _____

Communication Skills. The Examinee:

21. _____
22. _____
23. _____
24. _____
    _____
25. _____
26. _____
27. _____

SP CHECKLIST FOR MS. HANSON

History of Present Illness. The Examinee:

___1. asked about the location of the pain ("Lower part of my abdomen.")

___2. asked about the onset of the pain ("It started 3 days ago after my menstrual period.")

___3. asked about the quality of the pain ("It is dull.")

___4. asked about the intensity of the pain ("On a scale of 1 to 10 where 10 is the worst, this is an 8.")

___5. asked about any alleviating factors ("None.")

___6. asked about any aggravating factors ("Walking and moving make it worse.")

___7. asked about any association with nausea or vomiting ("No.")

___8. asked about a change in bowel movements ("No.")

___9. asked about any urinary complaints ("No.")

___10. asked about vaginal discharge ("Yes; but it is probably the end of my menstrual period.")

___11. asked about sexual history ("I have had only one partner for the last 3 years.")

___12. asked about any sexually transmitted diseases ("None.")

___13. asked about history of pregnancy ("No; I have always used birth control pills.")

___14. asked about use of condoms ("No.")

Physical Examination. The Examinee:

___15. listened to my abdomen with a stethoscope (after examinee performs this task, SP should give card with results: hypoactive bowel sounds).

___16. asked about the appendectomy scar clearly visible with inspection of my abdomen ("I forgot to tell you I had an appendectomy.").

___17. palpated my abdomen (SP will complain of severe pain on right lower side).

___18. attempted to elicit rebound tenderness (positive rebound tenderness elicited on right lower side).

___19. tried to elicit costovertebral angle tenderness (none).

___20. asked to perform pelvic examination (after examinee asks to perform this task, SP should give card with results: malodorous discharge, right adnexal, and cervical motion tenderness).

Communication Skills. The Examinee:

___21. discussed the initial impression with me (pelvic inflammatory disease or tubo-ovarian abscess).

___22. discussed the work-up for this problem (bloodwork, antibiotics, pelvic ultrasonagraphy, admission).

___23. explained that this could lead to infertility if not treated.

___24. explained that this was a sexually transmitted disease ("But my boyfriend is faithful to me; are you saying he's been with someone else?")

___25. explained that the sexual partner should be examined and treated.

___26. was empathetic.

___27. did not ignore or avoid my questions regarding my boyfriend's infidelity.

If you performed 19 of these 27 tasks, you passed this test station.

LEARNING OBJECTIVE FOR MS. HANSON:
DIAGNOSE PELVIC INFLAMMATORY DISEASE

Ms. Hanson presents with a three day history of severe right lower quadrant pain that is dull and constant. She is febrile with a temperature of 102.8° F. She uses birth control pills and would be at low risk for an ectopic pregnancy. Pyelonephritis is doubtful without urinary complaints and no costovertebral angle tenderness. Gastroenteritis is a consideration but the patient denies nausea, vomiting, and diarrhea.

As the interview progresses, Ms. Hanson admits that she does not use condoms because she has had a faithful sexual partner for three years.

On abdominal examination, Ms. Hanson is found to have a tender right lower quadrant and rebound tenderness. She has an appendectomy scar (even if the SP had been asked about previous surgery, she would have forgotten about the appendectomy until scar was mentioned by the examinee during the physical examination). Pelvic examination reveals cervical motion and right adnexal tenderness. There is a malodorous vaginal discharge which is sent for culture by the physician. The differential diagnosis is most likely pelvic inflammatory disease or tubo-ovarian abscess.

Pelvic inflammatory disease (PID) usually occurs after a menstrual period. Risk factors for the disease include multiple sexual partners and the use of an intrauterine contraceptive device. Hospitalization is required if the patient has a high temperature or if there is a possibility of a tubo-ovarian abscess. If untreated, PID may lead to infertility.

Ms. Hanson will ask her sexual partner to be examined and treated for sexually transmitted diseases. She will be educated and counseled regarding safe sexual practice including the use of condoms. Since the patient is very upset about her boyfriend's infidelity, the physician must be supportive and understanding.

OSCE Interstation Pearl: Be prepared to microscopically identify trichomonas vaginalis (motile flagella), Candida albicans (filaments and spores), and Gardnerella (clue cells or epithelial cells covered with many bacteria). Be able to recognize a gram stain of Neisseria gonorrhoeae (gram negative diplococci inside polymorphonuclear cells). Know that a gram stain containing many polymorphonuclear cells without a visible organism is consistent with Chlamydia.

CSA Patient Note Pearl: The differential diagnosis for this patient includes PID, tubo-ovarian abscess, ectopic pregnancy, complicated ovarian cyst, and endometriosis. Appendicitis would have been included in the differential diagnosis but the patient had an appendectomy. The diagnostic work-up includes pelvic examination with cultures, CBC, pregnancy test, and pelvic sonography.

Case 35

Case 35

You have provided gynecologic care for 50-year old Holly Faithful for over 10 years. She is a healthy patient who has had normal Pap smears and mammograms in the past. Her last check-up with you was 11 months ago.

She complains of episodes of diaphoresis which she feels may be the "hot flashes" of menopause. You know her to have no past medical history and she takes no medications. She does not smoke, drink, or use drugs. Her sister, who was also your patient, died of breast cancer two years ago. You have 15 minutes to speak to Mrs. Faithful. A physical examination is not required at this test station.

MY CHECKLIST

History of Present Illness. The Examinee:

1. _____

2. _____

3. _____

4. _____

5. _____

 _____

6. _____

7. _____

8. _____

9. _____

10. _____

 _____

Communication Skills. The Examinee:

11. _____

12. _____

13. _____

14. _____

15. _____

 _____

16. _____

 _____

17. _____

18. _____

19. _____

20. _____

SP CHECKLIST FOR MRS. FAITHFUL

History of Present Illness. The Examinee:

___1. asked about the onset of the hot flashes ("They started about 6 months ago.")

___2. asked about the duration of the hot flashes ("They last about 5 minutes.")

___3. asked about the frequency of the hot flashes ("They happen maybe 10 times a day.")

___4. asked what alleviates the hot flashes ("It helps if I open a window or turn the air conditioner on.")

___5. asked what aggravates the hot flashes ("Stress and the hot weather. They happen at night and wake me up from sleep.")

___6. asked about my last menstrual period ("No menstrual period for 12 months.")

___7. asked about any urinary problems i.e., incontinence, frequency, dysuria ("No.")

___8. asked about any vaginal dryness or itchiness ("Yes.")

___9. asked about any dyspareunia ("Yes. My husband has been afraid to initiate intercourse with me because I complain of pain.")

___10. asked about any feelings of anxiety or depression i.e., ("I am very anxious and on edge; I'm driving my husband crazy.")

Communication Skills. The Examinee:

___11. explained that it was menopause (plausible diagnosis).

___12. offered to help explain the situation to the husband.

___13. discussed the use of a topical or systemic estrogen for vaginal dryness.

___14. discussed the importance of calcium and vitamin D in the diet to prevent bone loss.

___15. discussed the importance of exercise to prevent heart disease and osteoporosis.

___16. discussed why estrogen use was important to prevent heart disease and osteoporosis.

___17. discussed the availability of medications other than estrogen for osteoporosis and hot flashes.

___18. discussed a special study to diagnose osteoporosis (bone densitometry or a DEXA scan).

___19. discussed estrogen use with the strong family history of breast cancer (not contraindicated).

___20. suggested a support group in the community for additional discussion.

If you performed 14 of these 20 tasks, you passed this test station.

LEARNING OBJECTIVE FOR MRS. FAITHFUL:
RECOGNIZE AND COUNSEL A PATIENT EXPERIENCING MENOPAUSE

Mrs. Faithful has been a healthy patient in your practice. At the age of 50, she is presenting with hot flashes and a 12-month history of secondary amenorrhea. Her husband is having difficulty coping with her mood swings and irritability. She is experiencing dyspareunia which is making her husband aloof and distant. Her presentation is consistent with menopause.

Mrs. Faithful is experiencing a normal event in life and needs support and reassurance from her physician. She should be made aware of the other symptoms of menopause such as urinary frequency, dysuria, and incontinence. Patients may become depressed or anxious during this time but there is no evidence that personality or mood changes are due to menopause.

A discussion about proper exercise and diet in the middle years will help prevent bone mineral loss and heart disease in the patient. Diet should be supplemented with 1000 mg of calcium and 200-400 units of vitamin D per day. Over the counter vaginal lubricants may help relieve vaginal dryness and dyspareunia. The gynecologist should offer to meet the husband to address his concerns about intimacy.

Hormone replacement therapy (HRT) requires careful discussion and consideration in a patient with a family history of breast cancer but its use is not contraindicated in this patient (the patient's mammograms have been normal in the past). Mrs. Faithful should be involved in every aspect of her care and in the estrogen replacement decision-making process. Other medications may be used for the hot flashes like alpha adrenergic agonist agents (i.e., clonidine). Women with early menopause or women at high risk for osteoporosis can have bone mass quantitated by dual energy x-ray absorptiometry (DEXA). Patients with poor bone density may be managed with estrogen or biphosphonates. Estrogens are available in patches, pills, and injectable forms.

Support groups may serve as an additional resource for Mrs. Faithful. She could enhance her knowledge of menopause and exchange experiences with similar women in her community.

OSCE Interstation Pearl: Estrogen alone is prescribed for women with previous hysterectomy (adding progesterone provides no additional benefit). Hormone replacement therapy or HRT (estrogen and progesterone) is given to patients with an intact uterus to prevent against endometrial hyperplasia and endometrial cancer. A baseline mammogram (followed by yearly studies) is recommended for women prior to initiating HRT.

Case 36

A 22-year old woman named Peggy Perky presents to the emergency room by ambulance. She is complaining of the sudden onset of abdominal pain. Her vital signs are:

Temperature	98.6° F
Blood pressure	95/60 mm Hg
Heart rate	110 beats per minute

You are the intern in the emergency room and the attending physician has asked you to see this patient in less than 15 minutes. Perform a focused history and physical examination in the time provided.

MY CHECKLIST

History of Present Illness. The Examinee:

1. _____
2. _____
3. _____
4. _____
5. _____
6. _____
7. _____
8. _____
9. _____
10. _____
11. _____
12. _____
13. _____
14. _____
15. _____

Physical Examination. The Examinee:

16. _____
   _____
17. _____
18. _____
19. _____
20. _____

Communication Skills. The Examinee:

21. _____
22. _____
23. _____
24. _____
25. _____

SP CHECKLIST FOR MRS. PERKY

History of Present Illness. The Examinee:

___1.   asked about the location of the pain ("It's in the left lower part of my abdomen.")

___2.   asked about the onset of the pain ("It started about 1 hour ago.")

___3.   asked about the quality of the pain ("Stabbing and tearing.")

___4.   asked about the intensity of the pain ("On a scale of 1 to 10, this is a 9.")

___5.   asked about the progression of the pain ("It is getting worse as we speak.")

___6.   asked about any aggravating factors ("None.")

___7.   asked about any alleviating factors ("Nothing really helps.")

___8.   asked about any radiation of the pain ("It goes to my left shoulder.")

___9.   asked about any urinary complaints ("No.")

___10.   asked about my last menstrual period ("It was 7 weeks ago.")

___11.   asked about any vaginal bleeding ("A small amount of bleeding after the pain started.")

___12.   asked about any gastrointestinal complaints i.e., vomiting or change in bowel movements ("No.")

___13.   asked about my sexual history ("My husband is my only sexual partner for 4 years; he is faithful.")

___14.   asked about contraception ("No method of contraception used.")

___15.   asked about my gynecologic history ("History of pelvic inflammatory disease 5 years ago.")

Physical Examination. The Examinee:

___16.   listened to my abdomen with a stethoscope (after examinee performs this task, SP should give card with results: diminished bowel sounds).

___17.   palpated gently on my abdomen (SP will complain of left lower quadrant pain).

___18.   palpated deeply on my abdomen (SP will complain of severe left lower quadrant pain).

___19.   tried to elicit rebound tenderness (positive rebound tenderness).

___20.   asked to perform the pelvic examination (after examinee asks to perform this task, SP should give card with results: left adnexal tenderness; mass 8 cm. in diameter palpable in left adnexal area).

Communication Skills. The Examinee:

___21.   discussed the diagnosis with me (plausible diagnosis is ectopic pregnancy).

___22.   discussed the next step in the management (bloodwork, pregnancy test, intravenous fluids, sonogram).

___23.   offered to speak to my husband and explain the situation.

___24.   was aware of my discomfort during the physical examination.

___25.   addressed all my concerns.

If you performed 18 of these 25 tasks, you passed this test station.

LEARNING OBJECTIVE FOR MRS. PERKY:
DIAGNOSE ECTOPIC PREGNANCY

The patient presented with the sudden onset of severe left lower quadrant pain that radiates to the shoulder not associated with gastrointestinal or urinary symptoms. She has some minimal vaginal bleeding that developed after the pain. She is afebrile but is hypotensive and tachycardic.

The plausible diagnosis is ectopic pregnancy. The pain and bleeding along with the history of amenorrhea, with no contraception use, is consistent with this diagnosis. The past history of pelvic inflammatory disease is a risk factor for ectopic pregnancy. Other risk factors for ectopic pregnancy include the use of an intrauterine device and a previous history of an ectopic pregnancy.

Tubo-ovarian abscess and pelvic inflammatory disease must be included in the differential diagnosis (even if promiscuity is denied) but, in these cases, the patient would most likely, be febrile and have no history of amenorrhea. A ruptured luteal cyst may present like an ectopic pregnancy but sonography (demonstrating the intra-uterine pregnancy) will distinguish between these two problems.

The radiation of the pain to the shoulder is due to diaphragmatic irritation from hemoperitoneum. Examination of the abdomen reveals rebound tenderness. Pelvic examination is remarkable for a tender adnexal mass. The "stat" pregnancy test will be positive in this patient.

Mrs. Perky will need a pelvic ultrasonography to confirm the adnexal mass and the absence of an intra-uterine pregnancy. Intravenous hydration and often blood transfusions, are needed to correct hypotension and tachycardia. Surgery for the ruptured ectopic pregnancy is performed after the patient is stabilized.

OSCE Interstation Pearl: You must be able to diagnose an ectopic pregnancy by sonography.

CSA Patient Note Pearl: The differential diagnosis for this patient includes ectopic pregnancy, tubo-ovarian abscess, pelvic inflammatory disease, ruptured corpus luteal cyst, appendicitis, endometriosis, and kidney stone. The diagnostic work-up includes pelvic examination, pregnancy test (urine pregnancy test may be negative but the serum beta hCG will almost always be positive), CBC, and pelvic sonogram.

Case 37

You are asked to see Mrs. Stacy Stevens in the emergency room. She is 24 years old and is 9 weeks pregnant. Her obstetrician, your partner, is attending a conference. The patient complains of vaginal bleeding and feels she may be having a miscarriage. Her vital signs are normal and there are no orthostatic changes. Please evaluate this tearful and frightened young woman in fifteen minutes.

MY CHECKLIST

History of Present Illness. The Examinee:

1. _____
2. _____
   _____
3. _____
4. _____
5. _____
   _____
6. _____
7. _____
8. _____
9. _____
10. _____
11. _____
12. _____

Physical Examination. The Examinee:

13. _____
14. _____
15. _____

Communication Skills. The Examinee:

16. _____
17. _____
18. _____
19. _____
20. _____
21. _____
22. _____
23. _____
24. _____
25. _____

SP CHECKLIST FOR MRS. STEVENS

History of Present Illness. The Examinee:

___1. asked about the onset of the vaginal bleeding ("It started about 5 hours ago.")

___2. asked about the quantity of the vaginal bleeding i.e., how many pads were soaked; is bleeding more or less than menstrual period? ("Just one pad like the first day of my period but I'm afraid.")

___3. asked about the progression of the bleeding ("I think it is slowing down; not getting any worse.")

___4. verified gestational age by asking the date of my last menstrual period ("Nine weeks ago.")

___5. asked if I had a pregnancy test or a sonogram ("Yes, I had both. The pregnancy test was positive and the sonogram revealed a baby was in the uterus.")

___6. asked about any abdominal pain or cramps ("Some cramps like my period.")

___7. asked what I was doing at the time the vaginal bleeding started ("Just watching television.")

___8. asked about sexual intercourse in the last 24 hours i.e., could this be postcoital bleeding ? ("No.")

___9. asked about my obstetrics history ("This is my first pregnancy.")

___10. asked about any recent stress ("None. Everything has been great; my husband and I are so happy.")

___11. asked about any tobacco use ("No.")

___12. asked about any illicit drug use ("No.")

Physical Examination. The Examinee:

___13. listened to my abdomen with a stethoscope (normal bowel sounds auscultated).

___14. palpated gently on my abdomen (no tenderness elicited).

___15. asked to perform a pelvic examination (after examinee asks to perform this task, SP should give card with results: cervical os closed; no effacement; uterus 10 weeks size; no blood, tissue or discharge present).

Communication Skills. The Examinee:

___16. explained the initial impression to me (threatened abortion is the most likely diagnosis).

___17. explained that this was a common problem early in pregnancy.

___18. explained the work-up (ultrasonography).

___19. explained that many women who experience this complication carry their pregnancy to term.

___20. advised bedrest for the next 48 hours.

___21. advised me to abstain from sexual intercourse for one week.

___22. told me to call immediately if further bleeding or cramps occurs.

___23. arranged for a follow-up appointment with me.

___24. offered to help discuss the problem with my husband.

___25. showed concern for me.

If you performed 18 of these 25 tasks, you passed this test station.

LEARNING OBJECTIVE FOR MRS. STEVENS:
DIAGNOSE AND COUNSEL REGARDING A THREATENED ABORTION

Mrs. Stevens has a minimal amount of vaginal bleeding during the first trimester of pregnancy. She is frightened that this is a sign of a miscarriage. She is not under any emotional stress and was not engaging in overactivity when the bleeding began. The bleeding is not due to other causes such as recent sexual intercourse (post-coital bleeding).

The differential diagnosis for first trimester bleeding includes threatened, incomplete and complete abortion. Approximately twenty-five percent of women will have some bleeding early in pregnancy which makes this problem a common complaint. The physician should verify gestational age and inquire about a pregnancy test or sonogram. Risk factors for miscarriage include tobacco and drug use.

First trimester bleeding is often associated with crampy abdominal pain. Mrs. Stevens had mild, crampy vaginal bleeding associated with abdominal pain. On pelvic examination, the cervical os is closed and there is no evidence of tissue or blood. The uterine size is consistent with a 10-week (AOG) pregnancy. The most likely diagnosis in this patient is a threatened abortion. Ultrasonography should demonstrate a viable fetus in this patient.

Mr. and Mrs. Stevens will be informed of the diagnosis. Since the fetus was visualized by ultrasonography, their chances of carrying the pregnancy to term are good. Restricting coitus and exercise for several weeks after bleeding has stopped is advised. The physician should offer support and reassurance to these anxious future parents.

OSCE Interstation Pearl: You must be able to diagnose an intra-uterine pregnancy by sonogram.

CSA Patient Note Pearl: The differential diagnosis for this patient includes threatened abortion, incomplete abortion, complete abortion, post-coital bleeding, ectopic pregnancy, and trophoblastic disease. The diagnostic work-up includes a pelvic examination, CBC, pelvic sonography, and a pregnancy test.

Case 38

A 30-year old investment banker named Victoria Billingsley has made an appointment to see you for her annual gynecologic examination. Her regular gynecologist retired to Florida and she is seeing you for the first time.

Besides her Pap smear, she wishes to be evaluated for worsening menstrual cramps. Her vital signs are normal. You have 15 minutes to speak with Ms. Billingsley and perform a focused physical examination.

MY CHECKLIST

History of Present Illness. The Examinee:

1. _____

2. _____

3. _____

   _____

4. _____

5. _____

6. _____

7. _____

8. _____

   _____

   _____

9. _____

   _____

10. _____

11. _____

12. _____

Physical Examination. The Examinee:

13. _____

    _____

    _____

Communication Skills. The Examinee:

14. _____

15. _____

16. _____

17. _____

18. _____

19. _____

SP CHECKLIST FOR MS. BILLINGSLEY

History of Present Illness. The Examinee:

___1. asked about the onset of the worsening menstrual cramps ("The last 10 months have been terrible.")

___2. asked about the severity of the cramps ("I have to miss work 2 days every month.")

___3. asked about any alleviating factors ("At this point, bedrest is all that works; I've tried over the counter medications and none of them work.")

___4. asked about any changes in the amount of menstrual flow ("The amount seems to be the same.")

___5. asked about my last menstrual period ("It was 8 days ago and I missed 3 days of work.")

___6. asked about my last Pap smear ("13 months ago and it was normal.")

___7. asked about my obstetrical history ("No history of pregnancies.")

___8. asked about previous attempts at pregnancy ("I was married for 5 years and used no contraception; I never became pregnant. My husband and I were not serious about having children at the time so we didn't seek help. I always thought I might be infertile")

___9. asked about a history of any gynecological problems i.e., endometriosis or sexually transmitted diseases ("Never.")

___10. asked about a family history of gynecologic problems i.e., endometriosis ("None.")

___11. asked about any dyspareunia ("Yes.")

___12. asked about my sexual history ("One partner for 2 years; monogamous; no method of contraception.")

Physical Examination. The Examinee:

___13. asked to perform a pelvic examination (after examinee asks to perform this task, SP should give card with results: tender, fixed retroverted uterus; indurated nodules in the cul-de-sac; left ovary enlarged; no adnexal or cervical motion tenderness).

Communication Skills. The Examinee:

___14. explained the probable diagnosis to me (endometriosis).

___15. explained what was needed to confirm the diagnosis (laparoscopy).

___16. explained the complications of endometriosis (infertility, chronic pain).

___17. explained the importance of follow-up for the problem.

___18. offered to give me ongoing support.

___19. asked me if I had any other questions or concerns.

If you performed 14 of these 19 tasks, you passed this test station.

LEARNING OBJECTIVE FOR MS. BILLINGSLEY:
RECOGNIZE INFERTILITY AND DIAGNOSE ENDOMETRIOSIS

Ms. Billingsley presents with the chief complaint of worsening menstrual cramps without changes in menstrual flow. She also complains of dyspareunia. She has no history of previous pregnancies or gynecologic problems. Her history is suspicious for infertility (5-year marriage with no contraception use).

Women with endometriosis present with a chief complaint of infertility or worsening menstrual cramps. Dyspareunia may also be the presenting problem. Often, there is a family history of endometriosis.

Detection of nodules (endometriomas) or an adnexal mass on pelvic examination is usually found in advanced cases of endometriosis. The physical examination in early or minimal disease may be normal. Ms. Billingsley will need laparoscopy for definitive diagnosis and to document the extent and stage of her disease. The patient will be counseled regarding the benefits of surgical intervention (remove endometriomas and lyse adhesions) to correct infertility and to alleviate the symptoms of endometriosis.

CSA Patient Note Pearl: The differential diagnosis for infertility (failure to conceive after one year of intercourse without contraception) includes the male factor (endocrine abnormalities, such as, hypopituitarism, drug or tumor induced hyperprolactinemia, thyroid and adrenal dysfunction), abnormal spermatogenesis (orchitis), anatomic problems, motility problems, and sexual dysfunction (impotence, retrograde ejaculation). The female factor may include problems with central ovulation (hyperprolactinemia, hypopituitarism), peripheral ovulation (ovarian resistance, premature ovarian failure), pelvic problems (endometriosis, adhesions, DES exposure, myoma, PID), and cervical problems (DES). The initial diagnostic work-up is based on the history of both partners and the pelvic examination but may include semen analysis, LH, FSH, and prolactin levels.

Case 39

Mrs. Mary Michaels is a 25-year old woman who presents to your office for a prenatal visit. She recently moved to your town and heard from her landlady that you were an excellent physician. The nurse informs you that her vital signs are the following:

Blood pressure	110/80 mm Hg
Heart rate	86 beats per minute
Respiratory rate	12 breaths per minute
Temperature	98.6° F

Please evaluate Mrs. Michaels in 15 minutes. A physical examination, other than an estimation of gestation by fundal height, is not required at this test station. A pelvic examination is not required.

MY CHECKLIST

History of Present Illness. The Examinee:

1. _____
   _____
2. _____
3. _____
   _____
4. _____
   _____
5. _____
6. _____
7. _____
8. _____
9. _____
10. _____
11. _____
12. _____
13. _____
14. _____

Communication Skills. The Examinee:

15. _____
16. _____
17. _____
18. _____
    _____
19. _____
20. _____
21. _____
22. _____
23. _____
24. _____
25. _____
26. _____
27. _____

SP CHECKLIST FOR MRS. MICHAELS

History of Present Illness. The Examinee:

___1. asked about my last menstrual period ("I can't remember. I'm not exactly sure. Can you tell me when I'm due to have my baby?")

___2. asked about my obstetrical history ("This is my first baby; no abortions or miscarriages.")

___3. asked about a history of sexually transmitted disease i.e., herpes, gonorrhea, chlamydia, syphilis, HIV("No.")

___4. asked about my other Ob/Gyn history i.e., menarche, regular periods, contraception, prior gyn surgery ("Menarche at 13 years old, regular periods, use condoms sometimes, no gyn surgery in the past.")

___5. asked about any pregnancy-related complaints i.e., abdominal pain, vaginal bleeding ("No.")

___6. asked about a history of medical problems ("None.")

___7. asked about a history of previous blood transfusions ("No.")

___8. asked about any prenatal care ("None. We could not afford it before but now my husband has a job.")

___9. asked about any tobacco use ("No.")

___10. asked about any alcohol use ("None.")

___11. asked about any illicit drug use ("None.")

___12. asked about my diet ("I try to eat 3 well-balanced meals a day.")

___13. asked about a history of congenital or birth problems in my family or my husband's family ("No.")

___14. asked if I felt fetal movements ("Oh yes. I started feeling them just a couple of days ago.")

Communication Skills. The Examinee:

___15. asked about support from my husband ("Yes. He is very much involved.")

___16. informed me that I was 20 weeks pregnant by palpation of my uterus/fundal height estimate.

___17. told me I would receive help from a nutritionist for optimal diet instruction.

___18. explained I would need blood drawn to check for previous infections i.e., hepatitis, rubella, syphilis, and HIV (I must consent to HIV testing).

___19. explained I would need blood drawn to check for anemia i.e., low blood count.

___20. explained I would need a sonogram to check the baby.

___21. explained I would need a pap smear done.

___22. explained I would need to give a urine sample to check for a urine infection without symptoms.

___23. explained that I would need to come to the doctor on a regular basis.

___24. explained the need for vitamins with iron for the baby.

___25. discussed community resources that prepare parents for labor and delivery.

___26. asked about a couple's appointment next time so he/she could meet my husband.

___27. solicited questions from me.

If you performed 19 of these 27 tasks, you passed this test station.

LEARNING OBJECTIVE FOR MRS. MICHAELS:
DETERMINE GESTATIONAL AGE BY FUNDAL HEIGHT
AND COUNSEL APPROPRIATELY

Mrs. Michaels presents to your office for her first prenatal visit. She denies using any substances which are harmful to the fetus including illicit drugs, alcohol, and tobacco. She has no past history of medical problems such as hypertension, diabetes, or asthma. She has no prior history of sexually transmitted diseases that might complicate delivery. Family history, in either parent, reveals no history of cerebral palsy, Down's syndrome, or multiple births.

During the first trimester, laboratory studies should include blood type with antibody screen, hepatitis B serology, treponema antibody, and rubella titers. An HIV test should be obtained with informed consent. A complete blood count is necessary to check for anemia and thrombocytopenia. Hemoglobin electrophoresis is necessary when indicated by the history. A physician should perform a Pap test and screen for gonorrhea and chlamydia. Urine culture should be sent to detect asymptomatic bacteriuria.

The patient should be counseled regarding diet and weight gain (no more than 30 pounds during the pregnancy) and made aware that moderate exercise and sexual intercourse are safe during pregnancy.

During the second trimester, the patient is offered testing for serum maternal alpha-fetoprotein (SMAFP) level (for detection of neural tube defects) and trisomies. Older women or high risk patients require genetic counseling. Fetal movements should be felt by the patient around the sixteenth week of pregnancy (possibly not until the 20th week, if primiparous). The third trimester requires screening for gestational diabetes mellitus.

The physician, through fundal height palpation, will be able to estimate gestational age. At 20 weeks of pregnancy, fundal height is at the level of the umbilicus. Routine ultrasound on every pregnant patient is not necessary but will be done on Mrs. Michaels since she has no previous prenatal care (late registrant).

Education and counseling is an integral part of following a pregnant patient. The father should be involved in visits and discussions regarding all aspects of the pregnancy including breast feeding, labor, and delivery.

Physical Examination Pearl: Be able to approximate gestational age by palpation of the fundal height.

Case 40

A 37-year old woman (AOG 30 weeks) G4P2 (2/0/1/2) presents to the emergency room with the complaint of vaginal bleeding. Her vital signs are as follows:

Blood pressure	130/70 mm Hg
Heart rate	80 beats per minute
Respiratory rate	18 breaths per minute
Temperature	98.5° F

The patient does not have any orthostatic changes.

Please evaluate this patient, Mrs. Polly Peterson, in fifteen minutes. Perform a focused history and physical examination on this patient.

MY CHECKLIST

History of Present Illness. The Examinee:

1. _____
2. _____
3. _____
4. _____
5. _____
6. _____
   _____
7. _____
8. _____
9. _____
10. _____
11. _____
12. _____

Physical Examination. The Examinee:

13. _____
14. _____
15. _____
16. _____

Communication Skills. The Examinee:

17. _____
18. _____
19. _____
20. _____
    _____
21. _____

SP CHECKLIST FOR MRS. POLLY PETERSON

History of Present Illness. The Examinee:

___1. asked about the onset of vaginal bleeding ("I woke up and found my bed soaked with bright red clotted blood.")

___2. asked about any associated pain ("I felt no pain but I did have some abdominal cramps.")

___3. asked about the quantity of blood loss ("It was very profuse but it has stopped now.")

___4. asked about a history of previous bleeding ("Some spotting during my 4th month.")

___5. asked about any problems in the course of this pregnancy ("No.")

___6. asked about the nature of the previous deliveries ("Second child by Cesarean section; one spontaneous abortion.")

___7. asked about previous surgical procedures ("None.")

___8. asked about tobacco use ("None.")

___9. asked about alcohol use ("None.")

___10. asked about illicit drug use ("No.")

___11. asked about other medical problems ("None.")

___12. asked about fever or chills ("None.")

Physical Examination. The Examinee:

___13. measured my fundal height by palpation (SP is approximately 29 weeks AOG; C-section scar is noted).

___14. performed Leopold's maneuvers (longitudinal lie, cephalic presentation, LOA, not engaged).

___15. listened to my abdomen for heart sounds with a doppler stethoscope (audible fetal heart sounds).

___16. gently palpated throughout the abdomen (uterus soft, no tenderness and no contractions).

Communication Skills. The Examinee:

___17. seemed concerned about my anxiety.

___18. explained the most likely diagnosis (placenta previa or abruptio placenta).

___19. explained the need for a sonogram to make the definitive diagnosis.

___20. explained that blood tests were needed to check clotting factors (CBC, PT, PTT, fibrinogen, fibrin split products).

___21. explained the plan (admission to the hospital, strict bedrest, fetal monitoring, and possible blood transfusions).

If you performed 15 of these 21 tasks, you passed this test station.

LEARNING OBJECTIVE FOR MRS. POLLY PETERSON:
DIAGNOSE PLACENTA PREVIA AS A CAUSE OF THIRD TRIMESTER BLEEDING

The most common causes of life threatening third trimester bleeding are placenta previa (implantation of the placenta over or near the internal os) and abruptio placenta (premature separation of a normally implanted placenta prior to fetal delivery). Less severe third trimester bleeding may be secondary to extrauterine sources, such as, cervical trauma, cervical dilatation, coagulation disorders, and vaginal or rectal lesions.

Mrs. Peterson is at increased risk for placenta previa given her advanced maternal age, multiparity, smoking history and prior cesarean section. Predisposing factors for abruptio placenta include advance maternal age, multiparity, diabetes, hypertension, prior abruption, smoking, alcohol, and cocaine use.

The presentation of painless, vaginal bleeding is the cardinal sign for placenta previa and differentiates it from abruptio placenta which may present with unremitting abdominal (uterine) low back pain.

Mrs. Peterson's vital signs are stable and she has no abdominal or uterine tenderness. In an abruptio, abdominal pain and uterine irritability may be present. Hemorrhage may be visible or concealed. Evidence of fetal distress, DIC, or hypovolemic shock may occur.

Transabdominal ultrasonography demonstrates the placement and the separation of the placenta and includes assessment of fetal well-being, gestational age, and localization of amniotic fluid.

For minor bleeding, bedrest is recommended. If uterine contractions are present, tocolytics can be used. Delivery must be by C-section for a complete previa. For severe bleeding, the patient must be stabilized and delivered by C-section. Subsequent management is dictated by maternal stability (bleeding may be unpredictable and persistent), fetal stability, and gestational age.

Physical Examination Pearl: A vaginal or rectal examination should NOT be done until placenta previa has been ruled out. The most gentle pelvic examination may provoke an uncontrollable hemorrhage.

CSA Patient Note Pearl: The differential diagnosis for third trimester bleeding includes placenta previa, abruptio placenta, cervical trauma, cervical dilatation, coagulation disorders, and vaginal or rectal lesions. The diagnostic work-up may include CBC, PT, PTT, and transabdominal ultrasonography. The pelvic examination may be contraindicated in patients with placenta previa.

Case 41

Your patient is a 16-year old adolescent named Linda Lovett. Her mother has scheduled this appointment because she feels her daughter is overly concerned with her weight. The mother is frightened that her daughter may have an eating disorder.

A physical examination is not required at this test station. The vital signs on this patient are as follows:

Blood pressure	85/60 mm Hg
Heart rate	48 beats/minute
Temperature	96° F
Respirations	12 breaths/minute

Upon entering the examination room, you see a cachectic-appearing young woman with thin, fine hair. She is approximately 5 feet 7 inches tall and weighs 105 pounds. Please evaluate Ms. Lovett in 15 minutes.

MY CHECKLIST

History of Present Illness. The Examinee:

1. _____
2. _____
3. _____
4. _____
5. _____
6. _____
7. _____
   _____
8. _____
9. _____
10. _____
11. _____
    _____
12. _____
13. _____
14. _____
15. _____

Communication Skills. The Examinee:

16. _____
17. _____
18. _____
19. _____
20. _____
21. _____
22. _____
23. _____

CHECKLIST FOR MS. LINDA LOVETT

History of Present Illness. The Examinee:

____1. asked about my weight loss ("I don't feel like I'm losing weight; I'm not sure why Mom is so worried.")

____2. asked about my diet ("I eat lots of fruits and vegetables; I stay away from fatty foods.")

____3. asked if I skip any meals ("Yes, sometimes breakfast or lunch; sometimes dinner. Fasting is healthy.")

____4. asked if I have secret food binges ("Yes, I have binge weekends.")

____5. asked about self-induced vomiting ("No.")

____6. asked about the use of laxatives or diuretics to help lose weight ("No.")

____7. asked if I count my caloric intake daily ("Yes, everyone should watch what they eat, shouldn't they? I try not to go above 1000 calories per day.")

____8. asked about ritualistic exercise ("I run 5 miles everyday.")

____9. asked me if I felt fat ("Just my thighs and arms are fat; the rest of me is alright.")

____10. asked me if I had a fear of gaining weight ("Yes; I really don't want to be fat.")

____11. asked if I was preoccupied with my diet and food ("Well, I do think about food everyday; I even collect recipes. I like to cook.")

____12. asked about my social life ("No time; I have to study.")

____13. asked about any sexual relationships ("None. I'm too busy.")

____14. asked about any signs of depression i.e., insomnia, crying ("No.")

____15. asked about amenorrhea ("No menstrual flow for 3 months; I think it's the stress of school.")

Communication Skills. The Examinee:

____16. discussed the initial impression with me (plausible diagnosis is anorexia nervosa).

____17. discussed the work-up with me (bloodwork, thyroid tests, electrocardiogram).

____18. discussed how hospitalization was needed.

____19. discussed the fact that treatment would include behavioral therapy and medication.

____20. discussed the entire family's need to participate in my care (family counseling).

____21. discussed my need for nutritional support.

____22. inquired about my understanding of the problem.

____23. was supportive.

If you performed 17 of these 23 tasks, you passed this test station.

LEARNING OBJECTIVE FOR MS. LOVETT:
DIAGNOSE ANOREXIA NERVOSA

Ms. Linda Lovett is a sixteen-year old high school student who wishes to become a successful attorney. Her dream is to attend an Ivy League college and be a corporate lawyer like her parents. She is described by family and friends as a goal-oriented perfectionist driven by success and achievement. She has little time for social relationships and is focused on performing well in high school.

This cachectic upper middle class young woman weighs 105 pounds which is less than eighty-five percent of her expected body weight. She limits her daily caloric intake and avoids foods high in fats and carbohydrates. She secretly food binges on weekends but denies self-induced vomiting or the use of laxatives and diuretics in an attempt to lose weight. She tries to remain thin by fasting and excessively exercising. She has a distorted image of her underweight body and considers specific areas (thighs and arms) to be obese. Recently, she has become amenorrheic. All the information obtained in the history is consistent with the diagnosis of anorexia nervosa.

Anorexia nervosa is a disorder of adolescents and is twenty times more common in women than men. These adolescents will present having lost a significant percentage of their expected body weight. Patients are preoccupied with food, their weight, and daily caloric intake.

Ms. Lovett feels she is a healthy, average teenager and denies her symptoms (denial of the problem is frequently seen in eating disorders). Her parents, however, are concerned about anorexia nervosa and have coerced their daughter into seeking psychiatric assistance. On presentation, the patient is hypothermic, bradycardic, and hypotensive. Her hair is fine and thin (lanugo). This presentation is consistent with severe malnutrition secondary to anorexia nervosa.

Before making the diagnosis of anorexia nervosa, medical conditions, such as, thyroid disease, diabetes mellitus, malignancy, and HIV must be excluded. The differential diagnosis of an eating disorder includes major depression and obsessive-compulsive disorder.

The treatment of anorexia nervosa includes family counseling, nutritional support, medication use, and hospitalization. Ms. Lovett will need these interventions to achieve and maintain an adequate weight. Death in anorexia nervosa may occur secondary to cardiac arrhythmias, electrolyte abnormalities, or suicide.

History-Taking Pearl: Try to differentiate between between anorexia nervosa and bulimia by history:

	anorexia nervosa	**bulimia**
weight control methods	decreased intake	self-induced vomiting and laxatives
weight	markedly decreased	may be near normal
binge eating	uncommon	common
ritualized exercise	common	rare
hypotension and bradycardia	common	uncommon
medical complications	hypokalemia and arrhythmias	hypokalemia, arrhythmias and esophageal rupture

Case 42

Case 42

Michael Minty, a 45-year old architect, has made an appointment to see you at the suggestion of his two sisters. The Minty sisters feel that Michael is despondent over the sudden death of his wife from a motor vehicle accident. They had been married less than one year at the time of the accident. The sisters are afraid that their brother will commit suicide.

You are the psychiatrist evaluating Mr. Minty. You have 15 minutes for this evaluation. No physical examination is required for this test station.

MY CHECKLIST

History of Present Illness. The Examinee:

1. _____
2. _____
   _____
3. _____
   _____
4. _____
5. _____
6. _____
7. _____
8. _____
9. _____
10. _____
11. _____
12. _____
    _____

Communication Skills. The Examinee:

13. _____
14. _____
15. _____
16. _____
17. _____
18. _____

SP CHECKLIST FOR MR. MINTY

History of Present Illness. The Examinee:

___1. asked how long ago my wife died ("4 months ago.")

___2. asked if I was angry about my wife dying ("Yes; I'm very angry about it. It took me 25 years to find the right woman to marry.")

___3. asked if I felt guilty about my wife's death ("Yes; I should have taken her to the store that night; it was raining.")

___4. asked if I had problems sleeping ("Yes; I sleep only 4 hours every night.")

___5. asked if I have any dreams about my wife ("Yes; I dream about her all the time.")

___6. asked about any loss of appetite ("Yes; I just don't feel like eating.")

___7. asked what I do in my free time ("I work on my wife's stamp collection; she would have liked that.")

___8. asked about withdrawing from the family ("I just need to be alone for a while, that's all.")

___9. asked me about any new relationships ("I'm not ready to date or initiate a relationship right now.")

___10. asked me about my work ("I was just promoted at work; everything at work is great.")

___11. asked about any alcohol use ("No.")

___12. asked about any drug use ("Absolutely not; a friend of mine gave me some sleeping pills but I refuse to take them; I dislike medications.")

Communication Skills. The Examinee:

___13. discussed the impression with me (normal grief reaction).

___14. explained that I will feel like participating in life again eventually.

___15. explained that the grief will recede eventually.

___16. explained to me that everything I am feeling is perfectly normal.

___17. offered to speak to my sisters about the problem.

___18. offered ongoing support.

If you performed 13 of these 18 tasks, you passed this test station.

LEARNING OBJECTIVE FOR MR. MINTY:
Diagnose normal grief reaction

Mr. Minty is experiencing a normal grief reaction. Since his wife's sudden death four months ago, he has difficulty sleeping and has lost his appetite. When he does sleep, he dreams of his wife (which is part of normal grieving) and the good times they shared together. He sometimes cries and he admits to feeling sad and lonely. He rarely leaves the house to visit relatives and has no desire to establish new relationships.

The patient feels guilty and angry about the death of his wife. He has taken on some of her hobbies in an effort to feel closer to her. Everything else in the life of the patient is stable. He was recently promoted at his job. He has not used drugs or alcohol during the period since his wife's death. He has withdrawn socially and does not wish a new relationship at this time but that is a normal part of grieving.

Mr. Minty's sisters are anxious and concerned about their brother. The patient's grief, however, is normal. Medications are not indicated. Mr. Minty must simply undergo the mourning process. As grief recedes, the patient will begin to participate in old and new relationships.

History-Taking Pearl: Grief reaction becomes abnormal when the patient develops extreme vegetative symptoms such as a profoundly depressed mood and a major sleep disturbance. The patient will feel worthless and hopeless and will have active thoughts of suicide. Remember that the 6 to 12 months often quoted as the timeframe for normal grieving may not apply to every situation.

OSCE Interstation Pearl: The three stages of grief may be discussed at this station. *Stage One* of grief occurs immediately after the death and consists of denial and disbelief. *Stage Two* may last up to six months and consists of extreme guilt ("I didn't do enough.") and extreme sadness. The patient becomes withdrawn and may have vivid illusions of the deceased. *Stage Three* of grief occurs when the patient recalls all the good times with the deceased, accepts the loss, and moves on with his/her life.

Case 43

A 26-year old woman named Tammy Tulip has made an appointment to see you at the suggestion of her primary care physician. She has seen her private doctor eight times in the last two months for chest pain and has had an extensive work-up including bloodwork (normal including lipid profile), an echocardiogram (normal), cardiac stress test (normal) and gastrointestinal studies (no esophageal spasm, GERD, or hiatal hernia).

Her private physician feels that Ms. Tulip must learn to relax and suggested your name for help and guidance. She continues to have frequent chest pain. Ms. Tulip has normal vital signs. You have 15 minutes to evaluate this patient. A physical examination is not required at this test station.

MY CHECKLIST

History of Present Illness. The Examinee:

1. _____
2. _____
3. _____
4. _____
5. _____
   _____
6. _____
7. _____
   _____
8. _____
9. _____
   _____
10. _____
11. _____
12. _____
13. _____
14. _____
15. _____

Communication Skills. The Examinee:

16. _____
17. _____
18. _____
19. _____
20. _____
21. _____
22. _____

SP CHECKLIST FOR MS. TULIP

History of Present Illness. The Examinee:

___1. asked about the onset of the chest pain ("It started maybe a year ago.")

___2. asked about the location of the chest pain ("Middle of my chest.")

___3. asked about the frequency of the chest pain ("Maybe 3 episodes per week.")

___4. asked about the duration of each chest pain episode ("It lasts 15 minutes.")

___5. asked what precipitates the chest pain ("It's unpredictable; I may be in the movies, eating dinner, or driving the car; it can happen anytime.")

___6. asked about any alleviating factors ("I just try to relax, breathe slow and it goes away on its own.")

___7. asked about any associative symptoms i.e., dizziness, palpitations, diaphoresis, paresthesias, trembling, hyperventilating, suffocation ("Yes; I get all of those things.")

___8. asked about a fear of dying or a sense of terror with the chest pain ("Yes.")

___9. asked if I was limiting or avoiding activities because of the chest pain ("I stopped going to the movies or to a restaurant because I'm afraid I may get an attack there.")

___10. asked about any family stresses i.e., recent family death, family illness, marital problems ("None.")

___11. asked about any job stresses ("I work as a toll collector; no stress whatsoever.")

___12. asked about any tobacco abuse ("No.")

___13. asked about any alcohol use ("One glass of wine every night.")

___14. asked about any illicit drug use ("No.")

___15. asked about any medication use ("My doctor gave me some pills for my nerves but I never use them.")

Communication Skills. The Examinee:

___16. explained the initial impression to me (plausible diagnosis is panic disorder).

___17. explained that my problem was treatable.

___18. told me that this was an exaggeration of a normal fear.

___19. explained the treatment to me (behavioral therapy, possibly medications, psychotherapy).

___20. advised me not to avoid the places where the panic attacks take place.

___21. showed concern for my problem.

___22. offered me ongoing support.

If you performed 15 of these 22 tasks, you passed this test station.

LEARNING OBJECTIVE FOR MS. TULIP:
DIAGNOSE AND TREAT PANIC DISORDER

Ms. Tulip has been to several physicians with the complaint of recurrent chest pain. She has no risk factors for cardiac disease and an extensive cardiac and gastrointestinal evaluation was unremarkable. Her episodes of chest pain are unpredictable and are associated with palpitations, dizziness, diaphoresis, trembling, hyperventilation, and paresthesias.

The cardiac episodes are so intense that Ms.Tulip feels death is imminent with each attack. She called the paramedics on several occasions. For a while, she thought she was going to die of a massive heart attack or just stop breathing. The patient is so frightened that she tries to avoid any location or function where previous attacks have taken place.

Ms. Tulip denies feeling stressed about her family or job. She denies substance abuse. She has been a nervous person all of her life and was once prescribed medication for her "nerves." She has experienced no traumatic event in her life that may have caused post-traumatic stress disorder.

Ms. Tulip is suffering from panic disorder. The disorder may be preceded by a previous stressful event in the life of the patient. The patient must not continue to avoid the places where previous panic attack episodes have occurred (may lead to agoraphobia). Treatment for this disorder includes behavioral therapy (relaxation, desensitization, controlled exposure) and cautious use of medications. Psychotherapy may help unveil the subconscious reason for the anxiety.

CSA Patient Note Pearl: The differential diagnosis for panic disorder includes hyperthyroidism, hyperventilation syndrome, mitral valve prolapse, pheochromocytoma, SLE, B12 deficiency, and neurologic diseases including multiple sclerosis and Wilson's disease. Panic disorder symptoms should be differentiated from drug-intoxication (cocaine, theophylline, amyl nitrite, amphetamines, anticholinergics) and drug withdrawal (alcohol, sedative hypnotics, antihypertensives). The psychiatric differential diagnosis for panic disorder includes hypochondriasis, malingering, depression, PTSD, simple phobia, and depersonalization.

Case 44

Eight weeks after having her first child, Mrs. Sadie Simmons makes an appointment to see you. Since the birth of her baby, Mrs. Simmons has been feeling emotionally drained. You have 15 minutes to evaluate the patient. A physical examination is not required at this test station.

MY CHECKLIST

History of Present Illness. The Examinee:

1. _____
2. _____
   _____
3. _____
   _____
4. _____
   _____
5. _____
6. _____
7. _____
8. _____
   _____
9. _____
   _____
10. _____
11. _____

Communication Skills. The Examinee:

12. _____
13. _____
14. _____
15. _____
16. _____
17. _____
18. _____
19. _____

SP CHECKLIST FOR MRS. SIMMONS

History of Present Illness. The Examinee:

___1. asked if my baby was healthy ("Yes.")

___2. asked if I was feeling anxious about caring for my baby ("Yes; this is all new to me; most of the time, I don't know if I'm doing it right.")

___3. asked about support from my husband ("He took on a second job to help with the bills; he really is tired when he comes home at night.")

___4. asked about communication difficulties with my husband ("I think he's stressed out about the baby; we don't talk as much as before.")

___5. asked if I felt less attractive to my husband ("Look at me; I gained so much weight.")

___6. asked about financial problems in the marriage ("We are just making ends meet.")

___7. asked about other family support systems ("My mother went home; she lives 1000 miles away.")

___8. asked me if I was feeling alone ("When the baby was first born, there were always visitors; now no one ever comes anymore.")

___9. asked me about mood changes i.e., sleep disturbances, nightmares, loss of appetite, headache, fatigue, forgetfulness ("I am tired all the time; I have no energy.")

___10. asked if I ever thought about harming the baby ("Oh no, never.")

___11. asked about a history of psychiatric problems ("None.")

Communication Skills. The Examinee:

___12. discussed the diagnosis with me (plausible diagnosis is postpartum depression).

___13. explained the role of hormones in this problem.

___14. explained that the work-up includes blood tests to check thyroid function.

___15. offered to speak to my husband and other family members to involve them in my care.

___16. offered me ongoing support.

___17. assessed my understanding of the problem.

___18. solicited my questions and concerns.

___19. scheduled a follow-up appointment.

If you performed 13 of these 19 tasks, you passed this test station.

LEARNING OBJECTIVE FOR MRS. SIMMONS:
DIAGNOSE POSTPARTUM DEPRESSION (PPD)

Postpartum depression may occur until one year after the birth of a child. The new mother lacks confidence and will have feelings of inadequacy regarding her ability to take care of the newborn. Support systems which may have been helpful earlier during the pregnancy or shortly after giving birth (parents and relatives) may no longer be present in the household. The mother will be fatigued, irritable, anxious and sleep deprived. She may be tearful and sad. Occasionally, patients with PPD present with symptoms of psychosis.

The household changes that occur with a new baby may affect the relationship between husband and wife. The new mother may feel less attractive to her husband. The husband may feel ignored and neglected by the busy mother. Financial problems may further contribute to the problems. The situation may be worse if the newborn is ill or born premature.

The risk of postpartum mood disturbance is increased in women with prior episodes of major depressive disorder. The treatment of postpartum depression includes improving the support system available to the new mother and enhancing communication between husband and wife. Medications are often required in the treatment of this disorder. There is an increased risk of infanticide with PPD and the physician must screen for this throughout the treatment period.

History-Taking Pearl: It is essential for the physician to ask the mother about "ideas" regarding the infant. A depressed mother may be delusional and think the infant is ill and kill the infant to prevent it from suffering in the future.

Case 45

Fifty-year old Albert Sullivan presents to your office with the chief complaint of insomnia. He is requesting a prescription for sleeping pills. He has normal vital signs. This is his first visit to your practice. You have 15 minutes to evaluate this patient. A physical examination is not required at this test station.

MY CHECKLIST

History of Present Illness. The Examinee:

1. _____
2. _____
3. _____
4. _____
5. _____
   _____
6. _____
7. _____
   _____
8. _____
   _____
9. _____
10. _____
11. _____
    _____
12. _____
    _____
13. _____
14. _____
15. _____

Communication Skills. The Examinee:

16. _____
17. _____
18. _____
19. _____
20. _____
21. _____
22. _____
23. _____
24. _____

SP CHECKLIST FOR MR. SULLIVAN

History of Present Illness. The Examinee:

____1. asked how long I have been experiencing the insomnia ("Almost 6 months now.")

____2. asked how many hours I sleep at night ("Maybe 2 hours every night.")

____3. asked if I have difficulty falling asleep ("No; I fall asleep immediately.")

____4. asked if I have difficulty staying asleep ("Yes; nightmares wake me up.")

____5. asked me to talk about my nightmares ("Vietnam; my entire platoon was killed except for me; I saw it happen.")

____6. asked me if I had feelings of guilt about surviving in Vietnam ("Yes.")

____7. asked me if I had flashbacks about the trauma I saw in Vietnam ("I can't get the thoughts out of my head. I relive the war, whether I want to or not, everyday.")

____8. asked me about feelings of depression i.e., hopelessness, sadness, loss of energy, inability to concentrate ("Yes; I have all of those.")

____9. asked me if I was emotionally distant from people ("My wife left me because of that.")

____10. asked me if I have withdrawn from all activities ("Yes; I stay home all day; I even lost my job.")

____11. asked about any periods of violence ("I hit my wife; that is why she left me. My temper is unpredictable. I was arrested for fighting a couple of times.")

____12. asked me if I felt anxious much of the time ("Yes; sometimes a car backfiring will cause me to jump up in fear. It sounds like a gun shot.")

____13. asked me if I use tobacco ("I smoke 3 packs of cigarettes a day.")

____14. asked me if I drink alcohol ("Maybe 2 beers a day.")

____15. asked me if I use illicit drugs ("No.")

Communication Skills. The Examinee:

____16. explained the initial impression to me (plausible diagnosis is post-traumatic stress disorder).

____17. explained that it is possible for this to occur many years after the traumatic event.

____18. explained that my violence was part of the disorder.

____19. explained that I would need medication.

____20. explained that I would need therapy (group and behavioral therapy).

____21. offered me ongoing support.

____22. addressed my nonverbal reactions (tearfulness).

____23. reassured me that I would improve.

____24. conveyed a sense of confidence.

If you performed 17 of these 24 tasks, you passed this test station.

LEARNING OBJECTIVE FOR MR. SULLIVAN:
Diagnose post-traumatic stress disorder (PTSD)

Mr. Sullivan presents with the chief complaint of insomnia. On further questioning, it becomes clear that the patient is unable to remain asleep because of nightmares. As a soldier in Vietnam, Mr. Sullivan witnessed the violent death of his entire platoon and 25 years later, he is suffering from post-traumatic stress disorder (PTSD).

PTSD may occur shortly or decades after experiencing or witnessing a violent traumatic event. The symptoms of this disorder include anxiety and depression. The patient is withdrawn and distant from loved ones. The patient feels guilty about surviving the trauma. He is plagued by recurring thoughts about the traumatic event in the form of flashbacks and nightmares.

Mr. Sullivan is prone to aggressive behavior and violent outbursts. He has been arrested for fighting and admits to spousal abuse. He is easily frightened by sounds that remind him of his wartime experience. These are symptoms of post-traumatic stress disorder.

The differential diagnosis of PTSD includes: major depression, mood disorder, malingering, and anxiety disorder. Substance abuse must be excluded as an etiology for the patient's behavior. The history of trauma causing PTSD must be of great magnitude (assault, motor vehicle accident, torture, fire, war, or natural disaster experience).

The treatment of PTSD includes behavioral therapy, group therapy, and the use of medications (anxiolytics, beta blockers, alpha adrenergic agonists, selective serotonin reuptake inhibitors [SSRI]). Even with intensive therapy, fifty percent of patients with post-traumatic stress disorder have a chronic persistent illness.

History-Taking Pearl: PTSD may develop within one week or as long as thirty years after the traumatic event (often the case in child abuse victims).

Difficulty sleeping is a common chief complaint and the examinee should differentiate between insomnia ("I can't sleep"), hypersomnia ("I sleep too much especially during the day"), and parasomnia ("My wife says I do unusual things when I sleep"). A person with insomnia should be asked whether he/she has difficulty falling asleep or difficulty staying asleep.

Case 46

A 52-year old female named Ms. Mary Meany presents to the emergency room complaining of severe abdominal pain. She has a temperature of 100.7° F and a heart rate of 110 beats per minute. Her blood pressure is normal. You are the surgical resident in the emergency room.

You enter the examination room and observe an obese woman lying on a stretcher squirming in pain. She appears to be uncomfortable and in some distress. Please evaluate Ms. Meany in fifteen minutes. Perform the appropriate history and brief physical examination.

MY CHECKLIST

History of Present Illness. The Examinee:

1. _____
2. _____
3. _____
4. _____
5. _____
6. _____
7. _____
8. _____
9. _____
10. _____
11. _____
12. _____
13. _____
14. _____
15. _____
16. _____

Physical Examination. The Examinee:

17. _____
18. _____
19. _____
20. _____
21. _____

Communication Skills. The Examinee:

22. _____
23. _____
24. _____
25. _____
26. _____

SP CHECKLIST FOR MS. MEANY

History of Present Illness. The Examinee:

___1. asked about the location of the pain ("It's on the right side under my ribs.")

___2. asked about the onset of the pain ("It started 4 hours ago.")

___3. asked about the progression of the pain ("It seems to be getting worse.")

___4. asked about the quality of the pain ("It feels like a big crampy pain.")

___5. asked about the intensity of the pain ("On a scale of 1 to 10 this is a 10.")

___6. asked about the radiation of the pain ("It goes to my right shoulder.")

___7. asked about any aggravating factors ("Deep breath, fatty foods, and water make it worse.")

___8. asked about any alleviating factors ("None that I can think of.")

___9. asked about any previous episodes ("Last year this happened but it went away after 2 hours.")

___10. asked about any nausea and vomiting ("Yes. I vomited once and I still feel nauseated.")

___11. asked about any fever ("I haven't had time to check.")

___12. asked about any change in bowel movements ("No diarrhea or constipation.")

___13. asked about any blood in my stools ("None.")

___14. asked about my past medical history ("None.")

___15. asked about any alcohol use ("None.")

___16. asked about my diet ("Fatty and greasy foods.")

Physical Examination. The Examinee:

___17. listened with a stethoscope over my abdomen (normal bowel sounds auscultated).

___18. palpated my abdomen gently (no pain on gentle palpation).

___19. pressed deeply over my abdomen (SP will complain of severe right sided pain under ribs).

___20. tried to elicit a Murphy's sign (positive pain with deep breath when right side is pressed).

___21. asked to perform a rectal examination (after examinee asks to perform this task, SP should give a card with results: no masses or tenderness; fecal occult blood test negative).

Communication Skills. The Examinee:

___22. acknowledged my discomfort during the physical examination.

___23. explained the initial impression to me (acute cholecystitis or gall bladder disease).

___24. discussed the plan with me (bloodwork, ultrasonography, and surgery).

___25. discussed prognosis (excellent).

___26. addressed my concerns about the surgery.

If you performed 18 of these 26 tasks, you passed this test station.

LEARNING OBJECTIVE FOR MS. MEANY:
DIAGNOSE ACUTE CHOLECYSTITIS

Ms. Meany is an obese woman who presents with severe right upper quadrant pain which radiates to her right shoulder and is accompanied by nausea and vomiting. She states that similar symptoms occurred last year but they resolved without medical attention. She denies hematemesis or change in bowel movements. She is not a diabetic. On presentation, she has a low grade temperature and is mildly tachycardic.

The patient denies alcohol use. Her diet consists of fatty and greasy food. The differential diagnosis after obtaining the history on this patient includes acute cholecystitis, pancreatitis, appendicitis, and ulcer disease.

On physical examination, the patient has severe right upper quadrant pain on palpation and has a positive Murphy's sign. The gallbladder is not palpable. The rectal examination is unremarkable. The most likely diagnosis after the physical examination is acute cholecystitis.

The work-up for this patient includes a white blood cell count looking for the leukocytosis which often accompanies cholecystitis. Liver function tests and pancreatic enzymes may also be elevated. Ultrasonography will visualize the gall bladder stones and identify changes seen with acute cholecystitis such as thickening of the gall bladder wall. Surgery is indicated in this patient and her prognosis is excellent.

OSCE Interstation Pearl: Be prepared to see an abdominal sonogram with gall bladder stones. Occasionally a KUB may be shown demonstrating a radiopaque gallstone (overall, the KUB is positive for GB stones 15-20% of the time).

CSA Patient Note Pearl: The differential diagnosis for this patient would be cholecystitis, pancreatitis, ulcer disease, hepatitis, and appendicitis. The diagnostic work-up would include a rectal examination with fecal occult blood testing, CBC, AST, ALT, alkaline phosphatase, bilirubin levels, amylase, lipase, and abdominal ultrasound.

Case 47

Tommy Trucker is a 35-year old tractor trailer driver who presents to the emergency room complaining of severe left sided back pain. You are the resident physician in the emergency room and are on your way to the cafeteria when the nurse informs you about the patient.

The patient will not lie down on the stretcher and is demanding pain medication. His blood pressure is 135/80 mm Hg and his heart rate is 100 beats per minute. He is afebrile.

You enter the examination room and find a patient pacing in the room. He is tilted to one side. He sees you and immediately asks for pain medications. He is threatening to go to another hospital if pain medications continue to be withheld. He is 6 feet tall and weighs approximately 250 pounds. He has snake tattoos on his arms and left cheek. Please evaluate Mr. Trucker in fifteen minutes. Perform the appropriate history and physical examination on this patient.

MY CHECKLIST

History of Present Illness. The Examinee:

1. _____
2. _____
3. _____
4. _____
5. _____
6. _____
7. _____
8. _____
9. _____
10. _____
11. _____
12. _____
13. _____
14. _____

Physical Examination. The Examinee:

15. _____
16. _____
17. _____
18. _____
_____
19. _____
_____
20. _____
_____

Communication Skills. The Examinee:

21. _____
22. _____
23. _____
24. _____
25. _____
26. _____

SP CHECKLIST FOR MR. TOMMY TRUCKER

History of Present Illness. The Examinee:

____1.　asked about the location of the pain ("The entire left part of my back and side.")

____2.　asked about the onset of the pain ("It started about 3 hours ago.")

____3.　asked about the quality of the pain ("It is like someone is punching me in the side.")

____4.　asked about the progression of the pain ("It is getting worse; I need pain medications.")

____5.　asked about any radiation of the pain ("It seems to be going into my left groin area.")

____6.　asked about any association with nausea or vomiting ("No.")

____7.　asked about any change in my bowel movements ("No.")

____8.　asked about any blood in my stool ("None.")

____9.　asked about any urinary complaints i.e., dysuria, frequency ("None.")

____10.　asked about any blood in my urine ("None.")

____11.　asked about any trauma to the area ("No.")

____12.　asked if this pain has ever happened before ("No.")

____13.　asked about any alcohol use ("Maybe a couple of beers a day.")

____14.　asked about any drug use ("Just some marijuana now and then.")

Physical Examination. The Examinee:

____15.　listened to my abdomen with a stethoscope (normal bowel sounds).

____16.　pressed deeply over my abdomen (no pain is elicited).

____17.　tapped on the left side of my back for any costovertebral angle tenderness (SP will jump off the examination table in pain).

____18.　asked to examine my inguinal area (after examinee asks to perform this task, SP will give card with results: normal inguinal examination).

____19.　asked to perform a rectal examination (after examinee asks to perform this task, SP will give card with results: normal rectal examination; fecal occult blood negative).

____20.　performed a musculoskeletal examination of my back i.e., range of motion, straight leg raising (normal examination of back; SP can bend in all directions easily).

Communication Skills. The Examinee:

____21.　acknowledged my distress and discomfort.

____22.　did not become frustrated or angry with me.

____23.　discussed my diagnosis with me (probable kidney stone).

____24.　explained the importance of a urine sample to check for blood in the urine.

____25.　explained the work-up to me (bloodwork, abdominal radiograph, urology consultation).

____26.　told me I will receive pain medications.

If you performed 18 of these 26 tasks, you passed this test station.

LEARNING OBJECTIVE FOR MR. TOMMY TRUCKER:
DIAGNOSE KIDNEY STONES (NEPHROLITHIASIS)

Mr. Trucker presents with severe left-sided flank pain that radiates to his back and groin area. He has no other associated complaints. He denies a history of trauma to the area or back injury. He is demanding pain medications and the emergency room staff suspects that the patient is drug-seeking.

You are asked to evaluate the patient and realize that his symptomatology is consistent with kidney stones even though the patient denies previous painful episodes (kidney stones are recurrent). He denies any gastrointestinal and urinary complaints. The abdominal and inguinal examinations are normal. There is no evidence of an acute abdomen, testicular torsion, or epididymitis. There is, however, left costovertebral angle tenderness which is consistent with pyelonephritis or a kidney stone. Examination of the back reveals no musculoskeletal physical findings.

The urinalysis of this patient will reveal microscopic hematuria without nitrites or leukocytes. The abdominal radiograph will show two kidney stones in the left ureter. The patient will receive vigorous hydration and analgesics. His renal function tests will be followed closely and a work-up for the etiology of his stones will be initiated (stones may contain calcium oxalate (35%), calcium apatite (35%), magnesium ammonium phosphate or struvite (20%), uric acid (5%), or cystine (2-3%). Most kidney stones will pass spontaneously.

You should be open-minded and nonjudgemental when evaluating this patient. You should elicit the appropriate history and perform the necessary physical examination on this demanding patient to arrive at the correct diagnosis.

History-Taking Pearl: Hematuria is a common chief complaint. If your doctor does not know the mnemonic for hematuria, "**SWITCH G.P.s**" (switch general practitioners):

S　=　stones, sickle cell disease, sickle cell trait, scleroderma, SLE, schistosomiasis, and sulfonamides
W　=　Wegener's granulomatosis
I　=　infections, instrumentation, iatrogenic (analgesics, anticoagulants, and cyclophosphamide), interstitial nephritis
T　=　trauma, TB, tubulointerstitial disease, tumor, and TTP
C　=　cryoglobulinemia
H　=　hemolytic-uremic syndrome, hypercalciuria, hemophilia, and Henoch-Schonlein purpura
G　=　Goodpasture's disease, glomerulonephritis
P　=　papillary necrosis, polycystic kidney disease, and polyarteritis nodosa
S　=　sponge disease (medullary sponge disease)

OSCE Interstation Pearl: An abdominal radiograph will be positive for several kidney stones. Keep in mind, however, that the size of a stone does not correlate with the severity of symptoms.

CSA Patient Note Pearl: The differential diagnosis for this patient includes kidney stones, pyelonephritis, testicular torsion, epididymitis, and musculoskeletal pain. The diagnostic work-up would include a genital examination, CBC, urinalysis, and a plain film of the abdomen. All first time kidney stone patients should have bloodwork sent for electrolytes, calcium, phosphate, and uric acid levels. Twenty-four hour urine collections for calcium, uric acid, phosphate, oxalate, and citrate are requested in patients with recurrent stones or with a positive family history.

Case 48

Case 48

You are asked to evaluate Mr. Johnny Guitar, a 50-year old musician in the emergency room complaining of abdominal pain. The patient was initially triaged to the fast track area of the emergency room for treatment of food poisoning but the intern working in that area feels something more is going on. You are the consulting surgeon. His vital signs are as follows:

Blood pressure	110/70 mm Hg
Heart rate	112 beats per minute
Respiratory rate	22 breaths per minute
Temperature	100.5° F

You have ten minutes to perform a focused history and physical examination on this patient. Please limit yourself to the time provided.

MY CHECKLIST

History of Present Illness. The Examinee:

1. _____
2. _____
_____
3. _____
4. _____
5. _____
6. _____
7. _____
8. _____
9. _____
10. _____
11. _____

Physical Examination. The Examinee:

12. _____
_____
13. _____
_____
14. _____
_____
15. _____
16. _____
17. _____
_____
18. _____
_____

Communication Skills. The Examinee:

19. _____
20. _____
21. _____
22. _____
23. _____
24. _____
25. _____

SP CHECKLIST FOR MR. JOHNNY GUITAR

History of Present Illness. The Examinee:

___1. asked about the location of the pain ("No special area; It's all over my abdomen.")

___2. asked about the quality of pain ("It is crampy and colicky; in music it would be called crescendo-decrescendo.")

___3. asked about the frequency of the pain ("It comes every 10 minutes or so.")

___4. asked about the duration of the pain ("It lasts maybe 1 minute then eases off like a contraction in labor.")

___5. asked about the onset of the pain ("Started yesterday.")

___6. asked about any nausea or vomiting ("Vomited 8 times since last night.")

___7. asked about any blood in the vomitus ("No.")

___8. asked about any change in bowel movements ("Have not had a bowel movement for 2 days.")

___9. asked about passing any flatus ("None.")

___10. asked about any fever ("None.")

___11. asked about my past surgical history ("I had an appendectomy at the age of 22.")

Physical Examination. The Examinee:

___12. listened to my abdomen with a stethoscope (after the examinee performs this task, SP should give card with results: high pitched bowel sounds; peristaltic rushes are audible).

___13. tapped or percussed over my abdomen (after examinee performs this task, SP should give card with results: tympanic with percussion).

___14. palpated gently over my abdomen (SP will guard the abdomen and complain of diffuse pain with gentle palpation).

___15. palpated deeply over my abdomen (SP will complain of severe pain with deep palpation).

___16. tried to elicit rebound tenderness (no rebound tenderness).

___17. asked to perform a rectal examination (after SP asks to perform this task, SP will present a card with results: no stool in vault; no masses or tenderness on rectal examination).

___18. asked to examine the groin area to check for a hernia (after examinee asks to perform this task, SP should give card with results: no hernia detected on examination).

Communication Skills. The Examinee:

___19. discussed the initial impression with me (plausible diagnosis is intestinal obstruction).

___20. explained that the cause of the obstruction was adhesions from a previous surgery.

___21. explained the plan (bloodwork, abdominal radiography, intravenous fluids, nasogastric tube, surgery).

___22. explained the prognosis (excellent).

___23. showed consideration for my discomfort.

___24. addressed my concerns about the nasogastric tube.

___25. was reassuring.

If you performed 18 of these 25 tasks, you passed this test station.

LEARNING OBJECTIVE FOR MR. JOHNNY GUITAR:
DIAGNOSE INTESTINAL OBSTRUCTION SECONDARY TO ADHESIONS FROM A PREVIOUS APPENDECTOMY

Mr. Guitar comes into the emergency room with the complaints of diffuse colicky abdominal pain and profuse vomiting. He is not passing any stool or flatus. On physical examination his abdomen is distended. He has high pitched bowel sounds and audible peristaltic rushing sounds. His abdomen is tympanic on percussion. Rectal examination reveals no masses and the absence of stool.

Mr. Guitar had an appendectomy over twenty-five years ago and with this surgical history is at risk for small bowel obstruction secondary to adhesions. Other etiologies for small bowel obstruction include an incarcerated hernia, a stricture due to inflammatory bowel disease, and a malignancy (large bowel obstruction may be due to malignancy, fecal impaction, volvulus, and diverticulitis). Physical examination of the groin area in this patient reveals the absence of a hernia.

An abdominal radiograph will demonstrate the lack of air in the rectum and the ladder-like pattern of a dilated small bowel with air fluid levels. A nasogastric tube should be inserted immediately to reduce any distension proximal to the obstruction and to relieve the vomiting. Intravenous fluid support is required and electrolytes should be monitored for evidence of dehydration. Strangulation with bowel necrosis is a complication of obstruction and may lead to perforation and sepsis. Mr. Guitar requires surgery to relieve the obstruction.

OSCE Interstation Pearl: An abdominal radiograph will demonstrate air-fluid levels, the "stepladder" or "string of pearls" dilated small bowel pattern and the lack of air in the rectum due to the intestinal obstruction. As the saying goes "never let the sun rise or set on an obstruction."

CSA Patient Note Pearl: The differential diagnosis for this patient includes: intestinal obstruction, paralytic ileus (no bowel sounds on physical examination), mesenteric ischemia, ileus, pancreatitis, and gastroenteritis. The diagnostic work-up would include a rectal examination with FOBT, inguinal examination looking for a hernia, CBC, electrolytes, and an abdominal radiograph.

Case 49

You are asked by the geriatrician to consult on a 77-year old man named Thomas Toomer who was admitted to the geriatrics service a few hours ago for acute abdominal pain. His vital signs are:

Temperature	101.6° F,
Blood pressure	100/70 mm Hg
Heart rate	120 beats per minute
Respirations	22 breaths per minute

You have 15 minutes to consult on Mr. Toomer. Please perform a focused history and physical examination on this patient.

MY CHECKLIST

History of Present Illness. The Examinee:

1. _____
2. _____
3. _____
4. _____
5. _____
6. _____
7. _____
8. _____
9. _____
10. _____
11. _____
12. _____
13. _____
14. _____

Physical Examination. The Examinee:

15. _____
16. _____
17. _____
_____
_____
_____
18. _____
19. _____
_____

Communication Skills. The Examinee:

20. _____
21. _____
22. _____
23. _____
24. _____
25. _____

SP CHECKLIST FOR MR. THOMAS TOOMER

History of Present Illness. The Examinee:

___1.   asked about the location of the pain ("It's in the left lower side of my abdomen.")

___2.   asked about the onset of the pain ("It's been going on for 36 to 48 hours.")

___3.   asked about the quality of the pain ("Crampy. Do you think I'll need surgery, Doc?")

___4.   asked about the frequency of the pain ("It's happening every 15 minutes. Like I'm having a baby.")

___5.   asked about the progression of the pain ("It seems to be getting stronger.")

___6.   asked about the radiation of the pain ("It stays on the left lower side.")

___7.   asked about any aggravating factors ("Nothing I can think of.")

___8.   asked about any alleviating factors ("Nothing makes it better. Will I need surgery to make it better?")

___9.   asked about any fever ("At home, I was 102° F. I also had chills; does that mean I need an operation?")

___10.   asked about any nausea and vomiting ("None.")

___11.   asked about a change in bowel movements ("I am having a little diarrhea.")

___12.   asked about any blood in my stools ("None.")

___13.   asked about any urinary complaints i.e., frequency, dysuria ("No.")

___14.   asked about my diet ("I eat junk food; no fruits, cereals, or vegetables.")

Physical Examination. The Examinee:

___15.   listened to my abdomen with a stethoscope (normal bowel sounds auscultated).

___16.   pressed gently on my abdomen (tenderness when pressing left lower side of my abdomen).

___17.   pressed deeply on my abdomen (severe tenderness when pressing left lower side; after the examinee performs this task, the SP should give card with results: tender and fixed sausage-shaped mass palpable in the left lower quadrant).

___18.   attempted to elicit rebound tenderness (positive rebound tenderness when letting go of left lower side).

___19.   asked to perform a rectal examination (after examinee asks to perform this task, SP should give card with results: no mass palpable in cul-de-sac; fecal occult blood positive).

Communication Skills. The Examinee:

___20.   explained the initial impression to me (diverticulitis, infection in my colon, abscess in my colon).

___21.   explained the work-up (intravenous fluids, bloodwork, radiographs, nasogastric tube, antibiotics).

___22.   explained that conservative management would be tried before surgery.

___23.   stated that surgery may still be necessary.

___24.   addressed my concerns about any surgery.

___25.   offered understanding of my emotions.

If you performed 18 of these 25 tasks, you passed this test station.

LEARNING OBJECTIVE FOR MR. THOMAS TOOMER:
DIAGNOSE DIVERTICULITIS

Mr. Thomas Toomer is an elderly gentleman who presents with crampy left lower quadrant pain associated with mild diarrhea. He is febrile and tachycardic. He denies nausea, vomiting, and urinary complaints. He dislikes physicians and has a great fear of surgery. He has been at home for two days trying on his own to get well in an effort to avoid a hospital admission.

On physical examination, Mr. Toomer has severe tenderness with rebound on palpation of the left lower quadrant. A mass is palpable and the fecal blood test is positive on rectal examination.

Bloodwork will reveal a leukocytosis and radiographic studies may reveal free air, ileus, or an abdominal mass. A computed tomographic study of the abdomen may reveal a collection in the colon consistent with an abscess. Diverticulitis is the most plausible diagnosis in this patient.

Conservative treatment with intravenous hydration, nasogastric suctioning and antibiotics may be attempted on this patient but if improvement does not occur, surgical drainage or resection of the infected area is required. The patient should increase the fiber in his diet after discharge in an effort to prevent future episodes of diverticulitis. Even with diet change, recurrent bouts of diverticulitis are common.

OSCE Interstation Pearl: Recognize an ileus and free air under the diaphragm on the radiographs. Remember that sigmoidoscopy and barium enemas are contraindicated in acute diverticulitis due to the risk of perforation.

CSA Patient Note Pearl: The differential diagnosis for this patient includes diverticulitis, appendicitis, ischemic colitis, and colon cancer (perforated). Gynecologic disorders (i.e., ruptured ovarian cyst) must be considered in female patients. The diagnostic work-up includes rectal examination with FOBT, CBC, abdominal film and, if needed, CT scan of the abdomen.

Case 50

A 32-year old man named Markie Mackey was assaulted outside his home. He was hit several times in the stomach with a baseball bat. Although he stated he was feeling fine, the paramedics insisted he come to the emergency room. His vital signs on arrival to the trauma center are the following:

Blood pressure	100/70 mm Hg
Heart rate	110 beats per minute
Respiratory rate	22 breaths per minute
Temperature	98.7° F

You have 10 minutes to perform a focused history and physical examination on this assault victim.

MY CHECKLIST

History of Present Illness. The Examinee:

1. _____
2. _____
3. _____
4. _____
5. _____
6. _____

Physical Examination. The Examinee:

7. _____
_____
_____

8. _____
9. _____
10. _____
11. _____
_____

12. _____
13. _____
14. _____
15. _____

Communication Skills. The Examinee:

16. _____
17. _____
18. _____
19. _____
20. _____
21. _____
22. _____
23. _____

SP CHECKLIST FOR MR. MARKIE MACKEY

History of Present Illness. The Examinee:

___1.   asked me if I was having any pain ("My stomach is a little sore.")

___2.   asked me if the pain radiated ("It seems to be going up to my left shoulder for some reason.")

___3.   asked me if I felt nauseated ("A little nauseated.")

___4.   asked me about any past medical history ("Never ill before.")

___5.   asked me about any medication use ("None.")

___6.   asked me about any allergies ("None.")

Physical Examination. The Examinee:

___7.   checked for orthostatic changes (after examinee performs this task, SP should give card with results: systolic blood pressure decreases by 20 mm Hg and heart rate increases by 20 beats per minute with standing or with legs dangling off the side of the bed).

___8.   listened to my lungs in at least 4 places (normal lung examination; no evidence of pneumothorax).

___9.   palpated my ribs (tenderness over ninth and tenth ribs on the left side).

___10.   listened over my abdomen with a stethoscope (normal bowel signs audible).

___11.   tapped over the left upper side of my abdomen (after SP performs this task, SP should give a card with results: increased dullness over the splenic area).

___12.   pressed gently throughout my abdomen (mild tenderness on palpation over the left upper side).

___13.   pressed deeply throughout my abdomen (mild tenderness over the left upper side).

___14.   attempted to elicit rebound tenderness (no rebound tenderness).

___15.   asked to perform a rectal examination (after examinee asks to perform this task, SP should give card with results: no tenderness; heme negative stools).

Communication Skills. The Examinee:

___16.   explained to me that I may have some internal bleeding.

___17.   explained that I may have ruptured my spleen.

___18.   explained the work-up to me (bloodwork, radiographs, vigorous intravenous hydration, transfusions).

___19.   told me I would need a needle in my abdomen to check for blood.

___20.   explained I would need surgery.

___21.   explained how I would probably keep most of my spleen.

___22.   addressed my concerns.

___23.   demonstrated empathy.

If you performed 16 of these 23 tasks, you passed this test station.

LEARNING OBJECTIVE FOR MR. MARKIE MACKEY:
DIAGNOSE SPLENIC RUPTURE FROM BLUNT TRAUMA INJURY

Mr. Mackey was assaulted several times in the abdomen with a blunt instrument. Although he feels minimum discomfort, the paramedics were correct in insisting that he come to the emergency room. The patient is tachycardic and hypotensive with orthostatic changes. These are signs of hypovolemia due to blood loss.

On inspection of the abdomen, there is no distension. The ribs over the spleen are tender to palpation and are most likely fractured. The area of dullness in the left upper quadrant is a sign of splenic enlargement from bleeding. There is mild abdominal tenderness on palpation but no rebound. These subtle physical findings can be seen with splenic rupture.

Occasionally, a splenic rupture may present with a palpable mass in the left upper quadrant accompanied by clear signs of peritonitis.

Abdominal radiographs in this patient may show the fractured ribs or an enlarged spleen. In the stabilized patient, computed tomography can better evaluate the extent of the splenic injury.

The hematocrit on this patient may fall rapidly requiring blood transfusions and vigorous hydration for stabilization. A diagnostic peritoneal lavage (DPL) will demonstrate blood in the abdomen (not organ specific however) and the patient will require a laparotomy. A good surgeon will make every effort to preserve as much spleen as possible (splenorrhaphy).

History-Taking Pearl: A simple mnemonic for all trauma patients is **AMPLE**:

A = Allergies
M = current Medications
P = Past medical history
L = Last meal
E = Events before the accident

Physical Examination Pearl: Left shoulder-strap pain is often a classic finding in splenic rupture. This is called Kehr's sign.

OSCE Interstation Pearl: Be able to identify the fractured ribs on the radiograph. A DPL is considered positive when there are >100,000 RBC/mm3 or >500 WBC/mm3 or the presence of bile, bacteria or amylase.

CSA Patient Note Pearl: The differential diagnosis for this patient includes splenic rupture or liver laceration (can occur with blunt trauma; the liver establishes hemostasis quickly and may stop bleeding on its own without surgical intervention). The diagnostic work-up includes CBC, DPL, urinalysis (for hematuria) and, possibly, a CT scan of the abdomen.

Section C: The Final Work-Out

Some Challenging Cases

These last two cases are rated difficult. If you find this final work-out simple, you are adequately prepared for any standardized patient encounter. Congratulations!

Case 51: an 18-year old woman with knee pain
Case 52: a 6-month old infant with severe diarrhea

Case 51

An 18-year old gymnast, named Olympia Ogelsby, presents to your office complaining of knee pain. She has normal vital signs.

You have fifteen minutes to perform a focused history and physical examination on this patient. Please limit yourself to the time provided.

MY CHECKLIST

History of Present Illness. The Examinee:

1. _____
2. _____
3. _____
   _____
4. _____
5. _____
   _____
6. _____
7. _____
8. _____
9. _____
10. _____

Physical Examination. The Examinee:

11. _____
12. _____
    _____
13. _____
    _____
    _____
14. _____
    _____
    _____
15. _____
    _____
    _____

Communication Skills. The Examinee:

16. _____
17. _____
18. _____
19. _____
20. _____

SP CHECKLIST FOR MS. OLYMPIA OGELSBY

History of Present Illness. The Examinee:

___1. asked about the location of the pain ("It hurts in the back of my knee and the side of my knee.")

___2. asked about the onset of the pain ("It started yesterday after practice.")

___3. asked what I was doing at the time the pain began ("It was right after a dismount; I think I landed in an awkward position.")

___4. asked if I heard any knee noises at the time of the injury ("Yes, the knee popped, it seemed.")

___5. asked if I'm experiencing any knee noises now i.e., popping, grinding, or cracking ("It seems to be making a popping sound.")

___6. asked what aggravates the pain ("Well, I surely can't do any gymnastics; walking makes it worse.")

___7. asked about any swelling ("Yes, it became swollen almost immediately; I put ice on it.")

___8. asked if the knee was buckling or felt unstable ("Yes, definitely.")

___9. asked if the knee was locking in the flexed position ("No.")

___10. asked about any previous knee injuries ("No.")

Physical Examination. The Examinee:

___11. checked my knee for a full range of motion (range of motion is full from 0–130°).

___12. checked for a knee effusion by the "bulge" or "ballottement" method (after the examinee performs one of these maneuvers accurately, SP should give card with results: moderate amount of effusion).

___13. performed the "Lachman's" maneuver i.e., with knee flexed to 15–30°, placed one hand on the tibia (thumb should be on tibial crest) and the other hand on thigh and pulled tibia anteriorly (after examinee performs this task, SP should give card with results: tibia slides anteriorly without there seeming to be an end point).

___14. performed the "McMurray's" maneuver i.e., with knee flexed, internally rotated the leg; then extended the knee; kept hand on knee to feel for clicks or locking (after examinee performs this task, SP should give card with results: no clicking or locking; normal McMurray's maneuver).

___15. performed the patellar inhibition test i.e., asked me to contract my quadriceps muscle forcefully against resistance applied to the superior pole of the patella (after examinee performs this task, SP should give card with results: contraction of quadriceps muscle produces no pain).

Communication Skills. The Examinee:

___16. discussed the diagnosis with me (most likely a tear of the anterior cruciate ligament).

___17. discussed the plan (orthopedics consultation immediately).

___18. explained the physical examination to me as it was being done.

___19. used language that I could understand.

___20. was empathetic when I tearfully asked about participating in the next Olympics competition.

If you performed 14 of these 20 tasks, you passed this test station.

LEARNING OBJECTIVE FOR MS. OLYMPIA OGELSBY:
DIAGNOSE THE MOST LIKELY ETIOLOGY OF A KNEE INJURY
BASED ON EXAMINATION

This eighteen-year old heard a popping sound then developed severe posterolateral knee pain after missing a dismount during gymnastics practice. Shortly afterwards, she developed swelling and was unable to walk. She feels her leg is buckling and is unstable. Her pain was not alleviated with rest, ice, compression or elevation (RICE). She has had no previous knee injury.

The most common cause of knee pain is the patello femoral syndrome (PFS) which is often called chondromalacia (chondromalacia implies an arthroscopic or pathologic diagnosis). This is a slowly progressive anterior knee pain often caused by downhill running or a direct blow to the patella. The patient will complain of pain when walking up or down the stairs and will have the "movie (theater) sign" (difficulty getting out of the seat and knee pain after sitting for a prolonged period of time). This problem may be accompanied by knee locking, clicking, grinding, and the knee giving way. There may be some accompanying weakness and effusion. On physical examination, the patient may have a positive patellar inhibition test (will refuse to contract the quadriceps muscle forcefully against resistance applied to the superior pole of the patellar due to worsened knee pain). The treatment of PFS includes decreasing activity, avoiding downhill running, ice, nonsteroidal anti-inflammatory agents, use of a knee brace, and physical therapy to improve strength and flexibility.

Traumatic knee injuries are usually due to "fixed foot" rotational injuries which may occur with hyperextension, changing direction suddenly during activity, or with sudden acceleration or deceleration activities.

A meniscus injury is often diagnosed by magnetic resonance imaging (an excellent study for cartilage). The person may present complaining of a swollen, tender, and warm knee. Arthrocentesis may reveal a clear effusion. The patient may have the "duck walk" sign (unable to walk in the squatting position) and a positive McMurray's sign. The knee may lock, pop, and buckle. The treatment of a meniscal tear includes RICE although some patients require arthroscopy and surgery.

The anterior cruciate ligament is the most injured ligament. The patient will complain of a popping sound at the time of the injury followed by intense posterolateral knee pain. The knee will immediately become swollen due to a bloody effusion. The patient may complain of popping, cracking, and a feeling of knee instability. On physical examination, there is a positive Lachman's maneuver. In athletes, this injury requires an immediate orthopedics consultation with possible surgical repair. MRIs poorly demonstrate ligaments and should not be requested first.

Ms. Ogelsby presents with the signs and symptoms of an injury to the ACL and has a positive Lachman's maneuver. You should immediately refer this future Olympic athlete to the orthopedics surgeon.

Physical Examination Pearl: You should be familiar with the 2 methods of evaluating the knee for effusion. The "bulge" sign is when you milk the medial knee upwards then tap the lateral knee. You will see the bulge of fluid return medially. The "ballottement" sign is when you apply downward pressure on the suprapatellar pouch then push the patella downward towards the femur. When you release the patella, it will float or spring back upwards.

CSA Patient Note Pearl: The differential diagnosis for knee pain includes arthritis, PFS, ligament injury, and a meniscal tear. The diagnostic work-up may include a plain radiography, arthritis screen (ANA, RF, ESR), Lyme titers, arthrocentesis, and an MRI.

Case 52

Case 52

A six-month old child is brought to the emergency room because of diarrhea. The parents are concerned that their baby, Brian Beasley, is becoming dehydrated. He appears weak and is slightly lethargic. The vital signs on Brian are as follows:

Blood pressure	80/40 mm Hg
Heart rate	160 beats per minute
Respiratory rate	48 breaths per minute
Temperature	100° F, rectally

The child's weight 2 weeks ago at his pediatrician's office was 6.0 kg. The nurse has the results of stat bloodwork and urinalysis revealing:

Na =	135 meq/L (136-145 meq/L)
K =	4.0 meq/L (3.5-5.0 meq/L)
Cl =	90 meq/L (98-106 meq/L)
HCO3 =	10 meq/L (23-28 meq/L)
BUN =	35 mg/dl (8-20 mg/dl)
Glucose =	70 mg/dl (70-105 mg/dl)

You have 15 minutes to interview the parents and perform a focused physical examination on Baby Brian. Please limit yourself to the time provided.

MY CHECKLIST

History of Present Illness. The Examinee:

1. _____
2. _____
3. _____
4. _____
5. _____
6. _____
7. _____
8. _____
9. _____
10. _____
11. _____

Physical Examination. The Examinee:

12. _____
13. _____
14. _____
15. _____
16. _____
17. _____
18. _____

Communication Skills. The Examinee:

19. _____
20. _____
21. _____
22. _____
23. _____
24. _____

SP CHECKLIST FOR BRIAN BEASLEY

History of Present Illness. The Examinee:

____1. asked about the onset of the diarrhea ("It started 2 days ago.")

____2. asked about the number of bowel movements per day ("Maybe 6 episodes daily.")

____3. asked about any blood in the stool ("No.")

____4. asked about any vomiting ("None.")

____5. asked about any fever ("None. I've taken his temperature every 4 hours.")

____6. asked about the urine flow i.e., a decrease in the number of wet diapers ("Very little urine output.")

____7. asked about any tears when crying ("No tears.")

____8. asked about the child's oral intake ("A few ounces of juice every 6 hours.")

____9. asked about any change in the personality of the baby i.e., irritable, lethargic ("Very sleepy and cranky.")

____10. asked about any past medical history i.e., diabetes ("No.")

____11. asked if any contacts are ill ("No one at home is ill.")

Physical Examination. The Examinee:

____12. weighed the child using the scale in the examination room (weight is 5.0 kg).

____13. examined the skin for tenting (tenting positive).

____14. checked for capillary refill (greater than 3 seconds).

____15. looked inside the mouth to check for dry mucus membranes (mucus membranes are dry).

____16. checked anterior fontanelle for depression (anterior fontanelle is sunken).

____17. checked the neck for rigidity (no rigidity).

____18. pressed gently on the abdomen (no tenderness and no masses).

Communication Skills. The Examinee:

____19. explained that the child was dehydrated.

____20. explained the treatment for the dehydration was intravenous fluids.

____21. explained that the child would be admitted to the hospital.

____22. used language that was easy to understand.

____23. demonstrated empathy.

____24. did not cause the child any unnecessary discomfort.

If you performed 17 of these 24 tasks, you passed this test station.

LEARNING OBJECTIVE FOR BRIAN BEASLEY:
DETERMINE THE SEVERITY OF DEHYDRATION IN A CHILD AND DETERMINE
APPROPRIATE INTRAVENOUS HYDRATION THERAPY

Six-month old Brian Beasley has had diarrhea (six episodes per day) for the last two days. He has no vomiting or fever. He has been irritable and refusing to drink fluids. The parents have noticed fewer wet diapers to change (normal urine output is 1cc/kg/hr) and lack of tears when the child is crying.

On physical examination, the child has lost 1 kg of weight since he was last seen by his pediatrician. The child was tachycardic, tachypneic, and hypotensive. Capillary refill was prolonged, the mucus membranes were dry, the skin demonstrated tenting and the anterior fontanelle was depressed.

Laboratory results revealed an isotonic dehydration. The doctor must be able to determine the severity of dehydration and correct the fluid, sodium, and potassium deficits appropriately.

The child has lost 1 kg since his last doctor visit, which is nearly 17% of his total body weight (1.0 kg/6.0 kg). Baby Brian is "severely" dehydrated. This category of dehydration may lead to shock and acute tubular necrosis and must be addressed immediately. Deficits along with maintenance fluids and electrolytes must be replaced using the following guidelines:

1. 20 cc/kg of a crystalloid solution (NS or LR) over 30 minutes until cardiovascular stability returns. If necessary this may be repeated.

2. calculate fluid deficit = (well weight - ill weight)(1000cc)
   1000cc fluid deficit = (6.0 kg - 5.0 kg)(1000cc/kg)

3. calculate sodium and potassium deficit:
   Na deficit = (135 meq/1000cc)(.6 ECF)(1000cc) = 81 meqs Na
   K deficit = (150 meq/1000cc)(.4 ICF) (1000cc) = 60 meqs K

4. calculate maintenance fluids = 100cc per kg = (100cc)(6.0kg well weight) = 600 cc

5. calculate sodium and potassium maintenance:
   Na maintenance = 3 meq/100 cc = 18 meqs Na/600cc
   K maintenance = 2 meq/100cc = 12 meq/600cc

6. replace ½ of fluid deficit and ½ of sodium deficit in the first 8 hours and the other ½ over the next 16 hours

7. replace maintenance requirements uniformly over 24 hours

8. K is corrected at a constant rate over 48 hours

Baby Brian will receive a 20cc/kg normal saline push (120cc) over a period of 30 minutes. During the first 8 hours, he will receive 1/2 of his deficit (500cc D5W with 40 meqs Na and 10 meqs of K) and 1/3 of his maintenance requirements (200 cc D5W with 6 meq of Na and 4 meq K). During the 8th–25th hours of treatment, Brian will receive 1/2 of the remaining deficit and 2/3 of the maintenance (400cc D5W with 12 meq Na and 8meq K).

OSCE Interstation Pearl: Know how to determine severity of dehydration: Mild is 2–3% of body weight lost or <50cc fluid lost/kg. The patient has dry mucus membranes. Moderate dehydration is 10% of body weight lost or 50–100cc/kg. Physical exam reveals dry mucus membranes, decreased skin turgor, depressed anterior fontanelle, sunken eyeballs, and tachycardia. Severe dehydration is >15% of body weight or >100cc/kg and may be accompanied by the additional findings of tachypnea and hypotension.

CSA Patient Note Pearl: The differential diagnosis for Baby Brian is dehydration, infection (especially meningitis), diabetic ketoacidosis, poisoning, and head injury. The work-up includes serum glucose, leukocyte count, blood urea nitrogen, and urine specific gravity. Other tests may include CT scan of the head, lumbar puncture, and blood cultures.

The Common Encounters for Each Specialty

Common Encounters in Family Medicine

Abdominal pain
Acute pericarditis
Adult health maintenance
Advance directives
Ambulatory management of HIV
Anemia
Anxiety
Asthma
Assessment of functional health status in the elderly
Behavioral disturbances
Care for common injuries (burns, bites, cuts)
Care of the newborn
Caring for the dying
Caring for the elderly
Cerebrovascular disease
Chest pain
Chronic obstructive pulmonary disease
Compliance with medications
Congestive heart failure
Conjunctivitis
Contraception/safe sex counseling
Dizziness
Dementia
Depression
Dermatological problems
Diabetes mellitus
Diarrhea
Elder abuse
Ethical issues in primary care
Exercise prescriptions
Family structure/family counseling
Fatigue
Fever
Growth and development of children
Headache
Heart disease
HIV testing and counseling
Home care and utilization of community resources
Hypertension
Low back pain
Marriage counseling
Menstrual irregularities
Musculoskeletal injuries
Nutrition prescriptions
Obesity
Occupational medicine
Office gynecology
Otitis
Peripheral vascular disease
Pharyngitis/sinusitis
Pneumonia
Post-myocardial infarction rehabilitation
Prenatal examination

Preventive cardiology
Seizure
Sexual abuse/assault
Smoking cessation and guidance
Somatization disorder
Stress management
Substance abuse
Suturing/minor surgery
Urinary tract infection
Vertigo
Well-baby care/well-child care

Common Encounters in Internal Medicine

Abdominal pain
Advance directives
Anemia
Back pain
Chest pain
Claudication
Confusion
Constipation
Cough
Diarrhea
Dizziness
Fatigue
Fever
Headache
Hearing loss
Hematemesis
Hematuria
Hemoptysis
HIV counseling and care
Impotence
"I need a physical exam."
"I need my blood pressure checked."
"I need my sugar checked."
"I passed out." (syncope)
Jaundice
Joint pain
Leg swelling (edema)
Lymphadenopathy
Melena
Painful urination (dysuria)
Palpitations
Rash
Rectal bleeding (hematochezia)
Shortness of breath (dyspnea)
Sore throat
Swollen thyroid
Tremors
Vertigo
Vision loss
Vomiting
Weakness
Weight loss

Common Encounters in Obstetrics and Gynecology

Abnormal pap smear

Abnormal uterine bleeding
Adnexal mass
Amenorrhea
Breast mass/breast disease
Calculation of gestational age and estimated date of confinement
Cancer screening
Chronic pelvic pain
Common complaints during pregnancy
Contraception and family planning
Detection of high-risk pregnancy
Detection of medical or surgical conditions which may complicate pregnancy
Disorders of lactation
Domestic violence
Drugs, tobacco, and alcohol in pregnancy
Dysmenorrhea
Dyspareunia
Ectopic pregnancy
Endometrial biopsy
Endometriosis
Fibroid uterus
First trimester bleeding
Genetic counseling
Hirsutism
Infertility
Menopause
Miscarriage/spontaneous abortion
Normal pregnancy
Nutritional counseling in pregnancy
Pelvic inflammatory disease
Placenta previa
Post-menopausal bleeding
Post-partum care
Premenstrual syndrome
Prenatal care
Sexual assault and abuse
Sexual dysfunction
Sexually transmitted disease
Urinary tract infection
Vaginal discharge
Vaginitis
Voluntary termination of pregnancy/induced abortion

Common Encounters in Pediatrics
Abdominal pain
Adolescent high-risk sexual behavior
Anemia
Breast feeding
Child abuse
Congenital heart disease
Cough
Cystic fibrosis
Dehydration
Developmental evaluation
Diarrhea/gastroenteritis
Earache/otitis media
Hearing loss
Hematologic malignancies
Hematuria

Infants with feeding problems
Infections in children
Joint pain
Language developmental problems
Nutrition guidelines and obesity
Orthopedic evaluation in a child
Perform age appropriate physical exam
Poisoning and ingestions
Proteinuria

Common Encounters in Psychiatry
Alcohol related disorders
Anorexia, bulimia
Bipolar disorder
Complications of psychiatric drugs
Delirium
Delusional or paranoid disorders
Dementia
Depression
Disassociative disorders
Normal grief
Obsessive-compulsive disorder
Panic disorder and phobias
Personality disorders
Post-traumatic stress disorder
Schizophrenia
Sexual disorders (erectile disorder)
Somatoform disorders
Stress reduction and management
Substance abuse
Suicidal patient

Common Encounters in Surgery
Abdominal mass
Acute abdominal pain
Breast mass
Burns
Electrolyte abnormalities in a post-op patient
Epistaxis
Gastrointestinal cancers
Head trauma evaluation
Hernia
Infections (e.g., cellulitis, diverticulitis)
Intestinal obstruction
Kidney stone
Multiple injury trauma evaluation
Post-operative fever
Post-operative shock
Vascular emergencies/use of doppler ultrasound

References

Andrew, B. The use of behavioral checklists to assess physical examination skills. *J of Med Educ.* 1977; 52: 589–591.

Annex to the proceeding of the AAMC's consensus conference on the use of standardized patients in the teaching and evaluation of clinical skills. *Acad Med.* 1993; 68: 437–483.

Asher, M.L. Asking about domestic violence: SAFE questions. *JAMA.* 1993; 269: 2367.

Barrows, H.S., Abrahamson S. The programmed patient: a technique for appraising student performance in clinical neurology. *J Med Educ.* 1964; 39:802–805.

Barrows, H.S. Simulated patients in medical teaching. *Canad Med Ass J.* 1968; 98: 674–676.

Barrows, H.S., Williams, R.G., Moy, R.H. A comprehensive performance-based assessment of fourth year students' clinical skills. *J Med Educ.* 1987; 62: 805–809.

Boulet, J.R., Ben-David, M.F., Ziv, A., Burdick, W.P., et al. Using standardized patients to assess the interpersonal skills of physicians. *Acad Med.* 1998; 73: supplement: S94–S96.

Brody, D.S. The patient's role in clinical decision-making. *Ann Int Med.* 1980; 93: 718–722.

Buckman, R. Breaking bad news. Why is it still so difficult? *Br Med J.* 1984; 288: 1597–1599.

Conn, H.L., Jr. Assessing the clinical skills of foreign medical graduates. *J Med Educ.* 1986; 61: 863–871.

Dawson, D.M. Entrapment neuropathies of the upper extremities. *N Eng J Med.* 1993; 329 (27): 2013–2018.

De Champlain, A.F., Margolis, M.J., King, A., Klass, D.J. Standardized patients' accuracy in recording examinees' behaviors using checklists. *Acad Med.* 1997; 72: S85–S87.

Educational Commission for Foreign Medical Graduates. Clinical Skills Assessment Candidate Orientation Manual. Philadelphia, Pennsylvania. 1998.

Engler, C.M., Saltzman, G.A., Walker, M.L., Wolf, F.M. Medical student acquisition and retention of communication and interviewing skills. *J Med Educ.* 1981; 56: 572–579.

Evans, B.J., Stanley, R.O., Mestrovic, R., Rose, L. Effects of communication skills training on students' diagnostic deficiency. *Med Educ.* 1991; 25: 517–526.

Ewing, J.A. Detecting alcoholism: the CAGE questionnaire. *JAMA.* 1984; 252: 1905–1907.

Fillenbaum, G.G. Screening of the elderly. A brief instrumental activities of daily living measure. *J Am Geriatr Soc.* 1985; 33: 698–706.

Folstein, M.F., Folstein, S.E., McHugh, P.R. Mini-mental state: a practical method for grading the cognitive state of patients for the clinician. *J Psychiat Res.* 1975; 12: 189–198.

Girgis, A., Sanson-Fisher. Breaking Bad News: Consensus guidelines for medical practitioners. *J Clin On.* 1995; 13: 2449–2456.

Grey, J. Global rating scales in residency education. *Acad Med.* 1996; 71 supplement: S55–S63.

Harden, R., Stevenson, M., Downie, W.W., Wilson, G.M. Assessment of clinical competence using objective structured examination. *Brit Med J.* 1975; 1: 447–451.

Harden, R.M., Gleeson, F.A. Assessment of clinical competence using an objective structured clinical examination (OSCE). *Med Ed.* 1979;13: 41–54.

Hodges, B., Turnbull, J., Cohen, R., Bienstock, A., Norman, G. Evaluating communication skills in the objective structured clinical examination format: reliability and generalizability. *Med Educ.* 1996; 30: 38–43.

Hoy, A.M. Breaking bad news to patients. *Br J Hosp Med.* 1985; 34: 96–99.

Katz, S., Ford, A.B., Moskowitz, R.W., et al. Studies of illness in the aged. The index of activities of daily living: standardized measure of biological and psychosocial function. *JAMA*; 1963; 185: 914–919.

King, A.M., Perkowski-Rogers, L.C., Pohl, H.S. Planning standardized patient programs: case development, patient training, and costs. *Teach Learn Med.* 1994; 6: 6–14.

Korsch, B.M., Gozzi, E.K., Francis, V. Gaps in doctor-patient communication 1. Doctor-patient interaction and patient satisfaction. *Pediatrics.* 1968; 42: 855–858.

Lachs, M.S., et al. A simple procedure for general screening for functional disability in elderly patients. *Ann Intern Med.* 1990; 112: 699–706.

Lang, A.E., Lozano, A.M. Parkinson's disease (first of two parts). *N Eng J Med.* 1998; 339: 1044–1053.

Lawton, M.P., Brody, E.M. Assessment of older people: self-maintaining and instrumental activities of daily living. *Gerontologist.* 1969; 9: 179–185.

Litvan, I. Parkinsonian features: when are they Parkinson disease? *JAMA*; 280 (19): 1654–1655.

Michel, P., Henry, P., Letenneur, L., Jogeix, M., Corson, A., Dartigues, J.F. Diagnostic screen for assessment of the IHS criteria for migraine by general practitioners. *Cephalagia.* 1993; 12: 54–59.

Petrusa, E.R., Blackwell, T.A., Rogers, L.P., Saydjari, C., Parcel, S., Guckian, J.C. An objective measure of clinical performance. *Am J Med.* 1987; 83: 34–43.

Petrusa, E.R., Blackwell, T.A., Carline, J., Ramsey, P.G., et al. A multi-institutional trial of an objective structured clinical examnation. *Teach Learn Med.* 1991; 3: 86–94.

Position paper from the American College of Physicians. Ethics manual, fourth edition. *Ann Intern Med.* 1998; 128: 576–594.

Quill, T.E., Townshend, P. Bad News: delivery, dialogue, and dilemnas. *Arch Intern Med.* 1991; 151: 463–468.

Quill, T.E. Partnerships in patient care: a contractual approach. *Ann Int Med.* 1983; 98: 228–234.

Regehr, G., MacRae, H., Reznick, R.K., Szalay, D. Comparing the psychometric properties of checklists and global rating scales for assessing performance on an OSCE-format examination. *Acad Med.* 1998; 73: 993–997.

Resnick, R., Smee, S., Royhman, A., et al. An objective structured clinical examination for the licentiate: report of the pilot project of the Medical Council of Canada. *Acad Med.* 1992; 67: 487–494.

Sanson-Fisher, R.W. and Poole, A.D. Simulated patients and the assessment of medical students' interpersonal skills. *Med Educ.* 1980; 14: 249–253.

Schnabl, G.K., Hassard, T.H., Kopelow, M.L. The assessment of interpersonal skills using standardized patients. In proceedings of the thirtieth conference on research in medical education. *Acad Med.* 1991; 66 supplement: S34–S36.

Stillman, P.L., Swanson, D.B., Smee, S., et al. Assessing clinical skills of residents with standardized patients. *Ann Intern Med.* 1986; 105: 762–771.

Stillman, P.L., Swanson, D.B. Ensuring the clinical competence of medical graduates through standardized patients. *Arch Int Med.* 1987; 147: 1049–1052.

Stillman, P.L., Regan, M.B., Swanson, D.B., et al. An assessment of the clinical skills of fourth year medical students at four New England medical schools. *Acad Med.* 1990; 65: 320–326.

Sutnick, A.I., et al. ECFMG assessment of clinical competence of graduates of foreign medical schools. *JAMA.* 1993; 270: 1041–1045.

Sutnick, A.I., Stillman, P.L., Norcini, J.J., et al. Pilot study of the use of the ECFMG clinical competence assessment to provide profiles of clinical competencies of graduates of foreign medical schools for residency directors. *Acad Med.* 1994; 69: 65–67.

Van der Vleuten, C.P.M., Swanson, D.B. Assessment of clinical skills with standardized patients: state of the art. *Teach Learn Med.* 1990; 2: 58–76.

Vu, N.V., Barrows, H.S., Marcy, M.L., Verhulst, S.J., Colliver, J.A., Travis, T. Six years of comprehensive, clinical, performance-based assessment using standardized patients at the Southern Illinois University School of Medicine. *Acad Med.* 1992; 67: 42–50.

Vu, N.V., Marcy, J.A., Colliver, S.J., Verhulst, S.J., Travis, T.A., Barrows, H.S. Standardized (simulated) patients' accuracy in recording check-list items. *Med Educ.* 1992; 26: 99–104.

Williams, R.G., Barrows, H.S., Vu, N.V., Verhulst, S.J., Colliver, J.A., Marcy, M., Steward, D. Direct standardized assessment of clinical competence. *Med Educ.* 1987; 21: 482–489.

Wooliscroft, J.O., Howell, J.D., Patel, B.P., Swanson, D.B. Resident-patient interactions: the humanistic qualities of internal medicine residents assessed by patients, attending physicians, program supervisors and nurses. *Acad Med.* 1994; 69: 216–223.

Wu, J., Pearlman, R. Consent in medical decision making: the role of communication. *Gen Int Med.* 1989; 3: 9–14.

PRACTICE CASES

Interviewing Skills

Enelow, A.J., Forde, D.L. and Brummel-Smith, K. 1996. Interviewing and Patient Care. 4th ed. New York: Oxford University Press.

Fillenbaum, G.G. 1988. Multidimensional Functional Assessment of Older Adults. Hillsdale, New Jersey: Lawrence Eribaum Associates.

Levinson, Daniel. 1987. A Guide to the Clinical Interview. Philadelphia, Pennsylvania: W.B. Saunders, Co.

Smith, Robert C. 1996. The Patient's Story: Integrated Patient-Doctor Interviewing. Boston, Massachusetts: Little, Brown and Co.

Physical Examination

Bates, Barbara. 1995. A Guide to Physical Examination and History Taking. 6th ed. Philadelphia, Pennsylvania: J.B. Lippincott Company.

Epstein, Owen, Perkin, G.D., de Bono, David P., Cookson, John. 1997. Clinical Examination, 2nd ed. St. Louis, Missouri: Mosby, Inc.

Seidel, Henry M., Ball, Jane W., Dains, Joyce E., Benedict, G.W. 1995. Mosby's Guide to Physical Examination, 4th ed. St. Louis, Missouri: Mosby, Inc.

Family Medicine

Mengel, Mark B., and Schwiebert, Peter L. 1995. Ambulatory Medicine: The Primary Care of Families. Norwal, Connecticut: Appleton and Lange.

Sloane, Phillip D., Slatt, Lisa M., and Curtis, Peter. 1993. Essentials of Family Medicine. Baltimore, Maryland: Williams and Wilkins.

Medicine

Kutty, K., Sebastian, J.L., Mewis, B.A., Berg, D.D., Kochar, M.S. 1998. Kochar's Concise Textbook of Medicine. Baltimore, Maryland: Williams and Wilkins.

Tierney, Jr., Lawrence, M., McPhee, Stephen J., Papadakis, Maxine A., eds. 1998. Current Medical Diagnosis and Treatment. Connecticut: Appleton and Lange.

Wilson, Jean D., Braunwald, Eugene, Isselbacher, Kurt J., Petersdorf, Robert, Fauci, Anthony, Root, Recaid K., eds. 1998. Harrison's Principles of Internal Medicine. 14th ed. New York: McGraw-Hill, Inc.

Obstetrics and Gynecology

Cunningham, F.G., MacDonald, P.C., Gant, N.F. eds. 1997. William's Obstetrics. 20th ed. Connecticut: Appleton and Lange.

Gabbe, S., Niebyl, J., and Simpson, W. 1996. Obstetrics Normal and Problem Pregnancies. 3rd ed. New York: Churchill Livingston.

Pernoll, M.L. 1991. Current Obstetrics and Gynecologic Diagnosis and Treatment. 7th ed. Connecticut: Appleton and Lange.

Scott, J.R., Disaia, P.J., Hammond, D.B., Spellacy, W.N. 1990. Danforth's Obstetrics and Gynecology. 6th ed. Pennsylvania: J.B. Lippincott Co.

Pediatrics

Behrman, Richard E., ed. 1996. Nelson's Book of Pediatrics. 15th ed. Philadelphia: W.B. Saunders, Co.

Hay, William W., Groothuis, J., Hayward, A.R., Levin, M.J. 1997. Current Pediatrics Diagnosis and Treatment. 13th ed. Connecticut: Appleton and Lange.

Fleisher, Gary R., Ludwig, Stephen, eds. 1993. Textbook of Pediatric Emergency Medicine. 3rd ed. Baltimore, Maryland: Williams and Wilkins.

Rudolph, Abraham M., ed. 1996. Rudolph's Pediatrics. 20th ed. Connecticut: Appleton and Lange.

Psychiatry

American Psychiatric Association. 1994. Diagnostic and Statistical Manual of Mental Disorders. (DSM-IV). 4th ed. Washington, D.C.: American Psychiatric Association.

Andreasen, Nancy C. and Black, Donald W. 1991. Introductory Textbook of Psychiatry. Washington, D.C.: American Psychiatry Press, Inc.

Frances, Richard J. and Miller, Sheldon I. 1991. Clinical Textbook of Addictive Disorders New York: The Guilford Press.

Gelder, Michael, Gath, Dennis and Mayou, Richard. 1996. Oxford Textbook of Psychiatry. 3rd ed. Oxford, England: Oxford University Press.

Kaplan, Harold I. and Sadock, Benjamin J. 1995. Comprehensive Textbook of Psychiatry. 7th ed. Baltimore, Maryland: Williams and Wilkins.

Wise, M.G. and Rundell, J.R. 1994. Concise Guide to Consultation Psychiatry, 2nd ed. Washington, D.C.: American Psychiatric Press.

Surgery

Schwartz, S.I., ed. 1994. Principles of Surgery. 6th ed. New York: McGraw-Hill, Inc.

Way, L.W. 1991. Current Surgical Diagnosis and Treatment. 9th ed. Los Altos, CA: Appleton and Lange.

Check out updated OSCE/CSA information at:
http://www.books.mcgraw-hill.com/medical/osce

Index of Practice Cases

OBSTETRICS AND GYNECOLOGY

PEDIATRICS

PSYCHIATRY

SURGERY

Index

A

AAMC (American Association of Medical Colleges), 3
Abdominal examination, 23–25
Abdominal pain, practice cases, 96–100, 170–174, 232–236, 242–245, 284–287, 294–301
Abortion, threatened, practice case, 246–249
Abuse, patient, 42–43, 46
    practice case, 180–184
Activities of daily living (ADLs), 25, 61
Acute pancreatitis, practice case, 170–174
Alcoholic patient, 43, 46
Alzheimer's disease
    informing patient of, 41, 46
    practice case, 58–61
American Association of Medical Colleges (AAMC), 3
AMPLE mnemonic for trauma patients, 305
Anaphylactic *versus* anaphylactoid reactions, 179
Angioedema due to shellfish ingestion, practice case,176–179
Anorexia nervosa, practice case, 262–266
Appendectomy, previous, intestinal obstruction secondary to
    practice case, 294–297
Arm and leg weakness, practice case, 116–119
Assault victim, 42–43, 46
    practice cases, 180–184, 302–305
Asthma, practice case, 198–202
Atrial fibrillation as risk factor for embolic stroke
    practice case, 116–119

B

Babinski sign, 24–25, 27, 118, 194
Back pain, practice cases, 192–196, 288–292
Bacteriological stains of body fluids, interpretation, 48
Bad news, delivering to patient, 41, 46
Barrett's esophagus, 129
Battered patient, 42–43, 46
    practice case, 180–184
Bell's palsy, 27, 149
Benign prostatic hypertrophy, practice case, 162–165
Blood pressure check, practice case, 90–94
Blood smears, interpretation, 48
Blunt trauma injury, practice case, 302–305
Blurred vision, practice case, 156–160
Breast examination, 24, 51
Breathing difficulty, practice cases, 198–202, 220–224
Brudzinski's sign, 24–25, 207
Bulimia, 266
Burning on urination, practice case, 142–145

C

CAGE questionnaire, 25, 43–44, 46
Cancer, informing patient of, 41, 46
Cardiac examination, 23, 25, 27, 51
Carpal tunnel syndrome (CTS), practice case, 186–190
Cases, practice. *See* Practice cases
Checklist, developing, 15–18
    example, 15–16
Chest pain, practice cases, 102–106, 272–275
Cheyne-Stokes respirations, 27

D

Children
    child abuse, 42–43, 46
    practice cases. *See* Pediatric patients, practice cases with
Cholecystitis, practice case, 284–287
Chronic cough, practice case, 112–115
Clinical Skills Assessment (CSA), 4–5
Communication challenges, 41–46. *See also* Communication skills
    alcoholic patient, 43–44, 46
    bad news, delivering to a patient, 41, 46
    battered patient, 42–43, 46
    confidentiality, 43, 46
    informed consent, 45–46
    non-compliant patient, 42, 46
    overtalkative patient, 43, 46
    patient decision to forego treatment, 41–42, 46
    patient's right to be informed, 42, 46
    patient with special emotional problems, 44–46
    smoker, 44, 46
    substance addicted patient, 44, 46
Communication skills, 3–4, 15, 18
    challenges. *See* Communication challenges
    component of CSA grade, 4–5
    five simple steps to effective communication, 29–33
    improving, 35
Community acquired pneumonia, practice case, 74–78
Confidentiality, 43, 46
Consent, informed, 45–46
Cough as presenting complaint, practice cases, 74–78, 112–115
CSA (Clinical Skills Assessment), 4–5
CTS (carpal tunnel syndrome), practice case, 186–190
Cullen's sign, 23, 25, 27, 172–173

D

Data gathering (DG), 4
DEATH (dressing, eating, ambulating, toileting, hygiene) mnemonic, 61, 136
Deep venous thrombosis (DVT), practice case, 108–111
Dehydration in an infant, practice case, 316–320
Dementia, practice case, 58–61
Depression, postpartum, practice case, 276–279
Depression, practice case, 166–169
Despondency, practice case, 268–271
DG (data gathering), 4
Diabetes, practice case, 156–160
Diagnostic test interpretation, 48
Diarrhea in an infant, practice case, 316–320
Directly observed therapy (DOT), 115
Discoid lupus, practice case, 120–124
Diverticulitis, practice case, 298–301
Domestic violence, 42–43, 46
    practice case, 180–184
DOT (directly observed therapy), 115
DVT (deep venous thrombosis), practice case, 108–111
Dysphagia, practice case, 126–130

E

Ear infection, practice case, 204–208

ISBN 0-07-135012-8

90000

9 780071 350129